Debatte im Oberhaus — **Einzelnummer 0,25 Goldmark**

JÜDISCHE RUNDSCHAU

Erscheint jeden Dienstag u. Freitag. Bezugspreis bei der Expedition monatlich 2,— Goldmark, vierteljährlich 5,75 Goldmark. Auslandsabonnements werden in der Währung der einzelnen Länder berechnet. Anzeigenpreis: 8 gesp. Nonpareillezeile 0,50 G.-M. Stellengesuche 0,25 G.-M.

Redaktion, Verlag und Anzeigen-Verwaltung: Jüdische Rundschau G. m. b. H., Berlin W15, Meinekestr. 10. Telefon: J 1 Bismarck 7165-70. Anzeigenschluß: Dienstag und Freitag nachmittags 4 Uhr. Redaktionsschluß Sonntag und Mittwoch nachmittag.

Postscheck-Konten: Berlin 17392, Basel V 9355, Belgrad 65032, Brüssel 39433, Budapest 59693, Danzig 1973, Haag 140470, Prag 59410, Riga 4155, Straßburg 16430, Warschau 190708, Wien 156030. Bank-Konten: Dresdener Bank, Depositen-Kasse Berlin, Kurfürstendamm 52; Rumänische Kreditbank, Cernauti (Rumänien); Anglo Palestine Co. in Haifa, Jerusalem, Tel-Aviv.

Nummer 27 | Berlin, 4. IV. 1933 | ח׳ ניסן תרצ״ג | XXXVIII. Jahrg.

Der Zionismus erstrebt für das jüdische Volk die Schaffung einer öffentlich-rechtlich gesicherten Heimstätte in Palästina. „Baseler Programm."

Tragt ihn mit Stolz, den gelben Fleck!

Der 1. April 1933 wird ein wichtiger Tag in der Geschichte der deutschen Juden, ja in der Geschichte des ganzen jüdischen Volkes bleiben. Die Ereignisse dieses Tages haben nicht nur eine politische und eine wirtschaftliche, sondern auch eine moralische und seelische Seite. Ueber die politischen und wirtschaftlichen Zusammenhänge ist in den Zeitungen viel gesprochen worden, wobei freilich häufig agitatorische Bedürfnisse die sachliche Erkenntnis verdunkeln. Ueber die moralische Seite zu sprechen, ist unsere Sache. Denn so viel auch die Judenfrage jetzt erörtert wird, was in der Seele der deutschen Juden vorgeht, was vom jüdischen Standpunkt zu den Vorgängen zu sagen ist, kann niemand aussprechen als wir selbst. Die Juden können heute nicht anders als als Juden sprechen. Alles andere ist völlig sinnlos. Der Spuk der sogenannten „Judenpresse" ist weggeblasen. Der verhängnisvolle Irrtum vieler Juden, man könne jüdische Interessen unter anderem Deckmantel vertreten, ist beseitigt. Das deutsche Judentum hat am 1. April eine Lehre empfangen, die viel tiefer geht, als selbst seine erbitterten und heute triumphierenden Gegner annehmen.

Es ist nicht unsere Art, zu lamentieren. Auf Ereignisse von dieser Wucht mit sentimentalen Salbadereien zu reagieren, überlassen wir jenen Juden einer vergangenen Generation, die nichts gelernt und alles vergessen haben. Es bedarf heute eines neuen Tones in der Diskussion jüdischer Angelegenheiten. Wir leben in einer neuen Zeit, die nationale Revolution des deutschen Volkes ist ein weithin sichtbares Signal, daß die alte Begriffswelt zusammengestürzt ist. Das mag für viele schmerzlich sein, aber in dieser Welt sich behaupten kann nur, wer den Realitäten ins Auge sieht. Wir stehen mitten in einer gewaltigen Umwandlung des geistigen, politischen, sozialen und wirtschaftlichen Lebens. Unsere Sorge ist: Wie reagiert das Judentum?

Der 1. April 1933 kann ein Tag des jüdischen Erwachens und der jüdischen Wiedergeburt sein. Wenn die Juden wollen. Wenn die Juden reif sind und innere Größe besitzen. Wenn die Juden nicht so sind, wie sie von ihren Gegnern dargestellt werden.

Das angegriffene Judentum muß sich zu sich selbst bekennen.

Auch an diesem Tage stärkster Erregung, wo im Angesicht des beispiellosen Schauspiels der universalen Verfemung der gesamten jüdischen Bevölkerung eines großen Kulturlandes die stürmischesten Empfindungen unser Herz durchzogen, haben wir vor allem Eines zu wahren: Besonnenheit. Stehen wir fassungslos vor dem Geschehen dieser Tage, so dürfen wir doch nicht verzagen und müssen uns ohne Selbsttäuschung Rechenschaft ablegen. Man müßte in diesen Tagen empfehlen: daß die Schrift, die an der Wiege des Zionismus stand,

Theodor Herzls „Judenstaat",

in hunderttausenden Exemplaren unter Juden und Nichtjuden verbreitet wird. Wenn es noch Gefühl für Größe und Adel, für Ritterlichkeit und Gerechtigkeit gibt, müßte jeder Nationalsozialist, der dieses Buch zu Gesicht bekommt, vor seinem eigenen blinden Tun erstarren. Aber auch jeder Jude, der es liest, würde beginnen zu verstehen; und würde daraus Trost und Erhebung schöpfen.

Theodor Herzl, dessen reiner Name in diesen Tagen durch ein Zitat aus einer Fälschung vor der gesamten deutschen Oeffentlichkeit befleckt wurde, schrieb in der Einleitung der genannten Schrift:

> „Die Judenfrage besteht. Es wäre töricht, sie zu leugnen. Sie ist ein verschlepptes Stück Mittelalter, mit dem die Kulturvölker auch heute beim besten Willen noch nicht fertig werden konnten. Den großmütigen Willen zeigten sie ja, als sie uns emanzipierten. Die Judenfrage besteht überall, wo Juden in merklicher Anzahl leben. . . .
>
> **Ich glaube den Antisemitismus, der eine vielfach komplizierte Bewegung ist, zu verstehen. Ich betrachte diese Bewegung als Jude, aber ohne Haß und Furcht.** Ich glaube zu erkennen, was im Antisemitismus roher Scherz, gemeiner Brotneid, angeerbtes Vorurteil, religiöse Unduldsamkeit — aber auch, was darin vermeintliche Notwehr ist. Ich halte die Judenfrage weder für eine soziale, noch für eine religiöse, **wenn sie sich auch noch so und anders färbt. Sie** ist eine nationale Frage, und um sie zu lösen, müssen wir sie vor allem zu einer politischen Weltfrage machen, die im Rate der Kulturvölker zu regeln sein wird."

Man müßte Seite um Seite dieser 1897 erschienenen Schrift abschreiben, um zu zeigen: Theodor Herzl war der erste Jude, der unbefangen genug war, den Antisemitismus im Zusammenhang mit der Judenfrage zu betrachten. Und er erkannte, daß nicht durch Vogel-Strauß-Politik, sondern nur durch offene Behandlung der Tatsachen vor aller Welt eine Besserung erzielt werden kann. Gegen nichts hat er so leidenschaftlich Stellung genommen als gegen das, was ihm jetzt unterschoben wird, nämlich gegen den Gedanken, die Juden könnten eine nichtöffentliche Weltverbindung herstellen oder irgend etwas tun, was bei den anderen Völkern irrtümlicherweise solche Vorstellungen erwecken könnte. In seiner Schrift „Leroy-Beaulieu über den Antisemitismus" schreibt er:

> „Wir Zionisten sind auf das deutlichste und entschiedenste gegen jede internationale Vereinigung von Juden, die, wenn sie wirksam wäre, den mit Recht verpönten Staat im Staate vorstellte und, da sie machtlos und nichtssagend ist, nur Nachteile bietet. . . . Nur das sei gesagt, daß wir zur Lösung der Judenfrage nicht einen internationalen Verein, sondern eine internationale Diskussion wünschen, das heißt: nicht Bündeleien, geheime Interventionen, Schleichwege, sondern die freimütige Erörterung unter der beständigen und vollständigen Kontrolle der öffentlichen Meinung."

Wir im Geiste Theodor Herzls erzogenen Juden wollen auch heute nicht anklagen, sondern verstehen. Und uns fragen, was unsere eigene Schuld ist, was wir selbst gesündigt haben. Immer hat das jüdische Volk in kritischen Tagen seines Schicksals sich zunächst die Frage vorgelegt, was seine eigene Schuld ist. In unserem wichtigsten Gebete heißt es: „Um unserer Sünden willen wurden wir aus unserem Lande vertrieben". Nur wenn wir kritisch gegen uns sind, werden wir gerecht auch gegen andere sein.

Die Judenheit trägt eine schwere Schuld, weil sie den Ruf Theodor Herzls nicht gehört, ja, teilweise verspottet hat. Die Juden wollten nichts davon wissen, daß „eine Judenfrage besteht". Sie glaubten, es komme nur darauf an, als Jude nicht erkannt zu werden. Man wirft uns heute vor, wir hätten das deutsche Volk verraten; die nationalsozialistische Presse nennt uns, und wir sind dagegen wehrlos, den „Feind der Nation".

Es ist nicht wahr, daß die Juden Deutschland verraten haben. Wenn sie etwas verraten haben, so haben sie sich selbst, das Judentum, verraten.

Weil der Jude sein Judentum nicht stolz zur Schau trug, weil er sich um die Judenfrage herumdrücken wollte, hat er sich mitschuldig gemacht an der Erniedrigung des Judentums.

Bei aller Bitterkeit, die uns beim Lesen der nationalsozialistischen Boykottaufrufe und der ungerechten Beschuldigungen erfüllen muß, für eines können wir dem Boykottausschuß dankbar sein. In den Richtlinien heißt es in § 3:

> **„Es handelt sich . . . selbstverständlich um Geschäfte, die sich in den Händen von Angehörigen der jüdischen Rasse befinden. Die Religion spielt keine Rolle. Katholisch oder protestantisch getaufte Geschäftsleute oder Dissidenten jüdischer Rasse sind im Sinne dieser Anordnung ebenfalls Juden."**

Dies ist ein Denkzettel für alle Verräter am Judentum. Wer sich von der Gemeinschaft wegstiehlt, um seine persönliche Lage zu verbessern, soll den Lohn dieses Verrats nicht ernten. In dieser Stellungnahme gegen das Renegatentum ist ein Ansatz zur Klärung enthalten. Der Jude, der sein Judentum verleugnet, ist kein besserer Mitbürger als der, der sich aufrecht dazu bekennt. Renegatentum ist eine Schmach, aber solange die Umwelt Prämien darauf setzte, schien es ein Vorteil. Nun ist es auch kein Vorteil mehr. Der Jude wird als solcher kenntlich gemacht. Er bekommt den gelben Fleck.

Daß die Boykottleitung anordnete, an die boykottierten Geschäfte Schilder „mit gelbem Fleck auf schwarzem Grund" zu heften, ist ein gewaltiges Symbol. Diese Maßregel ist als Brandmarkung, als Verächtlichmachung gedacht. **Wir nehmen sie auf, und wollen daraus ein Ehrenzeichen machen.**

Viele Juden hatten am Sonnabend ein schweres Erlebnis. Nicht aus innerem Bekenntnis, nicht aus Treue zur eigenen Gemeinschaft, nicht aus Stolz auf eine großartige Vergangenheit und Menschheitsleistung, sondern durch den Aufdruck des roten Zettels und des gelben Flecks standen sie plötzlich als Juden da. Von Haus zu Haus gingen die Trupps, beklebten Geschäfte und Schilder, bemalten die Fensterscheiben, 24 Stunden lang waren die deutschen Juden gewissermaßen an den Pranger gestellt. Neben anderen Zeichen und Inschriften sah man auf den Scheiben der Schaufenster vielfach einen großen Magen David, den Schild König Davids. Dies sollte eine Entehrung sein. Juden, nehmt ihn auf, den Davidsschild, und tragt ihn in Ehren!

Denn — und hier beginnt die Pflicht unserer Selbstbesinnung, — wenn dieser Schild heute befleckt ist, so sind es nicht unsere Feinde allein, die dies bewirkt haben. Viele Juden gab es, die sich nicht genug tun konnten in würdeloser Selbstverhöhnung. Das Judentum galt als überlebte Sache, man betrachtete es ohne Ernst, man wollte sich durch Lächeln von seiner Tragik befreien.

Aber es gibt heute bereits den Typus des neuen, freien Juden, den die nichtjüdische Welt noch nicht kennt.

Wenn heute in der nationalsozialistischen und deutschnationalen Presse häufig auf einen Typus des jüdischen Literaten und auf die sogenannte Judenpresse hingewiesen wird, wenn das Judentum für diese Faktoren verantwortlich gemacht wird, so muß immer wieder gesagt werden, daß dies keine Repräsentanten des Judentums sind, sondern höchstens geschäftlich von den Juden zu profitieren versucht haben. In einer Zeit bourgeoiser Selbstgerechtigkeit konnten diese Elemente auf Beifall auch bei jüdischen Zuhörern rechnen, wenn sie Juden und Judentum verhöhnten und bagatellisierten. Wie oft wurden uns Nationaljuden von dieser Seite die Ideale eines abstrakten Weltbürgertums gepredigt, um alle tieferen Werte des Judentums zu vernichten. Aufrechte Juden waren stets entrüstet über die Witzeleien und Karikaturen, die von jüdischen Possenreißern genau so oder in noch höherem Maß gegen das Judentum wie gegen Deutsche oder andere gerichtet wurden. Das jüdische Publikum beklatschte seine eigene Erniedrigung und viele versuchten, dadurch ein Alibi für sich zu schaffen, daß sie in den Spott miteinstimmten. Auch jetzt, in diesen schweren Tagen, glauben manche sich durch Fahnenflucht oder Anschmeißerei retten zu können. Der „Völkische Beobachter" vom 2. April berichtet schmunzelnd, daß die Boykottleitung von jüdischen Geschäftsleuten überlaufen wurde, die für sich eine Ausnahmebehandlung wünschten. Viele, so behauptet der „V. B.", hätten sich schnell taufen lassen, um sagen zu können, sie seien Christen. Glücklicherweise geht selbst aus der Darstellung des „V. B." hervor, daß solche Fälle vereinzelt waren. Aber die Zeit des Druckes ist noch nicht vorüber, wir stehen am Anfang, und darum muß von dieser Gefahr die Rede sein.

Denn die Gefahr, die größte Gefahr, die dem Judentum droht, ist die einer Verderbnis und Verkrüppelung des Charakters. Die Nationalsozialisten erklären in ihren Reden und in ihren Kundgebungen, daß sie Charakterlosigkeit mehr verachten als alles. Dr. Goebbels hat sich in seiner Rede am Freitag über die Wandlung der „jüdischen Presse" lustig gemacht, die so schnell umgelernt habe, daß die Redakteure des „Angriff" vor Neid erblassen müßten.

Wenn der Nationalsozialismus diese Sachlage erkennt, dann müßte er sich als jüdischen Partner ein Judentum wünschen, das seine Ehre hoch hält.

Er dürfte nicht jüdische Charakterlosigkeit fördern, um sie dann brandmarken zu können. Er dürfte dem Juden, der sich offen als Jude bekennt und der nichts verbrochen hat, seine Ehre nicht bestreiten. Ob dem so ist, wird sich bald erweisen: Man hat jetzt eine Prozentnorm für gewisse Berufe angekündigt

Zionism in Germany
1897–1933

THE SHAPING OF
A JEWISH IDENTITY

Stephen M. Poppel

THE JEWISH PUBLICATION SOCIETY OF AMERICA
Philadelphia · *5737/1977*

Copyright © 1976 by
The Jewish Publication Society of America
All rights reserved
First edition
ISBN 0–8276–0085–2
Library of Congress catalog card number 76–14284
Manufactured in the United States of America

Designed by Adrianne Onderdonk Dudden

With the exception of the photograph of Robert Weltsch, which he graciously provided himself, all other photographs of Zionist leaders, groups, and activities are reproduced through the courtesy of the Central Zionist Archives, Jerusalem. The illustrations from *Der Schlemiel* and the *Jüdische Rundschau* are reproduced through the courtesy of the Leo Baeck Institute, New York.

Frontispiece: *Zionism in 1933.* "Bear it with pride, the yellow badge!" Lead article in the *Jüdische Rundschau,* written by Robert Weltsch, responding to the Nazi boycott of Jewish businesses on April 1, 1933.

To my parents

CONTENTS

Illustrations follow pages 62 and 110.

ACKNOWLEDGMENTS

It is with pleasure that I take this opportunity to acknowledge the help that I have received in the course of this study of German Zionism. For financial assistance at various stages I am grateful to the Danforth Foundation for a Kent Fellowship; to Harvard University for a Sheldon Fellowship; to the Committee on West European Studies of Harvard University; to the late Mr. Theodore Schocken; and to the Madge Miller Research Fund of Bryn Mawr College. For their gracious helpfulness I am indebted to the staffs of the Harvard University Library, especially to Dr. Charles Berlin and the staff of the Hebrew Division; the Central Zionist Archives in Jerusalem, especially to Dr. Michael Heyman; the Jewish National and University Library in Jerusalem; the Leo Baeck Institute; the Schocken Library (Jerusalem); and the Weizmann Archive (Rehovot). A special word of appreciation is due to those German Zionists, whose names I have listed in the Bibliography, who consented to grant personal interviews and to those who gave their permission to quote from private correspondence.

For their kind interest I wish to thank the many people who by their willingness to discuss my work have thereby contributed to it, as well as those who have read earlier versions of this study and offered their suggestions for improvements. The present volume originated as a doctoral dissertation written under the direction of Professor David S. Landes, whose stimulating criticisms were always helpful. Finally, I would like to acknowledge the invaluable encouragement and support that I have received from my parents, friends, and teachers. To them I offer this book as a token of thanks.

PREFACE

The primary focus of this work is the German Zionist movement between 1897 and 1933. I have excluded the broader subject of Zionism among the German-speaking Jewries of the Austrian Empire and its successor states, where the political and ideological contexts and the conceptions of nationality were quite different from those in Germany. As for the delimiting dates, the year 1897 saw the beginning of formally organized Zionist activity in Germany with the foundation of the German Zionist organization, the Zionistische Vereinigung für Deutschland (ZVfD), almost simultaneously with the meeting of the first international Zionist Congress. The close of the period is marked by the establishment of Nazi rule in 1933, which effectively brought an end to assimilationism as a viable strategy and made emigration increasingly a subject of concern for all German Jews. At this point Zionism became less a matter of abstract ideological commitment than a program for immediate action. The more than six thousand Jews who left Germany for Palestine in 1933 amounted to over three times the number who had emigrated in the previous two decades. One no longer had to be a Zionist to consider departure advisable.

I have concentrated on the effects of Zionism on the German Zionists themselves, rather than on their efforts in behalf of Zion. This is not to deny the importance of German Zionism for the world movement, either in terms of material or human resources: the German Zionist contribution to fund raising was considerable, and German Zionists figured prominently in executive and administrative positions within the movement. Similarly, the focus on the Zionists who remained in Germany until 1933 is not intended to minimize the significance of the small number who actually settled in Palestine, many of whom played an important role there.[1]

Singling out German Zionism for detailed study is also meant as a corrective to the general pattern of Zionist historiography, which treats the world movement as a whole, moving from country to country only as necessary to trace the developments that led to the creation of the Jewish state. The studies of separate national Zionist movements that do exist often concentrate on political and organizational developments, though Yonathan Shapiro's analysis of American Zionism provides an important parallel to the present work insofar as it considers Zionism's latent function as an "ideology of survival for the Jewish community of the United States." The German movement has been treated in general terms in a history written by Richard Lichtheim, one of its leading members.[2]

While German Zionism is a subject of interest in its own right, it also has broad implications for both Jewish and German history, with sociological and psychological aspects as well.

In the context of the Zionist movement as a whole, German

Zionism typifies many of the features generally evident in
Diaspora Zionism.[3] Like other Zionist movements in the
West, German Zionism was marked by the tension resulting
from the apparent contradiction between continued residence
in the Diaspora, and the assertion of Jewish national distinctiveness and the commitment to the creation of a Jewish state.
Indeed, after the commitment to emigration was stated explicitly, this dilemma was particularly acute for German Zionism.
Moreover, as a postassimilatory movement, German Zionism
represented a reaction against liberal assimilationist ideology
and its narrow conception of Jewish identity—a reaction that
developed especially after World War I, received considerable
impetus with the establishment of the state of Israel in 1948,
and has grown particularly strong in certain circles in our own
time. Finally, German Zionism's self-conscious confrontation
with Arab nationalism in Palestine produced an important line
of approach that is of interest from the viewpoint of both
history and present policy in the Middle East.

While from the vantage of Jewish history Zionism appears
as a nationalist version of Jewish identity, seen from the perspective of German history German Zionism offers an interesting comparative foil as a Jewish version of German nationalism.
This is true both in German Zionism's appropriation of the
concepts and external forms of *völkisch* nationalism and in its
rejection of the expansionist nationalism of chauvinistic patriotism. Furthermore, the analysis of German Zionism's evaluation of Jewry's objective situation in Germany inevitably
touches on matters of interest to the German historian, such
as the nature of German political ideology and conceptions of
German society.

Indeed, the subject of the Jews in Germany has attracted a
considerable amount of scholarly attention of late. This has

been particularly noticeable in treatments of the Weimar Republic, where questions have been raised, directly or by implication, about the existence of specific or identifiably Jewish attitudes and about a distinctively Jewish cultural or economic role.[4] The problem is a difficult one, especially to the extent that the activities of assimilated German Jews were not generally guided by any specific consciousness of their Jewishness. Here German Zionism offers the advantage of providing an explicit and even assertive formulation of Jewish identity, as well as a group of Jews who consciously espoused it. The study of German Zionism also provides the opportunity, too little exploited, of examining the Jews of Germany from within, as they regarded themselves, rather than merely as they figured in the thoughts and actions of others.

There is yet an additional comparative dimension to be found in the study of German Zionism: the movement provides an example of the more general phenomenon of minority-group nationalism. In their attempt to formulate their own identity in terms of a putative national distinctiveness, German Zionists have their counterparts in any number of similar subgroups, both in past and contemporary society. Even in their more complex use of a nationalist ideology to rationalize and maintain their continued existence within a dominant culture, German Zionists were not alone.

The student of German Zionism is inescapably confronted by a scarcity of documentation—at least of the kind necessary for a study such as this one, which focuses on inner attitudes rather than external events. The files of the German Zionist organization, the ZVfD, were confiscated by the Gestapo late in 1938 and were evidently destroyed by the Nazis near the end of the war. Although official in nature, these may have contained a record of internal debates on policy as well as the consideration of broader issues of Zionist ideology. A limited reconstruction of this material is possible by referring to the files of other Zionist offices, now preserved in the Central Zionist Archives in Jerusalem, but this is no substitute for the full record, arranged in its original order, that an intact archive of the ZVfD would have contained.

The flight of the German Zionists from Germany led to a scarcity of personal documentation as well. A number of private archives have been preserved, generally those transferred from Germany to Palestine before 1933, but the valuable material these contain, such as diaries and personal reflective and introspective correspondence, make one all the more painfully aware of what is missing. Fortunately, a few prominent figures in the movement have produced written memoirs, though to the extent that these are retrospective they lose some of the vividness—and accuracy—that contemporary records would have provided. Interviews with surviving Zionists are also useful, but suffer some of the same shortcomings as memoirs.

In this situation periodicals and pamphlets, of which there are many, take on a special importance. Nevertheless, these present difficulties of their own. To the extent that they were intended for public consumption, they provide only limited access to the internal workings and deliberations of the movement and the individuals behind them. Moreover, the possible range of theoretical positions within German Zionism was not so broad that it could be expounded and argued for almost four decades without the debate becoming monumentally repetitious. The same holds for the polemic with assimilationism. Indeed, this was recognized by the unintentionally humorous remarks in the prospectus for the 1914 volume of the German

Zionist newspaper, the *Jüdische Rundschau*, which asserted that while

it is the ambition and pride of many newspapers to be varied and not repetitious, we regard it to be our most important task to say *the same thing over and over again*. For eighteen years we have been saying the same thing. We have been tirelessly repeating the same truths— which nevertheless have been recognized by only a minority of German Jews as the truths that they are—and we will not slacken in the future.[5]

Despite all these problems of documentation, the material that exists provides ample basis for presenting this study with confidence in the accuracy of its conclusions.

Zionism in Germany, 1897–1933

feld, the president of the German Zionist organization during the last decade of the Weimar Republic, to characterize Zionism as a "postassimilatory" phenomenon, a description that was as accurate when applied to Zionism in general as it was for the German movement itself. Indeed, to appreciate fully the historical significance of Zionism, it is necessary to turn back to the period before assimilation, before the modern problem of Jewish identity had emerged as an issue at all.

The Jewish Question in the Modern Period

The oustanding feature of the premodern Jewish community was its autonomy—in terms of law, culture, and values. Within the structure of medieval society the Jews had been established as a corporate group—much like the burghers of a town or the members of a guild. While the community depended for its existence on a charter or privileges granted either by the crown or a lesser lord, it enjoyed considerable freedom in the regulation of its internal affairs. To speak of the Jews in this period as a nation in a modern sense may be anachronistic, since Jewry was defined primarily by its adherence to Jewish law and, in Christian eyes, by its continued nonrecognition of Jesus as the Messiah. (Indeed, one clear indication of the essentially religious nature of this definition was the fact that conversation to Christianity was by itself sufficient to secure full acceptance into the dominant group.) Nevertheless, the restrictions prescribed by both Jewish and Christian religious law, which limited social intercourse between the two communities, had the effect of reinforcing the existence of an identifiable Jewish group, characterized by highly distinctive features of language, culture, and even occupational distribution. Furthermore, Jewishness involved a comprehensive identity which, as was typical of premodern consciousness generally, did not yet differentiate sharply between the religious and the secular. These facts, plus the memory of Jewish political independence in the biblical commonwealths and the expectation of its eventual messianic restoration, made the reality of a collective Jewish identity seem self-evident to members of the traditional community.[1]

The objective, visible existence of a Jewish group was one thing, but the subjective attitude of Jews toward their collective identity was quite another. The situation of the Jewish community, though "privileged" in a legal sense, was in reality far from favorable—the result of church doctrine that prescribed an abased condition for the Jews in witness of their rejection of Christ and supposed rejection by God. The potentially degrading—and proselytic—force of this policy was effectively blunted by the Jews' own sense of election and immediacy to God. Their confidence of their own place in the divine scheme of human history bred a corresponding certainty in the face of persecution and suffering. The Jews may have been oppressed, but they were never in their own eyes a pariah people. Thus traditional Jewish identity was self-assured at the same time that it was comprehensive.[2]

Medieval Jewish autonomy, therefore, was the product of forces both outside and within the Jewish community: a social and legal framework that fostered it and a subjective will on the part of the Jews to preserve their own identity. Its dissolution was the predictable consequence of the erosion of these two foundations. One general explanation for this collapse, viewed in terms of intellectual factors, can be found in the rise of religious toleration in Western Europe beginning in the late seventeenth century.[3] This may in turn be traced to the development of an attitude that is probably the surest basis for religious toleration—namely, religious indifference, an attitude that slowly but increasingly took hold among both Christians and Jews.

Another set of causes, more specifically political in nature, has been identified by the historian Salo Baron as the attack by the modernizing nation-state on the remnants of medieval society—specifically on the existence of corporate bodies that mediated between the state and the individual.[4] In the course of this attack it was necessary to eliminate Jewish communal autonomy as well, with what Baron suggests was a considerable loss for Jewry and against some Jewish opposition.

For the eighteenth century, Baron's theory of Jewish emancipation is best illustrated by the example that seems to have inspired it, the National Assembly's emancipation of the Jews in revolutionary France. There may be grounds for questioning this thesis, however, since despite any putative necessity for emancipation and despite the promise of the Declaration of the Rights of Man in August 1789 that "no one may be disturbed for his opinions, even in religion," the National Assembly was able to delay until January 1790 the emancipation of the acculturated Sephardic Jews of southern France and Paris, and that of the more traditional Ashkenazic Jews of Alsace until September 1791. Moreover, the attitude of the Enlightenment toward the Jews, as exemplified by the apparent anti-Semitism of Voltaire, was ambiguous; and Napoleon's imposition of certain restrictions on French Jewry for the decade beginning in 1808 presents additional difficulties for Baron's thesis.[5] In terms of the rhetoric of emancipation, however, Baron's thesis is amply substantiated by the celebrated declaration of the delegate Clermont-Tonnerre that "to the Jews as a nation everything must be refused; as individuals, everything must be given to them. They must be citizens. . . . There cannot be a nation within a nation."⁶

With regard to political modernization, eighteenth-century Germany presented a picture altogether different from France. On the map Germany appeared as a patchwork quilt of over three hundred sovereignties of vastly varying size, first consolidated only under the force of Napoleonic occupation. While the modes of government in these separate states varied, one important pattern was typified by the enlightened despotism of Prussia's Frederick the Great (1740–86). As for the Jews, their situation continued to be regulated by special legislation whose focus was, as it had been in medieval times, concern about their usefulness to the state, rather than any abstract human rights such as had been articulated in France.

In the realm of political theory, however, a current for change was becoming evident among the writers of the *Aufklärung,* the German Enlightenment. Foremost was Gotthold Ephraim Lessing, whose play *The Jews* (1749) reflected a new regard for the Jew based on principles of enlightened, universalist humanitarianism. Indeed, Lessing's intellectual comradeship and personal friendship with the Jewish philosopher Moses Mendelssohn appeared to symbolize the hope that Jew and Christian might meet as equals, unhampered by religious differences. The play *Nathan the Wise* (1779), Lessing's tribute to Mendelssohn, presented a parable of religious toleration in which Christianity, Judaism, and Islam are all recognized as sharing equally in the same eternal truths. "Are Christian and Jew sooner Christian and Jew than men?" Nathan asked, confident of a negative reply. Full of optimism, Mendelssohn counseled his fellow Jews only to "love, and you will be loved."⁷

In the light of the disappointments of later centuries, it is fair to point out a certain ambivalence toward the Jews already evident in Lessing's attitude. The protagonist of *The Jews* is extolled with the praise, "O how worthy of esteem the Jews would be if they were all like you."[8] The fact is, however, that not all Jews shared the exemplary virtues of a Mendelssohn; their acceptance by the Christian world would remain correspondingly problematic. Even in *Nathan the Wise* Lessing managed to blunt his moral—religious toleration—by a convenient revelation of mistaken identities in which the templar and the sultan, as well as the Jew's adopted daughter, are discovered to be long-lost relatives.

Nevertheless, the potential significance of the *Aufklärung*'s new sympathy for the Jews was enormous, for it was now theoretically possible for the Jews to find a place in society that was not primarily determined by their religion. To be sure, the question of what place this would be remained. Whereas during the Middle Ages physical survival had been the problem for the Jews, now the challenge was to maintain their own identity in a society founded on altogether new principles.

This problem, the "Jewish question" in its modern form, was of particular concern to the men of the Jewish enlightenment, known as the Haskalah. Its adherents (maskilim) were members of a small but important Jewish bourgeoisie that had begun to emerge in Germany around the middle of the eighteenth century. Indeed, by the 1770s and 1780s the Haskalah had taken on a fairly definite shape, centered in Berlin and Königsberg, with Moses Mendelssohn as its mentor, and *Hameassef*—the first successful modern Hebrew periodical—as its journal.

For these worldly Jews of the Haskalah, intercourse with the Christian world was a daily experience, and they strove to formulate an ideology that would comprehend and generalize their own experience. This involved nothing less than a complete redefinition of Jewish identity. Gone was an earlier comprehensive Jewishness; Judaism would now be limited to the realm of religion, eliminating any national dimension and leaving the maskilim free to enter a religiously neutral society whose supposed foundation was universal humanism, where religious differences were regarded as secondary and residual.

Meanwhile, the maskilim altered their conception of the Jewish religion itself, laying stress on the universal truths of ethical monotheism and eliminating or avoiding embarrassing notions of Jewish election and particularism. When pressed to justify the continued existence of Jewish religion, which presumably shared its essence with Christianity, Mendelssohn replied by distinguishing between a kernel of universalism and a husk of specific Jewish observances, ordained by God and therefore binding on Jewry. But by making the distinction, he opened the way for later religious reformers to attempt to preserve the kernel without the husk.

These theological changes were accompanied by a movement for social reform, as the maskilim, acting as carriers of modernization, sought to bring the bulk of German Jewry to the stage that they themselves had reached. The focus here was on educational reform, with the Free School established in Berlin in 1778 serving as a pilot project for the education of the new Jew. Emphasis was placed on practical, secular subjects, and important changes were made in the traditional religious core of the curriculum. Whereas in the past students had been expected to absorb Judaism by immersion in its classical texts, especially the Talmud, they now learned about Judaism from a certain remove, concentrating more on the Hebrew Bible, with its universal aspect as the Old Testament of Christianity, than on the Talmud.

The theory behind these reforms was articulated by the

maskil Naphtali Herz Wessely, who by 1782 declared outright that secular studies were to be given precedence over religious ones. Symbolic of this change was Mendelssohn's translation of the Torah into High German, transliterated into Hebrew characters, with the intention not of making the text accessible —there were already adequate Yiddish translations—but of fostering the knowledge of German among the Jews and eliminating their need to rely on these Yiddish versions. In condemning this translation Rabbi Ezekiel Landau of Prague accurately protested that the maskilim had completely inverted the accepted order of things, by making the Torah a handmaiden to serve secular learning.[9] (It is only one indication of the breakdown of traditional rabbinic authority that such a condemnation carried little of its former weight.)

The Haskalah's emphasis on practical education stemmed partly from its concern with the economic situation of German Jewry. Centuries of Christian restriction and oppression had left the Jews concentrated in petty trade or, worse still, in a state of poverty where begging was the only livelihood. Clearly, vocational reform was a prerequisite for any social integration of the kind that the maskilim believed they themselves had achieved; the question remained of how to proceed with an overall plan for integration. It was regarded as an expression of extraordinary sympathy and understanding for the Jewish plight when Christian Wilhelm von Dohm, writing at Mendelssohn's suggestion, admitted in his treatise *On the Civil Improvement of the Jews* (1781) that past Christian treatment was responsible for the present situation of the Jews and urged that they be relieved of legal and economic restrictions. To be sure, Dohm expected this reform to be justified retroactively by the energetic Jewish efforts at self-improvement that would follow. But he was at least willing to argue for the prior liberation of the Jews, in contrast to those who held that Jewish self-reform would have to precede any improvement in their political situation.[10]

Thus to the question of how the Jews could survive *as Jews* in the modern world, the maskilim had responded with a program of cultural and social reform that would secure their acceptance while retaining some measure of Jewishness. That contemporary German society was as open to their aspirations as they believed seems doubtful. The neutral society of the Berlin salons apparently was more a rarefied construct than a reality of sufficient scale to support Jewish integration into broader society. As limited as actual social integration may have been, however, the effects of the Haskalah's reforms on Jewish identity were enormous, for they not only reshaped the nature of Jewish self-conception, but also marked a vast alteration in Jewish self-regard. No longer was Jewishness the comprehensive affair that it had been in the past; now it was a limited matter of religion only—a religion that could be further modified without any necessary reference to traditional constraints. Judaism was shorn of its national dimension, and its particularisms were discarded in favor of universals that would be shared, it was hoped, by Jews and Christians alike. More important, the entire value orientation of the maskilim had shifted from traditional Judaism to the modern world around them, which was partly secular but ultimately Christian in its outlook. Thus these Jews ended by internalizing values long regarded as alien, as well as a generally negative evaluation of Judaism. Gone were the autonomy and self-assurance of the past. Now the goal was social integration rather than loyalty to tradition, and for this a large measure of adaptation was accepted as a necessary precondition. It is at this point in Jewish history, at the dawn of the modern period, that the Jew's self-image became conditioned by how he appeared to others and the characteristically modern attitudes of self-denial and self-disdain appeared. In short, this period is marked by the emergence of the problem of Jewish identity.[11]

Emancipation, Assimilation, and Zionism

The Haskalah's program for integration was based on an ideology of assimilationism, which assumed that Jewish integration would be brought by the Jews' success at acculturation, that is, by their assimilation of the culture and behavior patterns of the surrounding society. The integration sought was of several kinds—social, economic, and political—and it was expected that if all were not attained at once, they would still come in fairly close order.

Although the term "emancipation," which gained general currency in connection with Jewish affairs only in the 1830s, was sometimes loosely used to refer to all these different varieties of integration, properly speaking it is best reserved for describing the legal and political aspects of enfranchisement and citizenship. German Jews commonly spoke of acculturation as "assimilation," a usage that will be followed here, although some caution is necessary. In the first place, the term has acquired (partly as a result of later Zionist polemics) an unwarranted negative connotation implying that assimilation is akin to the complete abandonment of Jewishness, even to the point of religious conversion. But the departure from the Jewish community by many German Jews really marked a rejection of one of the major premises of assimilationism, which sought the integration of Jews *as Jews* and held that acculturation short of the total abrogation of Jewish identity would be sufficient for this end. In the second place, "assimilation" has been used to refer equally to both integration and acculturation, that is, to both the assimilation *of* the Jews by their surrounding society and the assimilation of the cultural milieu *by* the Jews. Besides being confusing, this double usage masks an important distinction—namely, that while acculturation was entirely dependent on Jewish efforts, integration was determined by the receptivity of the dominant society. Despite the hopes of the assimilationists, these two processes were not necessarily linked. Indeed, by the end of the nineteenth century it was precisely on this point that Zionism diverged from assimilationism, drawing as the lesson of modern Jewish history that emancipation had not been permanently secured and that it could not be.[12]

The question of whether Jewish efforts could influence Christian attitudes was one of the main themes of German Jewish history. To some extent this reflected the nature of Jewish emancipation in Germany, which was not the product of a relatively abrupt fiat, as in France, but instead became the subject of a protracted debate and was achieved only after a number of false starts. The contrast with France was mostly the result of the relatively halting progress of political modernization in Germany, which lacked any impulse as decisive as the French Revolution.[13]

To cite the example of Prussia, ultimately the home of the bulk of German Jewry: throughout the eighteenth century, Jews were admitted to residence only to the extent that they were of use to the state, and even then they were subject to harsh restrictions designed to limit population. In general Jews were forbidden to enter any occupation where they would compete with Christians and were directed to activities that bolstered Frederick the Great's programs for the economic

development of Prussia. Typically they were active in manufac-
turing, as well as minting and banking. Jewish proposals for an
improvement in their situation after the death of Frederick in
1786 were unsuccessful, and it was not until the general movement for reform that was launched in Prussia after its defeat
by Napoleon in 1806 that decisive action was forthcoming. By
an edict of 11 March 1812 the Jews of Prussia were eman-
cipated: they were granted all the rights and obligations of
citizenship, as well as free access to all occupations—except
military and public office. Unfortunately, much of this improvement was as short-lived as the defeat-induced reform
movement that had inspired it. With the final victory over
Napoleon in 1815 a wave of reaction swept through the German states, and the Jews found themselves effectively reduced
to their previous situation, at least as far as political rights were
concerned. Perhaps the most lasting result of the emancipation
of 1812 was the provision for the free choice of occupation,
which set the stage for strenuous efforts by reform-minded
bureaucrats to move the Jews into more diverse and productive
sectors of the economy than they had previously occupied.

A second brief episode of emancipation, under liberal auspices, came with the revolution of 1848, but this too was
undone in the ensuing period of political reaction. Indeed, it
was not until 1869, after Bismarck's forcible establishment of
the North German Confederation, that the Jews of these
states, including Prussia, were accorded civil rights. These
provisions were thereafter extended to all of Germany with the
foundation of the unified Reich in 1871. Despite this formal
emancipation, considerable restraints remained in effect that
blocked Jewish social advancement, such as the unattainability
of a prized reserve-officer's commission, the foreclosure of the
higher ranks of the civil service, and the near impossibility of

a Jew's winning a university professorship. Nevertheless, these irksome restrictions, though significant in a status-conscious society where the very positions denied the Jews were the most prestigious, were not unbearable; and they left open the careers in business and the professions that many Jews pursued. The Weimar constitution of 1919 confirmed both freedom of religion and the absolute separation of political citizenship from religious belief, and inaugurated a period when in practice Jews enjoyed a fuller degree of freedom than ever before. But this period also saw the emergence of the political and racial anti-Semitism that later, during the Nazi regime, would bring Jewish citizenship in Germany to an end with the Nuremberg Laws of 1935.[14]

It is of considerable significance that while the Emancipation Edict of 1812 dealt specifically with "the civil conditions of the Jews," every emancipation thereafter, whether long- or short-lived, came as the result of general provisions that separated civil rights from religion. That is, beginning with 1848 the situation of the Jews was essentially linked to the development of a modern, secular state, rather than being the subject of special legislation. In this sense the civil emancipation of the Jews came only with the general emancipation of society and politics from their premodern constraints. Indeed, the nature of Jewish emancipation seemed to confirm the strategy of assimilationism, which held that the Jew could find a place in a secular polity even while retaining his religious identity. It was this principle that shaped the Jew's conception of both himself and his religion throughout the modern period. Indeed, this is the ideology that has prevailed throughout the West, wherever Jewish communities have developed in modern, liberal states characterized by tolerance and religious pluralism. German Jews summed up the matter neatly in the phrase "German citizens of the Jewish faith," which so accurately described their self-conception that they incorporated it whole in the title of the organization that eventually embraced the great majority of German Jewry: the Centralverein deutscher Staatsbürger jüdischen Glaubens.[15]

Despite the eventual achievement of emancipation, the progress toward that goal had not been smooth, and while anti-Semitism persisted, integration could not be regarded as complete. At the same time that the supposed relation between assimilation and emancipation had provided a hopeful Jewry with a clear agenda, it also created a large potential for frustration and anxiety; for it implied that the Jews had it in their own power to influence the course of events. As long as the results they desired were not forthcoming, they could imagine that ever more strenuous efforts would hasten progress. This line of thought had been especially encouraged during the period before emancipation, when Christian writers stressed that Jews must deserve emancipation before it could be granted to them. The fact that emancipation ultimately depended on general political developments, not on Jewish merit, did not alter either their perception of the matter or the Jews'.

Even after formal, legal emancipation was established, other barriers remained. Thus there was every temptation for the Jews to continue trying to woo favor in Christian society, with the hope of winning acceptance. But the role of the suitor is not always dignified, and the assimilationists could find themselves in a position that struck some observers, particularly the Zionists, as unworthy and fawning. Indeed, for many of its adherents, Zionism was as much a movement for the restoration of their pride as Jews as for the reconstitution of Jewish nationality.

Although the hope for the messianic return of the Jews to Zion had been a main current in Jewish thought since the Exile, appearing as a central theme in the liturgy with which every Jew was familiar, it was not until the end of the nineteenth century that the modern Zionist movement took real form. Beginning in the middle of that century a number of important statements indicating a Zionist approach to the Jewish question appeared, drawn up by writers as different as the rabbis Yehudah Alkalai and Hirsch Kalischer and the socialist Moses Hess; but it took the Russian pogroms of 1881 to spark organized emigration from Europe to Palestine. These emigrants, Hovevei Zion (Lovers of Zion), contrasted sharply with earlier Jewish wanderers to the Holy Land, who had been motivated generally by traditional piety and depended largely on charity for support. The new settlers aimed rather at an economically viable and independent existence, and established the first modern and lasting Jewish agricultural settlements at such places as Zichron Yaakov, Rosh Pinna, and Petah Tikva. A central directing committee, established at a conference in Kattowitz in Upper Silesia in 1884, failed, however, to mobilize effective support for these new undertakings, which came to rely on subventions on a grand scale, particularly those of the Baron Edmond de Rothschild.[16]

Thus the movement was somewhat in disarray when it was dramatically galvanized by the appearance in 1896 of a pamphlet, *The Jewish State*, written by the Viennese journalist Theodor Herzl. Zionist folklore has it that Herzl was converted to Zionism when, as a reporter in Paris for the Vienna paper *Neue Freie Presse*, he witnessed the trial and degradation of the Jewish captain Alfred Dreyfus and the accompanying anti-Semitic bayings of the Paris mob, in what had been the first home of Jewish emancipation. Stunned by the apparent collapse of the assimilationist dream, we are told, Herzl penned his Zionist manifesto.

The factors that brought Herzl to Zionism were almost certainly more complex and deeper than myth would have it, going back both to his experience of anti-Semitism in Vienna and to psychological aspects of his personality.[17] But it is true that *The Jewish State* proclaimed what would become the classic Zionist analysis of the Jewish problem—whose major premise was the impossibility of assimilation:

The world echoes with cries against the Jews. . . . The Jewish question persists; it would be foolish to deny it. It is a vestige of the Middle Ages of which modern nations cannot rid themselves even with the best of intentions. . . . The Jewish question persists wherever there are an appreciable number of Jews. Where it is absent, it will be introduced by immigrants. Naturally we go where we are not persecuted, but our appearance brings persecution. That is true, and must remain true, everywhere, even in the most modern countries— witness France—as long as the Jewish question is not solved politically.

A political solution could be achieved only by recognizing that the Jewish question was a matter of nationality, not of religion. "We are a people," Herzl insisted, *"one* people," and he concluded that only by building their own state could the Jews determine their future with dignity, as equals in the community of nations.[18] Assimilationists might point to apparent progress in the West, but Zionists fixed on the failure of emancipation—both its failure to occur at all in Eastern Europe and its failure to bring full integration or to eliminate anti-Semitism in the West. In its repudiation of the whole strategy predicated on successful emancipation as the basis for Jewish existence, Zionism was indeed, as Blumenfeld had said, a postassimilatory phenomenon.

It was one thing to call for Jewish national and political restoration, but it was quite another to bring it about. To this task Herzl now turned, with the intention of establishing an internationally guaranteed chartered land company that would direct the orderly acquisition of land and the settlement of Jews in Palestine. The first step, however, was to organize the Jews themselves, and for this Herzl conceived of the grand gesture of an international congress of Jews. When he convened the first Zionist Congress in Basel in August 1897, the air was full of hope and expectation—but also of realism. Progress would have to be gradual and orderly if it was to be secure. Mass immigration to Palestine would have to await the necessary political arrangements, and so for the immediate future most Zionists would remain where they were. In the meanwhile, Zionism itself would provide a kind of spiritual abode for those who shared the newly restored sense of national identity that it offered. "Zionism," Herzl proclaimed, "is our return to Judaism even before our return to Zion."[19]

Nationalism and Identity

In the world at large—both Jewish and Christian—Herzl's enthusiastic message was generally greeted with indifference or hostility. Herzl had planned on gradual development, but he must have hoped for faster progress than was in fact achieved. When he died in 1904, at the age of only forty-four, the Zionist movement was still embryonic. Indeed, the realization of Herzl's plan for a charter would come only with the Balfour Declaration in 1917 and the League of Nations' subsequent establishment of the British Mandate for Palestine, with its provisions for Jewish settlement. Even after the way had been formally cleared for Zionist immigration, Zionists in the West tended to remain where they were, partly out of inertia, partly in recognition of serious practical impediments to settlement in Palestine. What was particularly remarkable in the case of the German Zionists was their continued reluctance to take action even in the wake of the so-called Posen Resolution, adopted in 1912, which required them to include emigration in their "life program." This raises all the more sharply the question of exactly what Zionism meant to its adherents who remained in the Diaspora.

2

TWO ZIONS

The success of the first Zionist Congress was as much a product of the separate Zionist efforts that it galvanized as it was a tribute to the organizing genius of Theodor Herzl, its convener. Herzl's grand gesture of creating a deliberative body to act as the representative of the Jewish people in its striving for national restoration has been justly recognized in his designation as the founder of modern political Zionism. But Herzl might have been just another pamphleteer calling for the return of the Jews to Zion if he had not been able to draw on already-existing currents of Zionist thought and action.

By the time the first Zionist Congress met in Basel at the end of August 1897, a Zionist organization, the National-jüdische Vereinigung, had already been established in Germany. This "National-Jewish Association," founded by Cologne lawyer Max Bodenheimer and ten others at a meeting in the wine-growing Rhine town of Bingen on 11 July 1897, represented the culmination of several years of Zionist efforts in Germany. Six years earlier, just a decade after the outbreak of widespread pogroms in Russia, Bodenheimer had published his first Zionist tract, *Wohin mit den russischen Juden?* To his question, "Whither with the Russian Jews?," Bodenheimer responded with the philanthropic version of Zionism that he would continue to advocate: oppressed Russian Jewry would find refuge in the land of the biblical Zion. Toward this end, in 1893 Bodenheimer founded the Association for the Promotion of Agriculture and Handicraft in Palestine, along with David Wolffsohn, a Lithuanian timber merchant living in Cologne whom Bodenheimer had met at the local Society for Jewish History and Literature, itself another one of Bodenheimer's creations. (Wolffsohn later succeeded Herzl as the head of the World Zionist Organization, though he proved to be somewhat lacking in Herzl's political adroitness.)

Bodenheimer had been unaware of Herzl until 1895, when in an attempt to broaden his Zionist connections, Bodenheimer made contact with the head of the London Friends of Zion, Colonel Albert Goldsmid, who brought Herzl to Bodenheimer's attention. The appearance of Herzl's *Jewish State* the next year moved Bodenheimer to write to the author in June 1896, thereby initiating an association that developed into a long-standing and close collaboration for the Zionist cause. The National-jüdische Vereinigung met for the second time in August 1897, during the Zionist Congress in Basel, and at its next meeting, at Frankfort on the Main in October of that year, it formally renamed itself the Zionistische Vereinigung für Deutschland (German Zionist Federation; hereafter ZVfD).[1]

A second important current of Zionist activity in Germany during these same years involved a relatively small number of Jewish university students in Berlin. The possibility of organizing separate Jewish fraternities in response to student anti-Semitism had been demonstrated in 1882 by the founding of Kadimah (Forward), the first Jewish nationalist student organization, in Vienna. The first steps in this direction were not taken in Germany until 1886, with the creation of a Jewish fraternity in Breslau. This group, the Viadrina, which was basically committed to assimilationism, was joined during the next ten years by like-minded Jewish fraternities from Heidelberg, Berlin, and Munich to form the Kartell-Convent in 1896. Fraternities oriented specifically toward Jewish nationalism had been somewhat slower to appear in Germany. A beginning had been made in Berlin with the founding of a group called Jung Israel–National-jüdischer Verein (Young Israel–Jewish National Association) by Heinrich Loewe in 1892. Loewe, one of the more energetic of the early Zionists, had been involved in one way or another with just about every Zionist undertaking in Germany around the turn of the century. By setting up a Palestine pavilion at the 1896 Berlin trade fair, shortly after his own return from a visit to Palestine, he had garnered a good deal of publicity for Jewish settlement there. Loewe had also been the only German-born member of an association of Russian Jewish students in Berlin, the Russisch-jüdischer wissenschaftlicher Verein, an experience that had doubtless encouraged him to establish the parallel Jung Israel fraternity for German Jewish students. Later Loewe served as the first editor of the ZVfD's official organ, the *Jüdische Rundschau.*[2]

A further step toward establishing Jewish fraternities was taken in 1893 by Bodenheimer's organizing a neutral-sounding Jüdische Humanitätsgesellschaft (Jewish Society for Humanitarianism). The group's first action was to form a political coalition with Jung Israel against the anti-Semitic Verein deutscher Studenten (Association of German Students) to compete in the elections for officers of the Berlin Academic Reading Room (Akademische Lesehalle), an informal student representative body. The Jewish coalition was joined by another ideologically neutral group, the Freie wissenschaftliche Vereinigung (Free Scientific Organization), which had been founded in 1882 as a "parity" or "free" fraternity. Indeed, anti-Semitism in German student life is eloquently attested to by the fate of such associations, which were theoretically open equally to Jews and Christians, but in practice were generally abandoned by even liberal Christians and came to include primarily Jews and baptized Jews only.

Against the background of these struggles between Jews and anti-Semites the decision was taken to create a major Jewish fraternity to counter the Verein deutscher Studenten. This was achieved in 1895 with the founding of the Jewish Students Association (Vereinigung jüdischer Studierender, renamed Verein jüdischer Studenten in 1900). This fraternity combined the membership of Jung Israel and the Humanitätsgesellschaft. The founding of the VJSt (although it had not yet taken the openly Zionist stance it would later adopt) represented an ideological commitment insofar as it constituted a rejection of the already-existing Jewish fraternity in Berlin, the assimilationist Sprevia. Nevertheless, it did share with all the other newly established Jewish fraternities the reluctant realization that anti-Semitism in Germany, particularly in the universities, had reached the point where the separate assertion of Jews as Jews had become necessary as a countermeasure.[3]

The tension in this situation is evident in the entries from these years in the diary of Adolf Friedemann, a leading figure in the early student Zionist movement and later in the ZVfD. This record of Friedemann's student life in Berlin is an exceptional document of introspective reflection about the significance of Zionism. Friedemann's analysis of the Jewish situation in Europe and his prescription for a Zionist solution bear a striking resemblance to the better-known Zionist vision presented in Herzl's diaries. Indeed, it is remarkable that the two accounts are so alike, both in tone and substance, and that the plight of European Jewry could independently evoke two such similar responses.[4]

In January 1894 Friedemann noted that when Bodenheimer had approached him the previous September to enlist him for a Jewish dueling fraternity *(schlagende Verbindung)*, he had declined because "almost all the Berlin free associations accept Jews," and he saw no need for a special group. Despite his reluctance to support an exclusively Jewish fraternity, Friedemann had assisted, as first vice-president, in organizing Bodenheimer's Humanitätsgesellschaft, which had the wholly acceptable goal of countering anti-Semitism and the safely altruistic purpose of "settling poor Jews in Palestine." The breaking point for Friedemann came in February 1894, when a blatant case of anti-Semitic discrimination in the rejection of a prospective Jewish member provoked him to resign from his fraternity. Two months later he reflected that "honor alone binds me to my people. What a career I could have if I allowed myself to be converted. So," he concluded, "I am an outsider." In June 1895 Friedemann took the final step by joining in establishing the Association of Jewish Students.[5]

The persistence throughout Europe of precisely the sort of anti-Semitism that Friedemann faced in Germany provided the point of departure for Zionist theory. A century after the French Revolution, over eighty years after the first abortive emancipation of the Jews in Germany, long after the Jews had abandoned the distinctive ways that had separated them from the general populace, the Jewish question remained unsolved.

Ultimately relief could be had, Zionists argued, only through Zionism's national approach and national solution. In the words of the Basel Program, adopted at the first Zionist Congress, Zionism sought "to create for the Jewish people a homeland in Palestine secured by public law." Jews who either "could not or would not assimilate" where they dwelled could find a home here. Over a year before the Zionist Congress, Bodenheimer had already presented a similar analysis with similar conclusions in the Theses that he had drafted for his newly created National-jüdische Vereinigung; these reappeared in the specific formulations of the Basel Program. Bodenheimer wrote that

the civil emancipation of the Jews within the other nations has not sufficed, as history shows, to assure the social and cultural future of the Jewish people. Therefore the final resolution of the Jewish question can consist only in the creation of a Jewish state; for only such a state will be in the position to represent the Jews as such in international law, as well as to receive those Jews who cannot or will not remain in their homeland. The natural focus for this state, to be created by legal means, is the historically consecrated soil of Palestine.[6]

Bodenheimer's concern with cultural renewal as well as with physical refuge was significant, since the Zionists of Western Europe found themselves in a situation very different from that of East European Jewry—Zionism's theory about the universality of the Jewish plight notwithstanding.

The Jews of Eastern Europe, still largely unemancipated, faced an immediate problem of physical survival against oppression and attacks, of which the Russian pogroms were only the most dramatic examples. Though some Zionists railed against the view generally held by Western Zionists, that Zionism was a transport venture to move East European Jews to safety, the truth was that (at least during the early years) German Zionists' efforts to foster emigration to Palestine were exerted largely in behalf of their less fortunate brethren to the East. As Adolf Friedemann put it in a ZVfD information brochure from 1903, "West Europeans will mainly provide the organizers for colonization," and he admitted that "naturally we are not about to initiate a mass emigration of German, French, [and] English Jews. We well know that only a small percentage will go."[7] This philanthropic version of Zionism was humorously, and accurately, characterized as a third-person affair: one man collected money from a second in order to send a third to Palestine.

Nevertheless, such charitable labor could be more meaningful to those undertaking it than might at first appear. It was not empty rhetoric when the official *Program of Zionism* asserted that Zionism was no mere "export enterprise for the consignment of masses of Jews, but rather the attempt to revivify the Jewish people." For behind the whole effort was a newfound identification between East and West European Jews, a common identity in their shared membership in a Jewish *Volk*. Ultimately, Friedemann claimed, the psychological benefit of Zionist philanthropic activity could be immense:

Zionism gives the Jew from the West [a sense of] his own dignity. . . . By reference to history and to a sense of race, it teaches him to discover a firm basis on which he can construct an integrated personality. . . . It shows how he can raise himself up and benefit himself by working for others less fortunate. It teaches him to feel himself to be at one with a totality that is akin to him in history, thought, and feeling. *Zionism reconciles us with ourselves.*[8]

Friedemann's emphasis on the psychological advantages of Zionism actually reflected the distinctive concerns of German Jewry. German Zionists had described the stark poverty and physical jeopardy of Jews living under czarist rule as a *materielle Judennot*, a material distress. German Jews by contrast, while enjoying relative material comfort and security, were faced with what the Zionists dubbed *geistige Judennot*, the spiritual, intellectual, and emotional distress of Jews who had abandoned their own culture and values—without, however, finding acceptance in German society. An early Zionist pamphlet recalled:

German Jews have been exhorted to assimilate so that things would go better. We have done so. We have assimilated up to the nose. We have aped all the manners and customs of the gentiles without asking what they are worth. We have denigrated our own customs and neglected our own culture.

But the effort had been in vain. What good had it done? "In the eyes of the gentiles we are still *Jews*, not believers in the Jewish religion, but children of a different nation. We have not held back from the brotherhood of nations, but *they* have never accepted us as fully belonging." Meanwhile, the rejection of Jewish advances had brought the sting of love unrequited. "We have wooed for the favor of the Aryan peoples long enough. . . . But the lady is coy, and the more one submits, the less it pleases her." What was worse, in courting German favor the Jews had stripped themselves of the very tradition and values that might have comforted them in their rejection. In this regard, Friedemann realized, the ghetto Jew had an advantage: "People no longer put us to the torch, but we no longer have the consolations of our fathers. The whole world is our ghetto." An early broadside lamented: "We have renounced our own individuality without realizing that we had thereby destroyed what was best within us."9

Zionism offered German Jewry refuge from this spiritual distress in the form of a spiritual Zion and an inner certainty that would protect the Jews against external abuse. In the new world of Zionism, Jews

once more know why they are Jews. They once again have hope for a Jewish future. They react with forceful pride against hostility from without. They implant in the hearts of their children an ideal that will preserve the coming generations from thoughtless mockery and shallow superficiality. . . . The pride of their own character gives them the strength to fight with vigor and dignity for their civil rights and against anti-Semitic attacks. . . . The moral conception of the Zionist program is to lead the Jews out of their spiritual distress . . . thereby restoring unity to the disintegrated Jewish soul.10

As Bodenheimer put it, there actually were two Zions—"the physical Zion for our starving brethren in the East" and "the spiritual Zion for the West European Jews who are enslaved within."11

To all this talk of spiritual distress there was, of course, an assimilationist rejoinder that reasserted its own ideology and denied the very existence of the problem that Zionism purported to solve. In truth, the bulk of German Jewry still held to the implied terms of emancipation, which demanded as the price for political integration what the director of the Central-verein, Ludwig Holländer, later frankly admitted was the abandonment of Jewish nationality and the transformation of Judaism into "a pure religious confession." Though integration on all levels was still incomplete, this was regarded as a transient difficulty, just as anti-Semitic residues were regarded as insignificant lapses from a supposedly prevailing liberalism.

Moreover, the Zionist sense of rebuff was by no means universally shared. Most German Jews either felt that they had secured the degree of acceptance that they sought, or expected to do so in good time. Even views on religious conversion, the ultimate act of assimilation, differed widely. Zionists might consider conversion to be an unworthy and even immoral subterfuge, a pointless mimicry certain to be discovered. But there were many Jews to whom their ancestral faith was a matter of indifference and for whom conversion may have been motivated by conviction rather than opportunism.

The assimilationist majority of German Jewry fell somewhere between these two extremes. (The Centralverein explicitly opposed apostasy.) Indeed, if by the end of the nineteenth century German Jews patterned their behavior and outlook after that of the surrounding society, this can perhaps better be ascribed to the gradual but certain working of a century of acculturation than to any moment-by-moment striving for acceptance. The attractions of European culture were not to be denied, and if this meant the loss of a comprehensive Jewish identity, then so much the worse for that identity—but not necessarily so much the worse for the Jews involved, who could regard their own acculturation as an achievement well worthwhile. To be sure, the Zionists tended to see things differently, and the question of why they did will be taken up in its turn. In the end, the choice between assimilationism and Zionism seems to have depended more on a combination of subjective perceptions and attitudes than on any objective reality.[12]

At the time, however, such an easy relativism was not possible, either for Zionists or assimilationists. While the Zionists described assimilationism as approaching moral bankruptcy, the assimilationists charged (with considerable justice from their point of view) that the Zionists were undermining the very foundation of their existence in Germany by affirming Jewish peoplehood and thereby lending apparent support to the stock slanders by anti-Semites—that the Jews were an unassimilable and potentially disloyal foreign body within the German nation. Indeed, there was assimilationist opposition to Zionism from the very birth of the movement. The gravity with which assimilationists regarded the Zionist threat was reflected in the public protest of a group of German rabbis, whose opposition to Herzl's plan to hold the first Zionist Congress in Munich forced him to convene it in the Swiss town of Basel instead.

But open conflict between the ZVfD and the Centralverein, at least until 1913, was limited mostly to skirmishes on the local level, with the Centralverein attempting to deny the fledgling Zionist movement any advantage that it might gain from public controversy.[13]

To the Centralverein's accusations that Zionism was endangering German Jewry politically, the Zionists responded with an argument that went to the heart of the definition both of Jewish identity and of the German polity. First, they claimed that the Centralverein's entire position was a false one, in that the German citizens of the Jewish faith whom it pretended to represent were in fact largely irreligious. Zionist wits made puns on the title of the Centralverein, suggesting that its members might more accurately be described as German citizens of Jewish *dis*belief, or even as Jewish citizens of the *German* faith —a dig at the more-than-German Germanness to which German Jews were prone. More serious was the Zionist contention, to be discussed more fully later, that since German society defined itself in nationalist and *völkisch* terms, Zionist recognition and cultivation of these aspects of Jewishness were more realistic than the assimilationist position and in the long run would provide a basis for Jewish existence in Germany more stable than liberal religious pluralism.[14]

As is often the case with closed systems of political ideology, these arguments seemed to reassure the Zionists more than they persuaded their opponents. And great as the outrage of critics was at this point, they were unfortunately destined for further distress. For the next logical development in Zionist ideology—one that evoked serious resistance even within the movement itself—was the insistence that there was only one Zion and that there alone could the plight of both West and East European Jewry be resolved. This effort to make Zionism into a first-person affair would surface dramatically in 1912. But meanwhile the ZVfD faced the task of building the movement in Germany.

3

BUILDING THE MOVEMENT

Before 1933 the Zionist movement included only a small minority of German Jewry. While the Jewish population of Germany hovered around 500,000 persons, at its peak Zionist membership totaled about 9,000 members before World War I and just over 33,000 for the period between the war and 1933. (After 1933 membership rose dramatically.) Even these figures may be somewhat inflated since they simply represent those who had paid the token Zionist membership fee, the shekel, named after the biblical coin and assessed in Germany at one mark. While some Zionists argued that the shekel should be accepted only from those who subscribed to Zionist principles, in practice this stricture was doubtless disregarded.

In view of the philanthropic stance of the ZVfD, it is likely that many who were listed among its members had simply made what they regarded as a charitable contribution; the committed membership would have been much smaller and the number of really active Zionists smaller still. Richard

Lichtheim, the historian of German Zionism, estimated in his memoirs that in 1909 only a third of the ZVfD's membership offered anything more than token support. A 1921 report estimates the number of organized members of local ZVfD branches at about half the total number of shekel-payers.[1]

In terms of gross membership the assimilationist Central-verein clearly predominated. In 1896, three years after its founding, the Centralverein included over 5,000 individual and 39 corporate members. In 1903 it reported 12,000 individual members in addition to 100 affiliated groups that represented more than 100,000 Jews. By 1913 the individual membership had climbed to over 35,000, passing 40,000 in 1916, and totaling more than 70,000 by the mid-1920s. The Central-verein's claim in 1924 that all told, including associated groups, it represented 85 to 90 percent of German Jewry seems essentially correct.[2]

It is obvious, then, that the advocacy of Zionism followed from a perception of the Jewish situation in Germany that was far from universal. Under the circumstances it is not surprising to discover a certain self-righteous tone of moral superiority on the part of the Zionists, who viewed the assimilationist position as not only shortsighted and self-deceiving, but also morally deficient. The Zionists regarded themselves as the vanguard of a new mode of German Jewish consciousness and consequently as something of an elite. Richard Lichtheim recalled, for example, that

between 1880 and 1900 it took special sensitivity and unusual independence of judgment to see the Jewish question in Germany in its historical perspective, and to dream of a renaissance on the soil of Palestine, which appeared . . . to almost all Europeans—Jews as well as Christians—to be completely fantastic and impossible. And nevertheless, scattered young German Jews suddenly saw, or felt, the problem of their existence in terms of this novel mode, and so became the avant garde of German Zionism.

Whether this self-congratulatory elitism was in fact justified is open to question, but it was certainly strongly felt. While Kurt Blumenfeld granted that the early Zionists were "men of average gifts," nevertheless they were convinced that they belonged to "an elite that would conquer Jewish life through its moral force."[3]

This sense of special inspiration was doubtless one source of the belligerent tone of early Zionist propaganda, as was the need for this new movement to capture the attention of German Jewry. Zionists evidently reckoned that there was nothing to be lost by presenting their case in all its starkness since Zionism owed its existence, after all, to certain inescapable divergences between the Zionist and the assimilationist analyses of the German situation. But excessive belligerence was avoided, at least until 1912. This tactical moderation was, for instance, an important reason for dissatisfaction with Heinrich Loewe's editorship of the *Jüdische Rundschau*, from 1902 to 1908. Loewe's contentiousness and even pettiness in dealing with anti-Zionist slights, and his tiresome stridency in attacking assimilationism may have been understandable in the absence of much positive news to report during these early years, but they were nevertheless a political liability. For one immediate aim of the ZVfD was to gain members, which meant not only winning adherents to Zionist doctrine, but also winning support for Zionism's philanthropic efforts in behalf of East European Jewry. And the continued emphasis on a palatable "third-person Zionism" was due as much to the fact that there was still hardly any other view in the minds of the Zionists themselves, as it was to the necessity for tact in dealing with non-Zionists. As Lichtheim put it: "To preach to German Jews the immediate avowal of the Jewish nation or . . . of emigration to Palestine would have appeared so absurd that not even the most audacious Zionist visionaries would have dared to do it."[4]

The Zionist Constituency

Except for the distinctiveness of perception and ideological commitment that made them join the Zionist group, the ZVfD membership was scarcely distinguishable in terms of sociological characteristics from the many Jews who remained outside the movement. The leadership was made up of businessmen and professionals, with an especially large number of lawyers. They were generally comfortable financially, being either middle or upper class. Lichtheim, who may have been slightly exceptional in this regard, at the age of twenty-four inherited a share in his father's estate that yielded an annual income of 16,000 marks. Now independently wealthy, he decided to devote himself to full-time Zionist work.

These active Zionists were amateurs in the literal sense and devoted large amounts of their time and money to the service of the organization. Before World War I, the physician Aron Sandler recalled, the burden of propaganda

had to be borne almost entirely by young members who made themselves available willingly. . . . We were engaged in our professional lives, and it cost no slight sacrifice when we were sent, often for a week [at a time] on [speaking] trips. . . . The present-day Zionist, accustomed to officials and offices, does not know what sacrifices of energy and ultimately of money were made then. . . . When at the beginning of 1914 I had to travel to Palestine for the founding of the first medical institute there, I went at my own expense.

Sandler's case was typical. Indeed, until the appointment in 1909 of Kurt Blumenfeld as the ZVfD's first party secretary *(Parteisekretär)*, the only paid help was clerical. As a group, the Zionist leadership were fairly close in age. In 1910, for example, most of the leading circle of Zionists were in their twenties or thirties, with the exceptions of the over-forty veterans such as Bodenheimer and Loewe.[5]

A clear picture of the composition of the Zionist membership at large is practically unobtainable. Membership lists have been lost, and with them the possibility of discovering any specific or detailed information about the status and backgrounds of the individuals who joined the ZVfD. The generalization that the ZVfD consisted of "a relatively large number of professionals [*Akademiker*], members of the petite bourgeoisie, and immigrant Jews from Eastern Europe" seems to be accurate. One indication of the composition of the professional component of ZVfD membership can be obtained by analyzing the scattered data available for the federations of Zionist student organizations. In 1907, 70 percent of the total membership (426), including alumni and those still in school, of the Bund jüdischer Corporationen (Confederation of Jewish Corps, one of the two major federations in existence at that time) were in the legal or medical professions. The comparable figure for 1932 for the membership of the Kartell jüdischer Verbindungen (the subsequently consolidated single federation) was 60 percent (out of 1,930 members). The picture can be only a general one, however, since not every professional member of the ZVfD would necessarily have been a member of a Zionist student organization previously.

As for geographical distribution, the movement predictably had its greatest support in the cities of major Jewish settlement, such as Berlin, Breslau, Frankfort on the Main, Hamburg,

Leipzig, and Munich. Of the cities with the largest numbers of Zionists during the 1920s, ten already had local ZVfD chapters *(Ortsgruppen)* by 1899. Cologne had been the headquarters of the ZVfD at the time of its founding because of Bodenheimer's residence there. But the activity of the Berlin chapter and the dominance in Jewish affairs of Berlin, the German city with the largest Jewish population, resulted in the ZVfD's central office being relocated in Berlin in 1904. The difficulty of maintaining communication between Cologne and the Executive Committee in Berlin was one reason cited by Bodenheimer in 1910 for his decision not to seek reelection as ZVfD president.[6]

One very important segment of the Zionist constituency were the so-called *Ostjuden*, Jews from Eastern Europe, whose numbers in Germany grew from 7 percent of the total Jewish population in 1900 to just under 20 percent by 1933. The reasons for Zionism's relatively greater attraction for *Ostjuden* than for native German Jews may appear obvious, if one assumes that the Zionist position had been self-evident to these emigrants from the areas of massive Jewish settlement in Eastern Europe, where the features of Jewish nationality—language and culture—were most visible. The *Ostjuden* would also have had a special philanthropic concern for friends and relatives who still remained in Eastern Europe. Furthermore, having suffered from anti-Semitism in its most direct forms, they might have been expected to be particularly sensitive to its presence and threat in German society.

But there were also strong forces working in the opposite direction. Germany represented a land of opportunity and relative freedom to the *Ostjuden*, and it is fair to assume that assimilation and integration appeared as primary goals. In addition, the *Ostjuden* would not yet have experienced the disenchantment with the promises of emancipation that had brought a few German-born Jews to Blumenfeld's "post-assimilatory" Zionism. Blumenfeld himself pointed out that during his effort before World War I to establish a more radical Zionist position,

precisely the young people who were born in Germany and whose intellectual development was bound up with German culture had acted much more decisively than the Zionists whose families had emigrated from Eastern Europe. To this latter group the thought of political freedom plainly seemed to be thoroughly compatible with the then current conditions in Germany.[7]

In any case, *Ostjuden* formed a large part of the Zionist membership and were a welcome support for the Zionist leaders, themselves mostly German-born, who encountered strong resistance among the native-born Jewish community at large. According to one Zionist organizer, "even in Berlin our meetings would have made a sorry impression if numerous *Ostjuden* . . . had not filled the room." It was appropriate, therefore, that part of the Zionist program be directed toward improving the conditions of the *Ostjuden* who had immigrated to Germany. Besides suffering from social discrimination and being subjected to special government regulations and restrictions as foreign citizens, these recent arrivals were often also barred from political participation in the *Gemeinden*, the legally constituted official Jewish communities. This opposition to the *Ostjuden* by longer-settled German Jews sprang partly from antipathy toward a group still unacculturated, partly from fears that the heavy influx of new immigrants would endanger the political security of Jews who had already established themselves in Germany. The situation was ironic, since the great bulk of German Jewry had at one time themselves migrated from the east. (The German Jewish reaction to Eastern European immigration had its parallels among other Western Jewries.)[8]

While it is clear that there was a political symbiosis between the Zionist leadership and its *ostjüdisch* constituency, there is no need to ascribe to political opportunism a policy that was clearly implied by the fundamental Zionist outlook. The Jewish people are one, Herzl had said, and Zionist ideology did not allow that these *Ostjuden*, who seemed closest of anyone to the true, living Jewish *Volk*, be excluded from the affairs of the German Jewish community in which they had come to live. And so either alone, or in coalitions such as the Jewish People's party of the 1920s, the Zionists fought for the rights of the *Ostjuden* at the same time that they took a leading role in social work among the immigrants.[9]

Efforts in behalf of the *Ostjuden* were, however, only one part of the Zionist program of ongoing work specifically directed toward German Jewry (*Gegenwartsarbeit*, in Zionist parlance); they also focused on Jewish culture. From the beginning of the movement it had been assumed that Jewish culture would command attention along with direct political activity, and that a Jewish cultural renascence would serve as an effective, independent force for the enhancement of Jewish national awareness. This had already been clearly stated, for example, in the Theses of the National-jüdische Vereinigung, which stressed the value that a knowledge of Jewish history would have in heightening Jewish self-awareness, now eroded by assimilation. In the same vein, in commenting on the second Zionist Congress in 1898, Bodenheimer singled out for praise the fact that gradually the view is gaining ground that the final goal of Zionism will be worthwhile only if the physical, spiritual, and moral regeneration of Israel [i.e., the Jews] proceeds apace as a natural progress of development. A common homeland without a common culture would be only partial and unsalutary.

The whole issue of Jewish culture proved to be unexpectedly problematic, however, when it became clear that Judaism could mean one thing to an assimilated Viennese journalist like Herzl and quite another to an Orthodox Zionist from Russia. Hence Herzl tried to skirt the issue altogether in the hope of avoiding dissension within the movement about the nature of Jewish culture and the role of Jewish tradition and religion.[10]

Partly in reaction to Herzl's treatment of the cultural question and partly in reaction to what was perceived as his autocratic leadership, a political opposition gathered, the "Democratic Faction," which insisted that "national cultural activity is an immediate consequence of the concept of Zionism and is an indispensable component of Zionist work." The conflict became an open clash at the fifth Zionist Congress in 1901, when Herzl appeared to block consideration of the Cultural Committee's report, which had been presented by Martin Buber, a delegate from Vienna and organizer of the Democratic Faction. Acting on their conviction of the importance of cultural work, leading figures in the Democratic Faction joined together to found the Jüdischer Verlag in Berlin. Beginning with its first publications in 1902, the Verlag served as the more or less official German-language publishing house of the Zionist movement and produced a book list of considerable cultural value. Buber's second major publishing venture, the monthly *Der Jude* (1916–26), also achieved notable success in establishing a high-level intellectual forum for the discussion of matters of Jewish interest.[11]

While both these projects were of great importance for German-speaking Jewry, and consequently for the Zionist movement in Germany, neither was a direct undertaking of the ZVfD. The ZVfD had made diverse efforts in the field of culture, but it was not until 1916 that it formally established a commission for cultural affairs. During World War I Salman Schocken, a Zionist businessman and bibliophile, had been involved in a project to provide reading material for Jewish internees and prisoners of war in Germany. (Russian Jews who had fled from czarist repression to the haven of Germany were interned as enemy aliens during the war.) In his report on this wartime cultural work to a special ZVfD delegates' meeting *(Delegiertentag)* in 1916, Schocken outlined a program of a more permanent nature. The plan, which aimed at nothing less than the reconstruction of Jewish learning in Germany, centered around a project to publish material of high quality that would be accessible to a wide readership. The *Delegiertentag* adopted Schocken's proposal and appointed a Committee for Jewish Cultural Work, which remained in existence for about a decade. During that time the committee managed to issue only ten volumes under its own imprint—a series of eight children's readers, a Hebrew-language textbook, and a volume of East European Jewish melodies. To be sure, one reason for the committee's falling short of expectations was postwar inflation; but it also failed to supply the necessary concentration of effort and support. Impatient with the committee's halting progress, in 1927 Schocken, its chairman, assumed personal responsibility for its last pending project, an anthology of Jewish readings, which later appeared as one of the first titles of the publishing house that he founded shortly thereafter.[12]

As was the case with Zionist philanthropy for Russian Jewry, all these activities of the ZVfD—membership building, fund raising, political efforts within the Jewish community in behalf of the *Ostjuden*, cultural work—only strengthened the view that Zionism was a matter for wholly domestic German consumption, with no necessary implications for actual emigration. But critics of this "third-person Zionism" resolved that it was time for a change.

4

THE RADICAL REORIENTATION
OF GERMAN ZIONISM

During its first years German Zionism had appeared on the whole to be a moderate affair, restrained in its demands on its members and conciliatory toward the far larger group among whom it sought additional adherents. To those who had shaped this policy of moderation, Zionists like Bodenheimer and Friedemann, there seemed to be every reason to continue on a course that had proved so successful in its avowed goals. As long as there was no real possibility for large-scale Jewish colonization in Palestine, given the resistance of its Turkish rulers, it appeared wisest to concentrate on fashioning a strong organization in Germany that would be capable of effective action when the opportunity came.

But there were others who, without disagreeing with this short-term goal, proposed a tack that was the very opposite of moderation. This self-styled radical group stressed that Zionist ideology was formulated to apply equally to all Jewries. The distinction between a geographical Zion for the physically suffering Jewish masses of the East and a spiritual Zion for the peculiar distress of German Jewry had effectively excepted German Zionists from the requirement of actual emigration. Now the radicals put forth the view that a restored Jewish national existence in Palestine was an ideal whose practical benefits should no longer be reserved entirely for the *Ostjuden;* German Zionists would have to accept it for themselves as well. Thus the "ascent" to Zion (*aliyah,* as it was called by its Hebrew term) was an equal obligation for all.

The radicals' stress on the particularist, national elements of Zionism was jarring to older members of the movement and even more shocking to non-Zionists, who had grown accustomed to the tact and moderation that had prevailed in the past. But the radicals argued that what appeared to be an extremist stance could have certain tactical virtues of its own.

This new strain of Zionist radicalism had in Kurt Blumenfeld its best exemplar and its chief advocate. Blumenfeld's life strikingly illustrated the postassimilatory Zionism that he himself had articulated. By background Blumenfeld was as deeply rooted in German culture as the most assimilated of German Jewry, a fact that later worked to his advantage. Blumenfeld was born, in 1884, to what he later described as a "Jewish family of German culture" whose social ties were primarily with Christians. Blumenfeld's father was a judge in East Prussia, at a time when the judicial corps was practically closed to Jews. His mother was a talented amateur musician and a patron of music, who came from a family in which "German convictions had displaced a Jewish tradition that had long since vanished."

Blumenfeld's early childhood was innocent of the "Jewish question" that would preoccupy his later years, and he recalled that he was made aware of a special Jewish identity only by two

confrontations with worlds significantly outside his own shel-
tered existence. One was the naïve admission by the family's
Catholic maid that she included in her confession the fact that
she was employed by the Blumenfelds, since it was a sin to be
in service to Jewish "deicides." The other was a chance encounter, while Blumenfeld was in the company of one of his
mother's musical acquaintances, with an East European Jew
who spoke only Yiddish, which Blumenfeld well understood
but feigned not to know lest he appear too Jewish. On reflection he regretted the incident and at that point realized, he
afterward claimed, that his fate indeed lay with the Jews of
Eastern Europe. It was no accident that when Blumenfeld
married, he chose as his wife an East European Jew, the first
who had ever entered the Blumenfeld household.[1]

Blumenfeld pursued the university career that was customary for a Jew of his class and standing, with the initial intention
of training for the law. These were also years, however, of
intensive activity in the Zionist student movement, and in
1909, when he was twenty-five, Blumenfeld abandoned his
preparations for a legal career to become the ZVfD's first party
secretary. As *Parteisekretär*, a combination of executive director and propagandist, it was Blumenfeld's task to make extensive speaking tours throughout Germany, publicizing the Zionist program while tilting with the anti-Zionist opposition that
his appearances almost invariably provoked. Blumenfeld
proved to be singularly talented in his role of Zionist champion.
A gifted orator with a magnetic personality, Blumenfeld succeeded in winning adherents to Zionism not so much by logical
suasion as by the force of his rhetoric. This approach fit with
his view of Zionism, which he regarded as more a "revelation"
than a matter of systematic doctrine.[2] His rhetorical skill was
captivating. As one critical observer put it, he was the kind of

orator who could deliver a moving speech about a flowerpot.

Coming as he did from a highly assimilated background, Blumenfeld was ideally suited to his self-appointed mission as the prophet of postassimilatory Zionism. German Zionism was postassimilatory in two senses, Blumenfeld argued. First, unlike the Jews of Eastern Europe, German Zionists had experienced the promise of emancipation and the process of assimilation—only to realize in the end that Zionism alone, with its restoration of Jewish nationality, offered a solution to the problem of their existence as Jews. Second, this postassimilatory Zionism had to take into account the fact that German Jewry's foundation in Jewish culture had been eroded, and that therefore the case for Zionism would have to rest on that Jewry's deep roots in German culture. Much of Blumenfeld's persuasiveness derived from his own broad grounding in German culture and his ability to bolster his arguments by reference to the familiar greats of German literature. Fichte, not the Bible or the Talmud, was his text for citation.

The extremism that Blumenfeld's critics charged him with may have been due in part to the zeal of the converted, but it may also have derived from the more mundane fact that Blumenfeld was a paid party functionary and could afford to be—was in fact expected to be—outspoken. But on the other hand, Blumenfeld would not have been chosen for his position had he not had a certain zeal for the cause to begin with. Indeed, Blumenfeld early distinguished himself as one of the outstanding younger Zionists, and he moved on from his post with the ZVfD to work for the World Zionist Organization in a series of different positions. From 1910 until World War I he continued his speaking tours, now in behalf of the world organization, and traveled extensively outside of Germany. During 1913 and 1914 he edited the Zionist organ *Die Welt.*

After the war he transferred his activity to propaganda work for the Keren Hayesod (Palestine Foundation Fund, which along with the Keren Kayemeth [Jewish National Fund] was one of the two major Zionist fund-raising agencies), whose executive directorship he assumed in 1933 after his final emigration to Palestine. In 1924 he won election as president of the ZVfD, an office he held until 1933, leading the movement in Germany through its final pre-Hitler decade.[3]

Blumenfeld's first formal attack on the moderate Zionist position came in the fall of 1910 at the ZVfD's *Delegiertentag* in Frankfort. In his address on Zionist "agitation methods" the new party secretary proposed a resolution that

the national character of our movement must be unambiguously stressed. In particular, decisive emphasis should be placed on the difference in principle [that lies] between Zionism, as the Jewish national movement [*Volksbewegung*] and all other Jewish organizations.

Blumenfeld later recalled that he intended this resolution, which was adopted almost unanimously, as a "declaration of hostilities" against philanthropic Zionism and against the older generation of Zionists who supported it. He concluded that one reason the resolution passed was that the delegates did not actually perceive its radical import. If true, it was not because of any secrecy on Blumenfeld's part, for he had already made his intentions clear enough in the article introducing the resolution, where he proposed radical innovation on two fronts. He asserted that a stark presentation of the Zionist position would bring a greater and more lasting advantage than any conciliatory approach:

Our . . . Zionist agitation has repeatedly committed the error of wanting to make Zionism "easy" for the general public. It attempts to ignore the problematic elements and to present matters as if all personal conflicts in the end consisted only of misunderstanding. The Zionists who have been won in this fashion, who in general must conceive of Zionism as a charitable work for the Jews of the East, are really of doubtful value for the achievement of our ultimate goal. Only men who are willing to bring endless sacrifices are capable of establishing a free people in a Jewish country. Such sacrifices can be brought only by someone who feels himself obligated [to work] for these goals for his own sake. . . . Only he will recognize the consequence that the final fulfillment of his Zionism lies in the return to Palestine, to the promised land.

In other words, Blumenfeld concluded, the Zionist enterprise could succeed only with the personal commitment of all its members to the ultimate goal of *aliyah*. Anyone who did not accept this was simply not a Zionist.[4]

The Posen Resolution and Beyond

Though there may have been confusion in 1910, there was no mistaking the meaning of the resolution that came before the 1912 *Delegiertentag* in Posen. The Posen Resolution—proposed by two members of the radical faction, Leo Estermann and Theodor Zlocisti, but clearly bearing Blumenfeld's stamp—declared that

in consequence of the overwhelming importance of Palestine[-oriented] work, both for the liberation of the individual personality and as a means for the attainment of our ultimate goal, the *Delegiertentag* declares it the obligation of every Zionist—above all the financially independent ones—to incorporate emigration to Palestine in his life program [*Lebensprogramm*]. In any case, every Zionist should establish for himself *personal* [economic] *interests* in Palestine.

The resolution was adopted, according to the picturesque account in the *Jüdische Rundschau,* "unanimously and with lively applause."[5]

In retrospect it is quite surprising that this resolution, which later threatened to divide the movement in two, passed at all. The only thing that is more surprising is that it passed with so little special notice at the time. Blumenfeld's speech introducing the resolution, "Education for Zionism," was not even summarized in the *Jüdische Rundschau*'s otherwise full account of the meeting, and the ensuing debate seems to have been entirely routine and placid. Despite the *Rundschau*'s report of acclamation, passage of the resolution may be ascribed in part to the fact that it escaped the notice of those who would have certainly advanced hostile objections. Adolf Friedemann's charge that it carried because of an "accidental majority" is perhaps not far from the truth. To be sure, Blumenfeld had spent over two years laying the ideological groundwork for the radical position, but it is also clear that he was capable of adroit on-the-spot maneuvering. Max Kollenscher, a delegate from Posen, recalled:

It may seem strange that precisely in Posen, in one of the strongholds of political Zionism [i.e., the Herzlean Zionism of Bodenheimer's generation], a decision such as this one was made—without any debate of principles and without contradiction. [This could happen only because] the decision was made on the basis of a spontaneous motion without being placed on the agenda. At the time of the vote, in the late afternoon, the *Delegiertentag* was poorly attended. We Posen delegates were busy with the preparations for the evening's festivities and were therefore no longer in the hall. In this way, unnoticed by most delegates, the resolution was adopted.[6]

No matter what tactics were responsible for its passage, the resolution was greeted at first with favorable comment. This focused not so much on the startling ideological innovation that seemed to obligate German Zionists to embark on *aliyah* as on the tactical advantage to be gained from taking such a radical stance. In reporting ZVfD President Arthur Hantke's closing remarks at the *Delegiertentag*, the *Jüdische Rundschau* commended the resolution for drawing a clear dividing line between Zionist and non-Zionist, on the grounds that "only the most radical representation of the national idea toward those on the outside can guarantee the triumph of the Zionist idea among German Jewry." Indeed, one reason that Blumenfeld succeeded was because his radicalism built on two notions of Zionist propaganda that were increasingly coming into favor. The first was that a strong line taken against non-Zionists would have a certain publicity value that would outweigh any possible alienating effect. Besides, it would offer a tactical advantage by providing opportunity for rejoinder against the anti-Zionist attacks that were sure to be provoked. These considerations seem to have motivated the frequent public appearances of Zionist orators and the sometimes contentious tone of the *Jüdische Rundschau*. In this regard Blumenfeld claimed that the significance of the resolution "lay above all in fundamentally confounding German Jewry's self-contentment." The second notion was a more recent attitude that only those converts who were committed to the full Zionist program were worth adding to the movement. Felix Rosenblüth commented in a 1911 review of Lichtheim's *Program of Zionism:*

Lichtheim wants to win total Zionists. Therefore the national character of Zionism is emphasized again and again with special decisiveness. He knows, to be sure, that the national idea provokes the greatest opposition to Zionism, but that it has at the same time an almost equally great agitational force.[7]

Although the Posen Resolution may have offered some tactical advantage, it was certain to upset the group of philanthropic Zionists against whom Blumenfeld directed it—and their protests were not long in coming. It is not surprising that at the first real confrontation over the resolution, at the ZVfD's Central Committee meeting in November, the clash between supporters and critics revolved around matters of style as much as ideological principles. The president, Arthur Hantke, had only praise for the resolution, partly precisely because of its radical tone, and defended it against the cries of outrage that it had provoked in the assimilationist camp:

Some of our members assert that we ourselves are responsible . . . for the open opposition with which we now have to deal. I cannot agree at all. The opposition was prepared in advance and obviously has used this resolution against us as a handy weapon. But the value of such a resolution lies in its effect on our supporters themselves, and this effect has been splendid, as we are already able to determine. . . . In principle our position vis-à-vis other organizations cannot be radical enough. For only if we set out as radicals will we triumph.

Blumenfeld in turn stressed the resolution's educational value as being

in *practical* terms one of the best things we have ever done. Our older and confirmed members obviously are not going to be weakened in their Zionist conviction even in an assimilated milieu. But we have to protect our younger Zionists . . . from losing their Zionist conviction and becoming disposed to compromise. . . . It is certainly extraordinarily regrettable that we have lost seventeen members in Dessau . . . but that would not have been possible if they had been firm in their Zionist conviction.[8]

On the opposing side Alfred Klee, who was concerned with cooperation between Zionists and non-Zionists and was later especially active in the affairs of the Berlin *Gemeinde,* took the content of the resolution much more seriously than its supporters seemed to. Not only would it hamper any joint efforts with non-Zionists in matters of common concern, but it also threatened serious political repercussions in that it limited room to maneuver in the general political arena:

The Posen Resolution represents a particularly inept tactic. . . . One can say [that] in a limited circle . . . but such a resolution, adopted by a *Delegiertentag,* means forging weapons for the opposition. . . . Because of the passage of the Posen Resolution it has become completely impossible for us to intervene in general German affairs, . . . to say in earnest that there is a sentiment among the Jews in favor of a swing to the Right, for through the resolution we have incurred the basic displeasure of the government. If the movers of the resolution had considered it [beforehand] . . . it might have been possible to formulate it more adroitly. . . . We must find such an interpretation to which all . . . active Zionists in Germany can subscribe. Otherwise, immeasurable harm will be caused. We could not ever again presume to turn to the Herrenhaus [the upper house of the Prussian parliament], for if the members knew of the resolution, they would prefer the gentlemen of the liberal camp [i.e., the Central-verein]. I cannot concede that the resolution has done us any good. . . . For the intensification of our Palestine work we do not need it at all.

As it turned out, Klee's fears appear to have been overdrawn, and there is no evidence of political damage such as he imagined. Still, he was correct in pointing out a difficulty that was, at least in theory, formidable.[9]

Adolf Friedemann, who would have more to say against the resolution later on, limited himself on this occasion to deploring the lack of realism that it betrayed and joined Klee in the hope that there was still a possibility of undoing the damage:

Herr Blumenfeld completely fails to appreciate what is possible and what is impossible. There can be great setbacks in Palestine. I regard it as a great misfortune that our youth has become so radical now. The setbacks that can come would hit these young people all the more strongly, and they will be exceedingly reproachful that we have uprooted them here and can give nothing to them there [in Palestine]. Where should we begin if we were now boycotted in public? We can still rectify the matter today by an authentic [mollifying] interpretation of the resolution.[10]

It is said that reigning ideologies are never so fully articulated as when they are called upon to defend themselves. Certainly this was the case with the philanthropic, vicarious version of Zionism that had dominated the German movement for more than a decade after its inception. The first flurry of protest against the challenge of Blumenfeld's radicalism was minor compared to the full-scale attack that was mounted at the next *Delegiertentag,* held in June 1914 at Leipzig, where the antiradical position was passionately expounded by its two principal spokesmen, Adolf Friedemann and Franz Oppenheimer. The actual debate at the Leipzig *Delegiertentag* was one of the few genuinely dramatic moments in the history of German Zionism. Challenged by a view that they regarded as wrong both in theory and in practice, members of an older generation of Zionists stood to defend their own understanding of Zionism, in a situation where compromise had been precluded in principle by the very nature of the radical position.

Friedemann's line of attack was to draw the consequences of the Posen Resolution explicitly and argue from them against the resolution itself. He condemned the radical position for its disregard of both the real situation of the Jews in Germany and conditions in Palestine, and charged Blumenfeld with indulging in meaningless and dangerous rhetoric:

For some time it has become the custom . . . to distinguish between good and bad Zionists—or, as we say politely, between good and better Zionists; by which the radicals, who make this distinction, always set themselves up as the better Zionists. . . . The Posen Resolution . . . demands that "every Zionist . . . incorporate emigration to Palestine in his life program" . . . but so far I am not aware of any compliance with this paper demand on the part of the movers of this resolution or of its most zealous supporters. [In fact, both Estermann and Zlocisti later emigrated to Palestine, the former in 1916 and the latter in 1921. As mentioned, Blumenfeld remained in Germany until 1933.]

Here in Germany the demand for a Jewish national culture is a bloodless ideal, an empty abstraction of theorizing minds. We live scattered in the midst of a great culture, which we imbibe . . . with our mother's milk. Culturally we can be Germans only. Goethe, Schiller, and Kant have been our teachers, and we cannot change our nature at will. . . . Even the propagandists of the extreme national sensibility have, as far as we can see, a completely minimal Jewish knowledge and a purely German culture. [The characterization of Blumenfeld was essentially correct.] Before they preach such theories, they might do well to improve their own knowledge. Nothing at all can come of theoretical good intentions. . . . Again and again I ask myself what the author [of the resolution] wanted, since even with the most careful observation, I see no preparations for emigration. This resolution . . . makes not only the somewhat sensible demand that we create interests for ourselves in Palestine . . . but at the same time also demands the shift of the center of gravity of our whole being over there. . . . There are only two possibilities. Either one takes this resolution seriously, in which case he has to shake his head over such a misapprehension of real conditions. Neither the country nor the people are ready for such demands. Or one regards it as an agitational phrase. And then he must decisively deplore such unpolitical rhetoric. . . . A tribe of fanatical young men will be raised who are intoxicated with this radicalism. It is the prerogative of youth to be radical, unconcerned with the consequences . . . [but] the more radically someone is brought up, the harder is his confrontation with the real world when he sets out in life. . . . And it is precisely with the most radical that a complete about-face comes soonest.[11]

In an earlier letter to Friedemann, Bodenheimer had offered his own critical remarks, essentially identical with Friedemann's, though set in somewhat more colorful language:

I find the rhetorical twaddle and drivel of Dr. Blumenfeld and his friends to be not radical at all, but [simply] foolish. These men toss off phrases about Jewish national consciousness and a Jewish purpose in life that they do not practice, . . . and happily are altogether unable to practice. A political movement must have a program that rests on the real necessities of life and not on a fantastic projection of what might be someday.[12]

Franz Oppenheimer in his turn mounted a critique of the Posen Resolution that generally paralleled Friedemann's, but was the more interesting of the two in that it was grounded on an explicit and systematic analysis of the nature of Jewish identity in Germany. Oppenheimer was an economist of some repute and had joined the Zionist movement in Herzl's day. His best-known contribution to Zionism was his early advocacy of a plan for the economic development of Palestine through collective agricultural settlements. Oppenheimer's personal view of Zionism was well summed up by his remark that it was "not a movement of Jews who desire to emigrate to Palestine, but a movement that desires the emigration of the Jewish people [as a whole]."

Oppenheimer's argument against the Posen Resolution rested on a distinction that he had first elaborated in an article several years earlier, where he contrasted the consciousness of clan *(Stammesbewusstsein)* with the consciousness of nation *(Volksbewusstsein)*—supposedly characteristic of West and East European Jewry respectively:

Clan consciousness [is] the consciousness of common descent [*Ab-stammung*], of common blood, or at least of a former common history with its common memories of suffering and joy, of heroism and great deeds. . . . But national consciousness arises from present circumstances, from a commonality of speech, of custom, of economic and legal relations and the like, and [also] of spiritual culture. . . . We [Western Jews] are collectively [either] Germans by culture [*Kulturdeutsche*] [or] French by culture, and so on . . . because we have the fortune to belong to cultural communities [*Kulturgemeinschaften*] that stand in the forefront of nations. . . . We cannot be Jewish by culture [*Kulturjuden*] because the Jewish culture, as it has been preserved from the Middle Ages in the ghettos of the East, stands infinitely lower than the modern culture which our [Western] nations bear. We neither can regress nor do we want to. But it would be impossible for the Eastern Jews to be Russian or Romanian . . . by culture. . . . They must be Jews by culture . . . for the medieval Jewish culture stands exactly as far above East European barbarism as it is beneath the high culture of Western Europe.

Therefore, Oppenheimer concluded, while "we are Germans . . . by nationality [*Nationaldeutsche*]" the Eastern European Jews are

Jews by nationality just as they are Jews by culture. Accordingly they both are and feel themselves as members of an alien people that dwells homeless among strangers—an alien people with its own language, religion, tradition [and] culture. [As for the] many of us in the West [who] likewise call ourselves "national Jews" with pride, a few may really be that: men of the propertied classes with a specially sensitive sense of honor, who perceive the social slight [that they suffer] as an unbearable humiliation; a few of the "disinherited," to whom their state gives nothing and proves completely disappointing; a few fiery heads who . . . throw out the baby with the bath water; a few who, so to speak, have already packed for the trip to Palestine.[13]

In the final analysis, Oppenheimer declared that despite the Posen Resolution's insistence on *aliyah*, he still regarded himself as a good Zionist because he stood by the Basel Program and its demand for a homeland for the Jewish people in Palestine.[14]

Oppenheimer's exposition of Zionist ideology eliminated the apparent contradiction posed by the Zionists in Germany who declined to make *aliyah*. To be sure, Oppenheimer's distinction between clan consciousness and national consciousness seemed labored; but, as Bodenheimer pointed out, even though the semantic difficulties were considerable, the underlying reality was undeniable:

[Although] our nationalism involves the establishment of a national center for the Jewish people in Palestine [it does not] acknowledge a fictitious nationality with the same substance as our German . . . consciousness. I have always taken the view that the substance of our German national feeling is distinctive. Unfortunately, we have in the German language no precise designation for this distinctive quality, so that if we do not want to use words like *Stammesbewusstsein* and *Volksbewusstsein*, which do not cover the concept [entirely], then we are forced to express both meanings by the word *Nationalgefühl* [a sense of nation].[15]

Oppenheimer's 1910 article had concentrated on matters of abstract ideology, but his attack on Blumenfeld at the 1914 *Delegiertentag* added the specific and personal accusations that Blumenfeld was playing the demagogue and that he had distorted the true Zionist doctrine expounded by Herzl. Like Friedemann's address, Oppenheimer's was charged with a sense of outrage and dismay at this new turn in Zionism, which appeared to be at once both wrong and dangerous. Oppenheimer charged that Blumenfeld

is enthused with his subject . . . so that he finds himself somewhat intoxicated. . . . As much as I am in agreement with Herr Blumenfeld's youthful inclination and as thrilling as I find his rhetoric, nevertheless I must wonder at anyone who has found anything in it besides disordered chaos. I knew exactly where the young delegates at the meeting would clap, and if I wanted to, I could also play on these sentiments. Applause came not at substantive thoughts but at the places where [Blumenfeld] consciously played on . . . his public. . . . We have been presented with feelings rather than thoughts.[16]

It is also clear that Oppenheimer feared that a radical stance like the Posen Resolution threatened to turn Zionism from a party, working for a definite political end, to a sect, concerned with orthodoxy of opinion, or, as Friedemann later put it, "a religious, hypercritical sect, with all its advantages and short-comings: unbounded devotion to an idea, purity of will, con-sciously intended exclusiveness, self-conceit, and . . . the ques-tioning of the spiritual motives of our fellows." But these were charges that Blumenfeld could bear with equanimity, for he regarded such a development as having a virtue of its own. As he later commented: "During their struggle with the other Jews the Zionists had almost completely isolated themselves, [but] one must be alone to gain clarity and certainty. There is no renouncing the valuable educational exercise of holding to a political line."[17]

As for the substance of the Posen Resolution, Oppenheimer contended that Zionism never before involved a commitment to *aliyah* and asserted that the claim that it did constituted an unwarranted innovation:

When I was approached . . . to join the Zionist movement I declined because I had not the slightest intention of leaving Germany. I was told that that was absolutely not required. Herzl himself tried to win me [for the cause]. I made no secret of my position on Zionism, to which Herzl replied, "You are a good Zionist." . . . The founder of political Zionism must have known what Zionism meant, and we have no obligations toward a Zionism with a new meaning. . . . I reject the Posen Resolution and am nevertheless a good Zionist.

In closing, Oppenheimer affirmed the indissoluble ties that bound him to German culture and that made emigration unthinkable:

I am not an assimilationist, but I am assimilated. I am a German and [at the same time] I am proud of being a Jew, proud of descent from seventy generations of proud men. . . . I am just as proud, however, to have grown up in the land of Walther and Wolfram, of Goethe, Kant, and Fichte, and to have absorbed their culture in myself. . . . My Germanness is something sacred to me. But whoever doubts my Jewish clan consciousness, against him must I defend myself as against a murderer. . . . [I do not regard Germany] merely as a place of abode [*Wohnland*]. Germany is . . . my home. . . . I have Jewish clan consciousness, German cultural consciousness, [and] Brandenburgian home consciousness [*märkisches Heimatbewusstsein*].

Oppenheimer's protestations could be made to appear pathetic and even ridiculous. One critic asked: "Why not [add] Berlin residential consciousness? and English parliamentary consciousness? and a feeling for French painting?"[18]

The conclusion of the debate at Leipzig was clearly an unfavorable one for Friedemann and Oppenheimer. Their resolution, that the officers and official press of the ZVfD refrain from identifying themselves with any one particular ideological trend, was actually a more specific challenge to Blumenfeld and the radical position than its literal formulation implied. ZVfD President Hantke declared that its passage would in effect be a vote of no confidence in the ZVfD leadership. But after passing an even more vaguely worded confidence resolution, the *Delegiertentag* moved to table the Friedemann-Oppenheimer measure by a vote of sixty-one to twenty-two.[19]

It is only fair to point out that despite Oppenheimer's charge that Blumenfeld was a sectarian extremist, the fact is that even under Blumenfeld's leadership, which was not always tolerant of divergent opinion, the ZVfD never really developed the features commonly associated with political sectarianism.[20] Within the ZVfD itself there was surprisingly little of the indefatigable debate about doctrine, the mutual vilification and excommunication that have been present in strongly ideologically oriented movements such as Marxism. Perhaps because the movement was constantly faced with real, immediate, practical problems there was never the excess energy available for extensive doctrinal dispute. Or it may be that despite all the apparent concern about ideology, this was really a secondary matter. The German Zionist organization was distinctive in being able to maintain its unity almost without exception despite the divisions, some very deep, that split the world movement. Within the ZVfD, which served as a kind of umbrella organization, groups as divergent as the Orthodox Jews of the Mizrachi faction and the socialists of Hapoel Hazair could operate together. This does not mean that there was no ideological debate at all, but only that in this context these divisions did not play a decisive role.

To be sure, the German movement did not develop in isolation from the World Zionist Organization, and the conflict over the Posen Resolution itself was part of a larger shift in Zionist orientation in the movement as a whole. Herzl had been committed to a course of purely "political Zionism," whereby a charter for Jewish colonization in Palestine would be secured through some form of diplomatic negotiation. Until then any gradual settlement of Palestine was to be avoided. In this Herzl was opposed by the adherents of "practical Zionism," who stressed the immediate need of many Jews to find refuge in Palestine and were less concerned with grand diplo-

Max I. Bodenheimer
(1865–1940)

Arthur Hantke
(1874–1955)

German Zionist Leaders

Felix Rosenblüth
(b. 1887)

Kurt Blumenfeld
(1884–1963)

Robert Weltsch (b. 1891) dictating an article in the offices of the Jüdische
Rundshau *(note the portrait of the Hebrew poet H. N. Bialik in the background)*

*Sammy Gronemann
(1875–1952)*

Adolf Friedemann
(1871–1932)

Richard Lichtheim
(1885–1963)

Founders of the Jüdischer Verlag (left to right: standing, Davis Trietsch, Chaim
Weizmann, E. M. Lilien; sitting, Martin Buber, Berthold Feiwel)

Zionist Groups and Activities

below: ZVfD Delegiertentag, *Hamburg, 1904*

bottom: Verein jüdischer Studenten *[Jewish Students Association], Leipzig, 1899. Note the dueling equipment.*

top: Verein jüdischer Studenten, *Munich, 1902. Note the student corps uniforms*

above: German Zionist students at the Tenth Zionist Congress, Basel, 1911 (with David Wolffsohn, President of the World Zionist Organization, in the center)

Verein Jüdischer Studenten, *Bonn, about 1915*

Jüdischer Turnverein Bar Kochba *[Jewish Athletic Association Bar Kochba]*, Berlin, *1912*

Young Maccabaea, Berlin, 1925

The Blau-Weiss engineering cooperative in Jerusalem, 1925

Hachsharah, *Zionist-oriented agricultural training, Germany, 1933*

macy than with the spiritual significance that a Jewish settlement in Palestine, no matter what the political circumstances,
would have for world Jewry.

Although Herzl died in 1904, it was not until 1911 that the
leadership of the Zionist movement passed decisively into the
hands of the practical Zionists. The passage of the Posen
Resolution in 1912 marked essentially the same shift, from
political to practical Zionism, from the older generation of
philanthropic Zionists to Blumenfeld's younger generation of
"radicals." The result, Blumenfeld claimed, was "a victory for
youth, a victory for Palestine-oriented Zionism over the *Gemeinde* politicians, . . . a victory of the carefree [*die Unbeküm-
merte*] over those whose temperate Zionism corresponded to
their social situation."[21] It was not, however, as it was supposed
to be, a victory for *aliyah*.

The passage of the Posen Resolution set off another serious
conflict, this time an external one, between the ZVfD and the
Centralverein, which was more significant for the disclaimers
that it called forth from the Zionist side than for any substantial consequences. Since its founding the Centralverein had
taken what could be construed as a moderate position toward
Zionism, refraining from any sustained and open attack even
though it unambiguously repudiated the Zionist principle of
Jewish nationality. As an organization devoted primarily
to defense against anti-Semitism through legal action,
the Centralverein had ample room in its ranks for Jews who
happened also to be Zionists, and many Zionists were in fact
members.

But in keeping with the implied condition of emancipation
that made a certain degree of acculturation a prerequisite for

political and social equality, the Centralverein demanded of its members a commitment to the cultivation of a Germanic consciousness. As stated in the organization's program,

the Centralverein deutscher Staatsbürger jüdischen Glaubens aims to gather German citizens of the Jewish faith, regardless of religious or political affiliation, in order to support them in the energetic protection of their civil and social equality, as well as to strengthen them in the unwavering cultivation of German conviction.[22]

On the face of it, this second intention might have seemed to have excluded Zionists from membership, given their theoretical commitment to the cultivation of the autonomous values of a national Jewish culture. As we have seen, however, this was hardly the case; many German Zionists proved to be as strongly oriented toward German culture as their assimilationist opponents in the Centralverein. It was precisely this common outlook that was Blumenfeld's target, and the sharp response of the Centralverein to the Posen Resolution was in part an indication of Blumenfeld's success. Arguing from its stated principles, in 1913 the Centralverein condemned and barred from membership Zionists who espoused a viewpoint that was essentially identical with the one for which Blumenfeld was agitating:

We demand of our members not merely the fulfillment of civic duties, but also *German conviction* and the application of this conviction in civic life. We do not want to solve the question of the Jews in Germany in an international manner. As Germans on the soil of the German fatherland we want to contribute to German culture and remain true to our community, which is hallowed by our religion and our history.

Nevertheless, the Centralverein was capable of distinguishing between philanthropic Zionists and radicals, and allowed that,

to the extent that the German Zionist strives to establish a secure homeland for the unemancipated Jews of the East, or to enhance the Jew's pride in his history and religion, he is welcome as a member. But from *that* Zionist, who denies a German national sensibility, who feels himself to be a guest of an alien host nation, and in terms of nationality regards himself as a Jew *only,* from him must we divorce ourselves.[23]

The Zionist defense against this excommunication was a curiously conciliatory one. At the special *Delegiertentag* called to consider the Centralverein's declaration, Alfred Klee was greeted with applause when he characterized it as essentially a moot statement, since

when one has read the resolution, one can conclude above all that no Zionist need withdraw. For there does not exist any Zionist such as the phantom that the Centralverein has conjured up, and which it is flaying. We German Zionists love our fatherland at least as loyally as the Jews who are members of the Centralverein.

Indeed, the resolution that the *Delegiertentag* adopted confirmed this fundamental compatability of Zionist and Centralverein outlooks, affirming that

the national Jewish conviction is the consciousness of belonging to the Jewish people, and the will to work for its preservation and development in the future through the establishment of a homeland in Palestine secured by public law. This conviction does not conflict with the interests of any state or any people. It can never prevent the German Zionists, in accordance with their historically determined position, from taking an active part in the political and cultural life of Germany.

The drafter of the Centralverein resolution, Ludwig Holländer, actually agreed with this disclaimer, conceding that "there is not the least reason to speak out against Zionism as it is presented in the Basel Program." There may be, he admitted, some Zionists who take the view that

we are not Germans, we are Jews; we do not belong to the German people, we are without roots here, we are the guests of a host nation. [But] neither the Zionist party as such nor the overwhelming number of German Zionists take this view, which is incompatible with Jewish emancipation. It is an open secret that the present leadership of the party, in contradiction to the view of a very large number of organized Zionists, strongly promotes the most extreme nationalism, apparently aided by its especially strong drawing power among the youth.[24]

In retrospect it may appear that Holländer might have intended his resolution in part as an intervention in the ZVfD to strengthen the hand of the antiradicals. Certainly the Centralverein action did much to highlight the differences that separated Blumenfeld and his opponents. In the end, however, the most significant fact may be that Blumenfeld, despite his objection to cooperation with non-Zionist organizations for fear of compromising Zionist principles, was nevertheless able to collaborate successfully when practical necessity demanded it. In his fund-raising work for the Keren Hayesod (Palestine Foundation Fund) after World War I, for example, Blumenfeld managed to secure the cooperation of non-Zionists without abandoning his own Zionist convictions. For Blumenfeld to be able to compromise while remaining at the same time a political radical was, as Chaim Weizmann, the president of the World Zionist Organization, quipped, "a good trick." To Blumenfeld's denial that it was a trick, Weizmann retorted:

"Maybe not for you, but for me, yes." Trick or not, Blumenfeld's adaptability in this regard indicated that at least one point of the radical program was less formidable in reality than on paper.[25]

5

THE FAILURE OF *ALIYAH*

Despite the turbulent ideological controversy that it generated, the Posen Resolution seems to have had little noticeable effect in the one area where its influence should have been most apparent: in the promotion of *aliyah*. Between World War I and the establishment of Nazi rule in Germany, Jewish emigration from Germany to Palestine reached a total of just over two thousand persons, less than a third of the number of such emigrants for the year 1933 alone.[1] During this same interval the German component of the total annual *aliyah* to Palestine hovered around 2 percent.

Before 1914 German *aliyah* had, if anything, been even more limited. The physician Elias Auerbach recalled that when he settled in Palestine in 1909 he was the first German Zionist to do so for reasons of personal Zionist motivation (two men had gone to Palestine because of their work in administrative posts, one for the World Zionist Organization and the other for the Jewish Colonization Association). In 1914 a Zionist petition to the German embassy in Constantinople concerning the *Sprachenkampf*—the struggle over the language of instruction in the new Haifa technical school—bore the names of twenty-seven German settlers in Palestine.[2]

To some extent these data on German *aliyah* are somewhat misleading. The fact that German settlers tended to be placed particularly in the bureaucratic, intellectual, and professional elites of the country gave them a greater influence in its developing affairs than their numbers indicate. For example, of the 27 persons who signed the 1914 petition, 12 belonged to the above categories. A similar distribution was evident in a list of 144 German Jews in Palestine that Brith Shalom (Peace Association), an organization devoted to Arab-Jewish cooperation, gathered in 1928. According to their office addresses, of the 85 members living in Jerusalem, 13 were functionaries of the World Zionist Organization and 10 worked at either the Hebrew University or the university library. Of the 49 living in Haifa, 14 listed professional occupations. This trend was even more pronounced in a list of former members of the German Zionist student organization living in Palestine. Out of a total of 102, 68 held professional positions, while only 23 were engaged in agriculture, with the rest listing other occupations that included trade and the crafts.[3] This occupational distribution is not in itself surprising, given the inclination of German Jews as a whole toward the professions. What is remarkable, however, is that the Zionist call for a normalization of Jewish life through the abandonment of this one-sided occupational distribution was so little heeded, even by the German Zionists who relocated in Palestine.

The German Jewish settlement in Palestine was problematic in other aspects as well. It was not just the Zionists who remained in Germany—such as Oppenheimer—who were convinced of the superiority of German ways and German culture. This attitude was shared by a few of the Zionists who went to Palestine and was evident in how they regarded both the native Arab population and the Jewish settlers coming from Eastern Europe. As early as 1916 Wilhelm Brünn, a physician who had been one of the few German Zionists to emigrate before World War I, complained of a widespread arrogance among the European settlers toward the Arabs that "was certain to end in a pogrom." He especially condemned the use of Blumenfeld's radical propaganda to instill the same chauvinistic spirit in the younger generation of German Zionists, and urged that "for heaven's sake none of them . . . come anywhere near Palestine."[4]

During the 1920s Fritz Loewenstein, former editor of the *Jüdische Rundschau*, wrote from Haifa that the Germans' arrogance toward the *Ostjuden* in Palestine was particularly unjustified, given their own inability to adapt to the situation there either in coping with the somewhat primitive local conditions or in learning Hebrew. (The extreme difficulty that the Germans had with the language was immortalized in the story of a German settler who after decades in Palestine was still unable to speak Hebrew. When asked if this did not embarrass him, he replied that, yes, he was terribly embarrassed, but that it was easier to be embarrassed than to learn Hebrew.) It was, explained Felix Rosenblüth, the president of the ZVfD from 1920 to 1923, a matter of specifically German virtues proving to be liabilities in difficult circumstances:

[There is] a certain inflexibility in the German Zionist type, whose disadvantages show up especially at times of economic or vocational crisis—a certain inability to adjust and adapt to new situations. The *Ostjude* has the advantage of his relatively greater rootlessness when it comes to accommodation. . . . In the case of many German Zionists a certain stiffness, which manifests itself to advantage in business affairs as stability, and a certain attachment to orderly circumstances, make for a greater despondency in the face of reverses and hardship.[5]

(German settlers in Palestine were often the targets of ridicule and even resentment by the East European majority. This was provoked both by a characteristic German stiffness and, especially with the arrival after 1933 of large numbers of not always enthusiastic immigrants from Germany, by the Germans' inclination to invoke memories of a better life in Germany. Hence the epithet *Bei-uns*-nik, from their refrain *"Es war so viel besser bei uns [in Deutschland]."* The epithet *Yekeh* was more commonly used and, while of obscure origin, was unmistakably derogatory. By one derivation it is a corruption of the German word for jacket, *Jacke,* in reference to the Germans' insistence on wearing suit jackets despite the hot Mediterranean sun. A folk etymology holds, however, that *Yekeh* is derived from a Hebrew acronym for *Y*ehudim *k*ashe *h*avanah, meaning "slow-witted Jews," in reference to the Germans' ponderous seriousness. The relations in Palestine between Germans and East Europeans may have owed some of their sharpness to resentment accumulated in Europe, where the *Ostjuden* had been the targets of scorn.)

There was, however, at least one problem that both German Jew and *Ostjude* suffered from alike. Like the biblical Israelite returning from Egypt, each bore the indelible scars of long exile. "Each brings," said one observer, "his own *golus* [exile] with him."[6] The generation of the desert would have to be replaced by a younger one before a shared, normalized Jewish identity could develop in Palestine. Until then, even for the Zionists who did move to Zion there was no balm in Gilead.

That some German Zionists did make *aliyah* does not necessarily testify to any special or decisive influence wielded by the
Posen Resolution, and the few Zionists who emigrated would
likely have done so in any case.[7] Meanwhile, those who stayed
in Germany seemed unmoved by their formal commitment to
include *aliyah* in their "life program." So the question remains
of why the resolution, confirmed in the face of serious and
determined opposition, had so little practical consequence.

The simplest answer is that, like much of the radical program, this verbal commitment was largely a matter of rhetoric.
"The resolution," recalled one delegate at Posen, "was an
empty demonstration, since no one thought any differently
about his personal attitude toward Palestine afterward than he
did before." Talk of including *aliyah* in one's "life program"
had a certain elegant vagueness that allowed for nominal support without requiring any immediate action. As Elias Auerbach put it, writing from his home in Palestine:

If it had been clearly and distinctly stated [in the resolution] that
every Zionist had to take upon himself as soon as possible the personal realization of his Zionism, that is, settlement in Palestine, the
enthusiasm would certainly have been much diminished.[8]

Indeed, throughout the history of German Zionism there
was a general gap between rhetoric and reality, as well as
between rhetoric and action. To be sure, the divergence between rhetoric and reality had a definite positive value in a
movement bent on overcoming obstacles that sober realism
would have regarded as insurmountable. To mention only one,
Zionism was unique among nationalist movements, whose goal
typically is sovereignty over the territory in which the national
population is concentrated, in that it first had to gather to-

gether a Jewish nation that had been dispersed around the world. Only then could it begin the difficult task of building a homeland in Palestine. That this attempt to "make the impossible possible with unknown methods" could actually succeed was a source of gratified awe for the Zionists themselves. Zionist wit Sammy Gronemann quipped on the occasion of his first visit to Tel Aviv: "I was forced to admit, to my amazement, that all the lies I had been telling for decades [of Zionist work] were nothing but the absolute truth."[9]

The gap between rhetoric and action, a common failing in human affairs, was a more serious one. Like millenarian reformers whose overarching vision makes them insensitive to more immediate needs, the Zionists enjoyed a certain partial insulation from reality that resulted from the very scope of their ideology. Unlike the Centralverein, which considered specific cases of anti-Semitism to be aberrations from a liberal norm, the Zionists regarded anti-Semitism as a given. But particular examples that confirmed this view paradoxically lost something of their specific outrageousness. It was not until the beginning of the 1930s, in fact, that anti-Semitic excesses in Germany drew the direct and sustained attention of the *Jüdische Rundschau*.[10]

The very grandeur of the Zionist vision drew it away from action in another aspect as well. *Aliyah* became a remote ideal that very few would achieve, but toward which all might strive. "Emigration to Palestine is the goal of our life," Blumenfeld affirmed, but he also conceded that "Zionism is the way to Zion, even if only a few Zionists reach its end." That this striving itself might become the norm was the point of the story about a Zionist who had visited Palestine frequently, but could never bring himself to settle there because, as he put it, life would be empty without his longing for Zion. The Posen

Resolution, explained Richard Lichtheim, was a declaration of intention, a statement of what the Zionist should regard as the "highest ideal" of life, even though it was certain that not every Zionist would be able to make *aliyah,* or even invest in Palestine.[11]

The remoteness of the ideal of *aliyah* was reflected in the ease with which it was postponed. At the Posen *Delegiertentag,* Blumenfeld had already asserted, in apparently fearless self-contradiction, that "our work is not yet ready; it begins with the next generation." "The colonization of a country is a difficult and lengthy proposition," Lichtheim explained in *The Program of Zionism.* "It requires gradual progress and cannot be achieved overnight." Even after the Balfour Declaration brought the possibility of full-scale Zionist development in Palestine, Salman Schocken lamented that for those in their middle years "the [British] Mandate came too late" for them to be able to join personally in the upbuilding of Palestine.[12]

Confidence in the zeal of the coming generation and its ability to take up the burden of Zionism in Palestine may have been somewhat ill-founded. One member of the Zionist student movement protested that the German Zionists would never be able to succeed in Palestine because of their aversion to agricultural labor. "Do we want our wives to become peasants?" he asked. "Do we want to marry peasants?" This projection, however, proved to be overly skeptical. After World War I the Hechalutz (Pioneer) movement provided Zionist-oriented agricultural training *(hachsharah)* for large numbers of young people, many of whom actually emigrated. According to one estimate, between 1919 and 1930 almost 1,000 of these *chalutzim* left for Palestine, although about 425 eventually returned.[13] To be sure, the significance of the *chalutz* movement for German Zionism was limited by the fact that a great many of these pioneers were *Ostjuden* for whom *hachsharah* in Germany was only a way station to Palestine. (*Hachsharah* programs acquired a special importance after 1933, as they allowed German refugees to qualify for entry into Palestine under the quota allotted for agricultural laborers.)

Nevertheless, the attitude persisted that while farming in Palestine was fine for Jews who had no other choice, it was hardly a fitting occupation for Zionists from Germany. In his greeting to the 1920 *Delegiertentag*, Otto Warburg, the president of the World Zionist Organization, made the point quite explicitly:

It should be said that there should be no great expectations of the German Zionists as agricultural workers. For this purpose we have countless masses in the East, who can accomplish much more. As immigration increases it will be difficult to employ all these people in agriculture. Should we let our young people emigrate [to take up] agriculture too? The Eastern Jews have more possibilities because their needs are more modest and they are more accustomed to agricultural labor. The German Zionists [can] find other vocations that can be learned better right in Germany—not especially in agriculture and gardening, but also in industry and as middle-level bureaucrats. . . . For this the better preparation can be found not in the East, but right here in Germany.[14]

And so despite the affirmation of the Posen Resolution that there was only one Zion, with a direct claim on the presence of all Zionists, the old familiar distinction between Eastern and Western Zionist persisted. For the *Ostjude, aliyah* was a matter of necessity; but for the German Zionist it remained a luxury, a matter "above all," as the Posen Resolution put it, for "the financially independent ones."

For those who remained behind, meanwhile, activity in the organization itself could become something of a surrogate for *aliyah.* As long as it was impracticable for German Jews to emigrate to Palestine, wrote one German Zionist, "we must quiet our longing in Zionist activity. In the community of Zionist workers we can hope for a life that offers us a certain substitute for Palestine."[15]

Zionists and World War I

The outbreak of World War I, with its serious disruption of all Zionist activities, has sometimes been advanced as a reason for the Posen Resolution's failure, but this argument is not convincing. Certainly it is true that before the war Jewish immigration to Palestine had to face serious Turkish restriction, so that at the time that it was passed the resolution must have been understood to have had no immediate applicability. But the war itself brought a British declaration of support for Zionist aspirations in Palestine, the Balfour Declaration of 1917. This and the establishment of the British Mandate in Palestine after the war seemed to clear the way at last for an immediate realization of the Zionist program.The *Jüdische Rundschau* expressed these new expectations in its forecast for the 1918 *Delegiertentag:*

Speeches about Palestine at previous *Delegiertentage* had the character of theoretical addresses, since the problems of colonization seemed to most German Zionists to be problems for the next generation. This has changed completely. Herzl's dream, the achievement of the political preconditions for the colonization of Palestine on a grand scale, appears now to be realized. And so the demand for the practical realization of Zionism unavoidably faces the Zionists of the whole world . . . —the German Zionists as well.[16]

There is no denying that unexpected difficulties arising under the British Mandate barred any such decisive action. But the minimal German participation in postwar immigration indicates that it was the German Zionists' own disinclination to move to Palestine, not British obstruction, that was the cause.

While its part in the failure of the Posen Resolution was only marginal, World War I was the occasion for an important episode in the history of modern German Jewry: the contact between Jews serving in the German army on the eastern front and the densely settled Jewish population of the occupied territories. Heretofore these *Ostjuden* had been encountered only as uprooted immigrants trying to make their way in Germany. But now German Jews had the opportunity to discover the integral and vibrant world of East European Jewish culture. For some the experience only confirmed their former negative judgment. But others, by far the majority, "were gripped by the strength and warmth, by the piety and idealism that they discovered underneath the crust of need and poverty." Here was a living Jewish community whose vitality could only serve to demonstrate to German Jewry how much it had lost in the process of assimilation. Even the non-Zionist philosopher Franz Rosenzweig was moved to write that

I felt something I rarely feel. I felt pride in my race, in so much freshness and vivacity. . . . I can well understand why the average German Jew no longer feels any kinship with these East European Jews: actually he has very little such kinship left; he has become philistine, bourgeois.

This confrontation with East European Jewry, speaking its own language and living in its own districts, seemed to confirm the Zionist vision of the reality of the Jewish people, and it drew new adherents at the same time that it bolstered the conviction of already-committed Zionists.[17]

The administrative problems of dealing with the Jews in the occupied territories, coupled with the desire of German Jews to give aid to their brethren in the east, called forth a cooperative effort between German Jewry and the German government: the Committee for the East (Komitee für den Osten). The domestic civil truce of wartime apparently extended to the conflict between the ZVfD and the Centralverein, and Zionists and assimilationists joined this coalition of Jewish organizations, which served to mediate between the *Ostjuden* and the military authorities, and to foster their social welfare. The Zionist contingent of the committee included men like Bodenheimer, Friedemann, and Oppenheimer, members of the older nonradical Zionist faction, who were inclined toward cooperation with non-Zionists. The entire enterprise provided a welcome opportunity for Jews to demonstrate both their patriotism and the congruence of Jewish interests with German war aims. Zionists made a more specific effort in this direction by attempting to elicit from the German government a statement of sympathy for Zionist aspirations in Palestine. Here the Zionists had the advantage of America's neutrality and the exaggerated estimate in some German government circles of American Jewry's ability to influence their own country's alignment in the war. On the other hand, Germany was unwilling to offend its Turkish allies. In any case, shortly after Britain's publication of the Balfour Declaration, Germany followed with a carefully worded statement of conditional support for limited Zionist settlement in Palestine. The strategy came to naught, however, with Germany's defeat and the consequent dismemberment of the Ottoman Empire under Allied auspices.[18]

On the whole the war enjoyed as much support among German Jews, Zionists and assimilationists alike, as it did among Germans in general. It had seemed at first that anti-Semitism would finally be submerged in the wartime unity of

German society. Jews flocked to the colors with the same enthusiasm as their compatriots in a war that was the first— and also the last—in which Jews were allowed to serve as officers in the army. Nevertheless, a residual anti-Semitism persisted, surfacing most dramatically in the army's "Jewish census" of 1916, which sought to determine the truth or false-hood of charges that Jews were shirking military service, espe-cially in the dangerous front lines. That the census was con-ducted at all was taken by German Jewry as a massive affront to its loyalty and devotion. Further developments only confirmed the anti-Semitic nature of the enterprise, with some Jews being withdrawn from frontline positions on the day of the census. The results, withheld from the public by the War Ministry, were later leaked for tendentious use in an anti-Semitic volume.

The fact is that Jewish military service and casualty rates deviated from the overall average only insofar as Jewish demo-graphic structure was specifically urban and middle class. Nevertheless, this did not prevent the postwar spread of the destructive libel of Jewish military evasion and Jewish responsi-bility for the "stab in the back" of a collapse on the home front that supposedly brought Germany's defeat. The charge prompted the formation of a Jewish veterans' organization, the Reichsbund jüdischer Frontsoldaten, devoted specifically to countering this slander, though with little success in those quarters where it was most tenaciously held. Altogether the experience only seemed to confirm the Zionists' contention that anti-Semitism was ineradicable.[19]

To be sure, Jewish attitudes were no more monolithic than were those of any other sector of German society, and the war fostered pacifist, as well as belligerent, attitudes. Indeed, such pacifism might be expected to be a concomitant of the Jewish nationalism of Zionism, which presumably transcended the specific lines of cleavage established by the war. On the whole, however, such attitudes were no more evident in the Zionist camp than they were among the Social Democrats, a German party whose first loyalty was supposedly to the international brotherhood of the working class.

Nevertheless, the exceptions, though few, were significant to the extent that they existed at all. One was Robert Weltsch, the postwar editor of the *Jüdische Rundschau*, whose proposals for accommodation with the Arabs in Palestine were partly influenced by a pacifist outlook bred of World War I. Another was Adolf Friedemann, who recorded in the secrecy of his diary a month after the war's outbreak his deep sorrow at the idiocy of the war and his skepticism at the unbridled and uncritical enthusiasm of German Jews for their fatherland. Friedemann wrote that there was

anti-Semitism everywhere. . . . I had never believed that the war would destroy the enmity toward us in a single blow. But at least during the hostilities all this meanness should have been stilled. It is even less gratifying to see how the strivers after decorations and medals are surfacing everywhere. Moreover, one racks one's brains as to why in these conditions Jews are automatically so enthusiastic for the victory of German arms. It is certainly natural that for the sake of the Jews and of culture we hope for the destruction of the Asiatics [*Vernichtung der Asiaten*]. But Frenchmen, Belgians, Englishmen were friendly to the Jews, are great nations of culture, and protect the rights of the poorest exiles, whom the Reich banishes. And is it not a matter of indifference in what language a child says "Father"? What would be lost if a piece of land, like Alsace, should come under French rule again?[20]

Friedemann's sentiments were as unusual as they were poignant.

One other consequence of the war, perhaps the most obvious one for German Zionism, was the shift of the center of the world Zionist movement away from Germany. With Herzl's death in 1904 the headquarters of the World Zionist Organization had moved from Vienna to Germany, first to Cologne, the home of David Wolffsohn, Herzl's immediate successor, and then to Berlin, the home of Otto Warburg, who was elected to replace Wolffsohn in 1911. The outbreak of war posed a serious problem for an international organization with headquarters in Germany, and in an effort to maintain its neutrality the World Zionist Organization opened an office in Copenhagen. The final victory of the Allies and the establishment of the British Mandate in Palestine drew the focus of Zionist activity to London, which became the site of the Zionist Executive from 1920 until its removal to Jerusalem in 1936. Meanwhile, the German language, which had been the accepted working language of the movement, began to give way to English and Hebrew.

As for the Posen Resolution itself, it would seem that the German Zionists, specifically the radicals, simply did not mean what they said. Whatever ideological conflicts or tactical considerations led them to formulate and approve this "radical" position, their actions indicated that, with few exceptions, they never really intended the extreme negation of Jewish life in the Diaspora that the resolution expressed. "Palestine and the Diaspora," said ZVfD president Arthur Hantke, "are the two pillars on which the Judaism of the future must rest."[21]

In fact, in all but one regard the radical reorientation of German Zionism seemed to have been ineffectual—but the exception was an important one. In arousing within German Jewry a massive, organized opposition to Zionism, Blumenfeld was successfully employing a typical and familiar radical gambit. The demand "For us or against us" was guaranteed to secure publicity at the same time that it bolstered the faithful in their commitment to the cause. The flurry of attacks and counterattacks that followed the Centralverein's 1913 anti-Zionist resolution brought Zionism to the attention of a public that had long proved itself deaf to Zionist propaganda.

If in the end the radical posture seems to have been largely a matter of rhetoric, this fact only poses more forcefully the question of just what the significance of German Zionism was. Blumenfeld's attempt to turn Zionism from a third-person into a first-person affair was scarcely successful, at least regarding *aliyah*. But in a deeper sense German Zionism had been a first-person affair all along.

A Weltanschauung *is an intellectual construction which solves all the problems of our existence uniformly on the basis of one overriding hypothesis, which, accordingly, leaves no question unanswered and in which everything that interests us finds its fixed place. It will easily be understood that the possession of a* Weltanschauung *of this kind is one of the ideal wishes of human beings. Believing in it one can feel secure in life, one can know what to strive for, and how one can deal most expediently with one's emotions and interests.*

—Freud, *"The Question of a* Weltanschauung"

Ideology. . . *mean[s] an unconscious tendency underlying religious and scientific as well as political thought: the tendency at a given time to make facts amenable to ideas, and ideas to facts, in order to create a world image convincing enough to support the collective and the individual sense of identity. Far from being arbitrary or consciously manageable (although it is as exploitable as all of man's unconscious strivings), the total perspective created by ideological simplification reveals its strength by the dominance it exerts on the seeming logic of historical events, and by its influence on the identity formation of individuals (and thus on their "ego-strength").*

—*Erik Erikson,* Young Man Luther[1]

6

IDEOLOGY AND IDENTITY: THE FUNCTIONS OF GERMAN ZIONISM

If the defining feature of the modern Jew was the failure of his traditional understanding of himself and his place in the world, then nowhere was this crisis of identity more severe than in Germany. Led by the promise of emancipation to refashion himself in a more acceptable mode, the Jew nevertheless found himself rebuffed by a Germany that professed to recognize only the old goods from which the new pattern had been cut. However German the Jew himself might feel, to others he seemed Jewish. "Among ourselves," one critic observed, "we Jews may have the impression that we speak as Germans to Germans. *We* have the impression. But no matter how much we feel ourselves to be completely German, the others feel us to be entirely non-German." "To the non-Jewish world," remarked Kurt Blumenfeld, "the Jew remains a Jew, no matter what his religious label." It was this inescapable reality that

Blumenfeld dubbed the "objective Jewish question [*Juden-frage*]." This was what the nineteenth-century anti-Semite Friedrich Rühs had meant when he protested that "if the Jews are now supposed to be not Jews at all, but Germans, then there is no telling nations apart anymore."[2]

Here, then, was a clash of a most disconcerting sort between the Jew's self-image as a German and his appearance as a Jew, in a matter where to see oneself as others did was an issue more of psychological necessity than ethical propriety. The peculiar nature of the situation was neatly captured in a Zionist parable from the turn of the century in which a stranger to Germany, ignorant of Jews and Germans alike, is pictured as meeting that curious entity, the German citizen of the Mosaic persuasion. The stranger notices

among the Germans [some] people who seem to be distinctive and peculiar. If he confronts one and asks, "Dear sir, to what nation do you belong?" the proud reply will be, "I am a German." He will speak further with the man and will notice that he is different from a German not only in appearance, but also in his manner of speaking and thinking. Once again he will ask, "Are you really a German?" The Jew will then feel somewhat uncomfortable and say, "I am a German of the Mosaic faith." "Curious religion that, which curves the nose, forms the eyes so strangely, and alters the whole being of a person so fundamentally." The whole business will strike the stranger as peculiar, and he will scout out the next best German and ask, "What is that man there? He says he is a German of the Mosaic faith." "That's supposed to be a German?" will be the indignant reply. "That's a Jew!"

The tale did not end there, however, but went on to suggest that the Jew's self-disdain, which stemmed from his attempt to assimilate and shed his distinctive Jewishness, drew in turn the disrespect of non-Jews. Hence there was supposedly a clear progression first from self-denial to self-hatred, then from self-hatred to being hated by others. As our stranger concluded: "So that must be a fine nation, the nation of Jews, if a person has to be ashamed to belong to it. One must take care with these people." The moral was thus a lesson in the genesis of anti-Semitism:

The stranger, who could be the most enlightened person, has learned in a half hour the art of being an anti-Semite. Here one sees a bit of the origins of anti-Semitism. Those who do not own up to being Jewish concede that the Jew is something inferior . . . something contemptible.[3]

Indeed, by the twentieth century this attitude of abnegation had gone so far that the very word "Jew" came to be regarded by both Christians and Jews as a term of abuse:

It was considered tactless or outright hostile to say of someone that he was a Jew, and naturally every Jew avoided doing so in polite company. . . . If the word "Jew" had really shrunk to a mere invective without any positive content it seemed more proper not to use it.[4]

Hence the currency of the polite euphemism *Israelit*, and against that the conscious choice of *Jude* by writers such as Gabriel Riesser in the nineteenth century and Martin Buber in the twentieth, who sought thereby to sound a note of Jewish self-assertion.

Instead of the curse of self-disdain Zionism offered to the Jew the liberation of self-affirmation, the opportunity to present himself forthrightly as a Jew without finely differentiated reservations based on religious and civil affiliations. It sought "to imbue every Jew with pride in his origins, his illustrious history, and his magnificent spiritual treasures, so that he will not—as unfortunately is often the case—regard his own Judaism as a disgrace." Furthermore, just as the Jew's low regard of himself supposedly drew the scorn of others, it was now expected that his self-affirmation would induce their respect:

Only when we once again become full Jews [declared an 1898 Zionist broadside] will we be full German citizens. From that moment on, when we discard the ridiculous phrase about "Germans of the Jewish confession"—in which no one really believes—will we be clearly creative. Only when we proudly and openly confess, "We are the sons of the Jewish people [*Stamm*], but we have participated, as much as you, in all the achievements of culture; we have cooperated in all tasks for the [common] weal, we are German citizens of Jewish birth!"— only then will the honorable anti-Semite—and there *are* such—have respect for us. He will not love us, but he will respect us. No man can be forced to love, but even an opponent can be compelled to grudge respect.[5]

This early confidence that Zionism's affirmation of Jewishness would disarm anti-Semitism in Germany unfortunately proved to be overly optimistic. But there is no question that Zionism was effective in enhancing the self-image of its adherents and thereby resolving, at least for them, the difficult problem of German Jewish identity.

Conversion to postassimilatory Zionism typically began when a long-held assimilationist view came increasingly into doubt, and it was consummated in a final, often apparently sudden, displacement of assimilationism by a transforming Zionist commitment. The experience could be an overwhelming one, and the memoirs of those who underwent it call to mind their close parallels in the literature of religious conversion.

Richard Lichtheim's Zionist conversion, to cite one example, seems practically archetypal. Both in tone and substance it captured the passion and enthusiasm shared by the few

German Jews who suddenly came to realize the truth of Herzl's dictum: "The Jews are a people, one people." Lichtheim, the son of a wealthy and thoroughly assimilated family, had been raised in the exclusive, fashionable milieu of Berlin West, a district especially favored by families like his own. It was the closed world of the "non-Jewish Jew," in which Jews socialized with one another unaware of either their own Jewishness or the absence of Christian social partners. After a period of growing disquiet with the life around him, Lichtheim came upon Zionism. His account of the experience is worth citing at length:

The outward event that brought about my conversion [*Bekehrung*] to Zionism was my meeting with a student who introduced me into a Zionist circle and gave me Herzl's writings to read. After a few days of reading, of reflection and discussion, the transformation was complete. I became a Zionist. . . .

The Zionist analysis of the Jewish situation impressed me very soon as evident, *since I had already discovered or suspected much of it through my own observation. . . .* The great enlightenment came over me . . . when I found stated outright, with compelling lucidity, in the introductory chapters of Herzl's "Jewish State" *my own inner experience of the nature of anti-Semitism and the national character of the Jewish question.*

Here were the answers to all the questions that I had for years posed for myself and my acquaintances. Not through assimilation and baptism, but through independent achievement in one's own land would the relationship between Jews and other peoples be normalized, and anti-Semitism overcome. Neither the imitation of an alien manner nor adaptation to the surrounding world . . . was capable of solving the personal problem that every Jew carried around with him. This solution had to come from within, from one's own nature. *Here, and only here—in Zionism—could the Jewish personality finally develop free and unbroken.*

To be sure, this created a new problem—the question of the content of a Judaism that had to be secularized, and that had to enter into the family of nations anew. But that was not so important to begin with as the consciousness of belonging to the Jewish people, and the manly bearing that was a consequence. *It was a matter of affirming myself and thereby becoming free. . . .*

Everything in the views of my acquaintances that had appeared flawed, dubious, and false now found its explanation. I achieved a distance from the cosmopolitan, aesthetic "Berlin W." of my earliest youth and turned away from it. This glass cage held me no longer. I had found the way through the glass wall into the open.

What my family had for a hundred years regarded as the solution for the Jewish question had proven itself an error. Assimilation succeeded for scattered individuals, *but only at the cost of self-abandonment.* It was no solution for the hundreds of thousands of Jews who still wavered between ghetto and European culture. But it was also no solution for me, since I had discovered that not simply my individual will, but a four-thousand-year history had made me irrevocably a Jew. *My avowal of Zionism was the avowal of myself.* That was the solution to the Jewish question. There could be no other.[6]

Here was an experience that was repeated time and again— the growing and painful awareness of the severity of the "Jewish question" and the inadequacy of previous attempts to solve it, the realization that Zionism articulated feelings that had been hitherto inchoate, and the liberating power of Zionism's sweeping vision. Once both the disaffection with assimilationism and a predisposition toward Zionism were established, it was striking how a single, specific event was sufficient to precipitate conversion. As with Friedemann, it was often some final encounter with anti-Semitism, suddenly perceived as more grievous than the many that had been glossed over in the past. Or, as in Lichtheim's case, it could be an exposure to Zionist doctrine or theory as expounded in discussion or reading. Herzl's manifesto *The Jewish State* had a tremendous impact on those who were sensitized to its message, and it was responsible for many a conversion, as were Herzl's posthumously published diaries. Other writings might have the same effect. The historian Gershom Scholem, for example, came to Zionism through his reading of Graetz's classic *History of the Jews.* [7]

Like many great truths, the wisdom of Zionism could appear in unexpected places that seemed to depend more on the vision of the reader than the intention of the author. For Max Bodenheimer, whose youth and student days had been marked by sharply felt incidents of anti-Semitism, the immediate impulse for conversion to Zionism came with his chance reading of a German police chief's work on thieves' dialects and their borrowings from Yiddish. Bodenheimer suddenly realized that to have preserved their own language over the generations the Jews must have been more than simply a religious group, they must have been a nation. The consequences of this conclusion were overwhelming:

The Zionist idea was the result of a sudden inspiration. It was like a light that suddenly broke forth within me. The remarkable character of this phenomenon shook my whole being. I felt like a slave for whom the road to liberty suddenly opens, like a prisoner who by a miracle finds the tool to break his chains. The state of mind into which this thought transported me can hardly be described. Whereas shortly before I had wrestled with the decision to abandon Judaism and seek refuge from Jew-hatred in new surroundings where my origin was unknown, I was now filled with a holy zeal to serve the cause of my people. Perhaps it came from the fact that I suddenly recognized the futility of such an assimilation for the people as a whole, perhaps also because my feeling of honor resisted such a flight from the community into which I had been born. At any rate the change was inexplicable to myself, especially since it had nothing to do with religion. . . . Perhaps I was already on the verge of this recognition, and only a slight puff of wind was needed for one banked fire to burst into flame.[8]

Among those who came to Zionism after a break with an assimilationist past, the familiar pattern of dramatic Zionist

conversion seemed almost universal. It spanned the whole
Zionist political spectrum. At the pole opposite Bodenheimer
was Kurt Blumenfeld, who testified that

everything that had been embryonic for years now was expressed so
self-evidently by Zionism that I experienced my decision for Zionism
as a final destiny.... When I [attempted to] substantiate my Zionism
I always felt that I had come to my insights not through any system
or through reason, but through a revelation [*Offenbarung*] that over-
came me again and again. I trusted it because through it I succeeded
in bringing many people . . . to an unexpected turning point.

Nor was the phenomenon limited to leading Zionists, whose
memoirs happen to be the most accessible. From the ranks of
the movement comes the testimony of one member that Zionism was "more than a political program . . . [it was] a call to
a completely new life"; or of another that "now that I plunged
into this movement with all the zeal of the newly converted,
I began to see everything through Zionist lenses."[9]

Here, then, lay the real personal significance of Zionism for
its adherents in Germany—not as the vehicle for fund raising,
charitable work for the *Ostjuden,* or the promotion of *aliyah,*
but as the source of a coherent, integrated, and compelling
world view; in short, as the source of a viable and supportive
identity. Zionism was, Robert Weltsch recalled, "only in a
limited sense an emigration movement." Rather, it was "a
movement based on a world view [*eine weltanschauliche Bewegung*] that stood up for a national Jewish center in order to give
the Jews an identity."[10]

What is remarkable about Zionism's transforming power is
that it seemed to operate quite apart from any specific intellectual or ideological content, aside from the abstract affirmation
of Jewish nationality. (Lichtheim's Zionist confession makes

this quite clear.) Nevertheless, its nebulousness does not seem to have impaired its ability to effect in its advocates a personal transformation that was the equivalent of a spiritual rebirth. An alumnus of the Zionist student movement testified:

We did not become more "Jewish." We did not emigrate to Palestine in masses, but we found in ourselves a new strength. We found a new meaning in our lives and in the realm of our spiritual and social being. We were men who were saved by Judaism from anomie, rootlessness, and pallid aestheticism. The wonder of an inner rebirth was consummated in us.[11]

Once again the similarity to religious conversion, with its fundamental and sweeping reorientation of personality and identity, is apparent. So it is not surprising to notice the Zionists' natural use of a religious vocabulary to describe their experience of transformation, even though it may have had no specific connection with the Jewish religion itself. Lichtheim spoke of the religious phenomena of "conversion" *(Umkehr* and *Bekehrung)* and "vocation" *(Berufung),* while Bodenheimer, despite his claim that his conversion had "nothing to do with religion," cited his "holy zeal" for the Zionist cause. We find one Zionist describing his conversion as his "Day of Damascus," while another wrote that "a light glimmered in the darkness, not only in the sense of a new revelation, but also in the sense of spiritual salvation."[12]

In the light of all this religious illumination it seems fair to suggest that Zionism may have served as a surrogate for religion. In fact there is clear indication of this in some instances, both for Jews who had abandoned earlier religious ties and for those who until their Zionist conversion had been estranged from formal Judaism. Felix Rosenblüth belonged to the first group, having had an Orthodox upbringing and having been religiously observant until the age of twenty. He himself remarked that Zionism could be "a sublimation of Orthodox fanaticism into a more nonreligious form." Bodenheimer, who went through a short period of Orthodoxy after his conversion to Zionism, was an example of the second group.[13]

The transforming experience of Zionist conversion has another parallel: adolescent identity crisis and identity resolution, where old commitments fall into doubt in a crisis of uncertainty that may be resolved in a new sense of self. In its most dramatic form this reshaping of identity can be felt by those who experience it as the equivalent of a second birth. For many young Zionists this theoretical parallel described the historical fact. The turn toward Zionism could serve as an act of rebellion against parental authority and parental values in the relatively authoritarian context of German society, where the clash between generations was especially intense. (This adolescent revolt writ large was the basis for the distinctive German youth movement, whose Zionist counterpart will be examined later.) By its recognition of Jewish peoplehood, Zionism represented a dramatic repudiation of the liberal, assimilationist values of adult Jewry, which was likely to appeal to youth seeking an avenue for revolt. There was even a certain daring in Zionism's acceptance of the *Ostjuden,* and the free association of native and immigrant Jews that was possible within the movement and that could scandalize one's elders.[14]

Spiritual Zionism

It should not be altogether surprising that Zionism could provide its adherents with an identity, since the role of ideological commitment in individual self-definition is familiar. What

is curious about German Zionism, however, is that it rationalized a *continued Jewish existence in Germany* on the basis of
an ideology of national separatism. That is, while non-Jewish
Germans regarded the Jews as a distinct and unassimilable
people, this was the very thing that the Zionists chose to affirm,
restating positively what in the context of assimilationism had
been a condemnation. But paradoxically, in asserting themselves as members of an independent Jewish *Volk,* one that
was as valid as the German *Volk,* the Zionists seemed to have
found a stable basis for remaining in Germany—in psychological if not in political terms. This was evident not only in the
fact of the Zionists' remaining in Germany, but even more
specifically in their explicit testimony to the consequences of
Zionist allegiance. Kurt Blumenfeld argued that

the Jew can live in Germany freer of conflict if he recognizes the
problematic nature of the Jewish situation and does not occupy
himself with pointless opposition to anti-Semitism, but rather faces
the non-Jewish German unabashed, with open visor. The alleged
dangers of so-called double loyalty are the product of an anxious
imagination.[15]

This was certainly a peculiar result in view of the Posen
Resolution's insistence on the importance and necessity of
aliyah. But even discounting the prescriptive value of that
resolution, whose real significance was quite different from its
apparent one, the problem still remained: in *theory* Zionism
seemed incompatible with a Jew's remaining in Germany.
Consequently, anyone who did remain might appear to be
guilty of sheer hypocrisy at worst or, at best, of blind self-
contradiction. Certainly this was the case if one took the
Zionist's own rhetoric at face value.

There was, however, one other possible explanation for the

German Zionists' inaction. In the movement at large the issue of *aliyah* was a matter much in dispute, and of the two contending views—"negation of the galuth" and "affirmation of the galuth"—the latter offered support for what was in effect the actual position of the German Zionists.

Galuth means "exile," specifically the Jews' long exile from Zion, and its very use instead of the more neutral Diaspora ("dispersion") indicates an attitude toward Jewish life outside of Zion that was somewhat negative to begin with. "Negation of the galuth," however, involved a judgment that was both absolute and normative. This view contended that given the ineradicability of anti-Semitism, a solution to the "Jewish problem" was impossible in the Diaspora, and that nothing of value for the development of Jewish tradition or culture could come of Jewish Diaspora existence. The result was a strictly political and territorial construction of Zionism: only in their own land, speaking their own language, would the Jews be able to establish a normal, free, and creative existence. Jews who regarded themselves as Jews would move to Zion. All others who remained in exile would be absorbed into their host nations. Jakob Klatzkin, one of the principal champions of this position, wrote:

The national center, the concentration [of Jews] in Palestine, will accelerate the gradual withering away of the galuth. It will put an end to this excruciating agony. It will permit a valid assimilation into the Diaspora, into the everyday world of the gentiles. At the same time a Hebrew[-speaking] Palestine will issue a proclamation: Here national rebirth, there national death.[16]

The opposing view, generally associated with its principal exponent, Ahad Haam, held that such a theory was unrealistically stark in its statement of alternatives and that it failed to take proper account of the Jewish will to survive, even in the unfavorable conditions of the Diaspora. While Ahad Haam argued that objectively the Diaspora could and would continue to exist, he conceded that as a subjective matter a negative attitude toward it was appropriate. "With few exceptions," he wrote, "all recognize that the position of a lamb among wolves is unsatisfactory, and they would gladly put an end to this state of things if it were possible."[17] Thus the dispute was not over ultimate ends, but rather over shorter-range possibilities. Hence the phrase "affirmation of the galuth" was, strictly speaking, a misnomer. It meant simply that as long as the galuth remained in existence, the quality of Jewish life therein ought to be enhanced as much as possible. Therefore, Ahad Haam argued, a Zionism that was oriented entirely toward territorial and political nationalism would be inadequate.

He proposed instead that Zion be regarded primarily as a spiritual center, providing spiritual support for Jewish life in the Diaspora. Thus while Jewish settlement in Palestine could serve as an immediate refuge for persecuted Jews and could continue to be the ideal destination for all Jews, there was nothing in this "spiritual Zionism," as it was called, that required any Jew to pack his bags and emigrate to Palestine.

It should be clear that this was the view of Zionism that actually prevailed in the German movement, not the one implied by occasional flurries of radical rhetoric. Lichtheim stated in his semiofficial *Program of Zionism* of 1911:

The real meaning of a Jewish center in Palestine lies . . . in the effect that it will exert on the spirit of Judaism. . . . Zionism seeks to form a national core for Judaism that will influence, lead, and develop Judaism elsewhere. . . . More important than the material improvement [in the lives of Jewish settlers in Palestine] are the *spiritual* repercussions of the Jewish settlement. The fact of its existence will demonstrate to all the Jews of the world the possibility of a renaissance of Judaism.

In the same vein the ZVfD's pamphlet *What Does Zionism Want?* proclaimed that

this new Jewish culture [in Palestine] will become of decisive significance for those who remain behind in the Diaspora. Palestine and the Diaspora will stand in a constant reciprocal spiritual relationship. Just as the Diaspora will provide the men and the means for the upbuilding of Palestine, so on the other side will Palestine be the source of energy for the Diaspora. Palestine will rekindle the spiritual life of the Diaspora.[18]

The doctrine could be a complex one, and it was not always presented with such straightforward clarity. Blumenfeld's pronouncements on the subject, for example, reflected not only the logical difficulties intrinsic in "spiritual Zionism" but also the strength of his own ties to German culture and his reluctance to abandon it. As he summed up the matter in retrospect, within the world movement the position of German Zionism regarding negation and affirmation of the galuth

was special, in that its negation of the galuth was bound together with a clear appreciation of the significance of German culture and of German spiritual life. The Zionist recognition of the "Jewish question" led more and more strongly to our separation from a world that was not ours.

Regarding this view, however, the criticism of an anonymous Zionist opponent of Blumenfeld's was legitimate:

What [must] the great masses think of the proclamations of "affirmation of the galuth" and "negation of the galuth"? As long as they see that we and our children remain in the galuth and that of the few who depart . . . to emigrate to Palestine quite a large percentage return; as long as they hear our declarations about the torn anguish of our souls in the galuth and the intolerability of life in the galuth, but see us living here quite contentedly, just as assimilated as they are themselves, we cannot reckon that we are going to win any "great masses."[19]

The unfortunate truth is that what was really a theoretically integrated and consistent survivalist ideology for Jewish life in Germany could easily seem, especially when overdrawn, to be an exercise in hypocrisy.

Zionism's striking success in providing its adherents with a viable version of German Jewish identity did not detract from the fact that the competing assimilationist version seemed to function equally well for the overwhelming majority of German Jewry. Zionist denunciations notwithstanding, assimilationism was not equivalent to cringing self-abnegation, and it could involve—as it did in the Centralverein—an affirmation of Jewishness and an enhancement of Jewish self-respect that was equal in significance to Zionism's, though different in content.[20]

Given the fact that these two ideologies had such similar results in practice, it would be of considerable interest to know why an individual chose one rather than the other, and what set Zionism's adherents apart from the assimilationists. Unfortunately, these are questions with no clear answers. Apart from the commitment to Jewish nationality, Zionist ideology was sufficiently vague that it is difficult to determine exactly wherein lay the strengths of the special identity it provided. Furthermore, though the data are admittedly scanty, the lack of any evident correlation between the espousal of Zionism and particular sociological variables makes it impossible to identify any causal factors that would have drawn an individual specifically to Zionism. In the matter of cultural background, for example, the bulk of the Zionist membership was of recent East European origin, but there were also a great number of longer-settled German Jews, especially in positions of leadership. Similarly, as far as can be determined, neither economic class nor religious outlook seems to have made any difference. Jewish "notables" of the professional and rentier classes could be found in both the Zionist and assimilationist camps, as could the whole range of religious belief from traditional Orthodoxy through atheism (although insofar as liberal reform was specifically assimilationist, it would have been present on that side only). To the extent that Zionist commitment was a product of adolescent rebellion it is true that it offered a clear contrast to the established assimilationism, but other channels for revolt against the bourgeois liberalism of adult Jewry were available, such as socialism and political radicalism. So even here there is no telling exactly what made a person opt for Zionism.[21]

The problem of distinguishing between Zionists and assimilationists is further complicated by the fact that in terms of practical activity there was so little difference between the lives of members of the Centralverein and those of the ZVfD. This was true even for a "professional" Zionist such as Blumenfeld, whose involvement in organizational work was comparable to that of his counterparts in the Centralverein—save, of course, for the content of their respective speeches. Even in their intellectual outlook the Zionists were as deeply rooted in German culture as any of their fellow Jews. And there is no reason to believe that the Zionists had the monopoly on Jewish learning and Jewish culture that their propaganda at times seems to have claimed.

In sum, there may be no differentiating between the ZVfD

and the Centralverein in terms of their abstract functional significance as sources of equally viable, though theoretically opposed, versions of German Jewish identity. Zionists thought themselves more at ease than the assimilationists, but assimilationism seems to have functioned perfectly well for those who continued to espouse it. Nevertheless, it must be granted that one of Zionism's claims was correct: whether a Jew was regarded as fully German or not was indeed a matter for non-Jewish Germans to determine, and the decision was often a negative one. Whether the Zionist analysis of all aspects of the Jews' situation in Germany was this accurate is a different question. Therefore, it is fair to inquire how far the Zionist view actually comported with the reality of German conditions, both as they appeared then and as they appear to us in retrospect.

7

ZIONISM, ANTI-SEMITISM, AND GERMAN POLITICS

The conflict between the Zionists and their ideological opponents sprang less from a dispute about the value of German culture, on whose worth both sides were generally agreed, than from divergent views on the nature of the Jews' situation in Germany. To be sure, they differed in that the assimilationists might carry acculturation to its limit and completely eliminate even nominal attachment to Judaism. But the official, representative institutions of German Jewry—both the Centralverein and the organizations and spokesmen of the liberal Judaism that the majority of German Jews professed—were by their very nature opposed to such an extreme. (Recognizable in American terms as something between Conservative and Reform Judaism, this liberal Judaism was the denationalized, "modernized" religion that the Centralverein's German citizens for the most part had in mind when they characterized themselves as being "of the Jewish faith.") By way of establishing the limits beyond which assimilation might not go, Eugen

Fuchs of the Centralverein explained that if assimilationism meant

casting off the vestiges of the ghetto, breaking with what has withered and died, breaking with caftan and earlocks, then no one will have any objection. But if assimilationism means breaking with the sanctified custom[s] . . . of our fathers, or abandoning the manifestations of the Jewish spirit and the Jewish heart, Jewish feeling and the Jewish sense of family, if it means giving up one thing and adopting the other, not because it is better, but because it is the other, then this assimilationism will be abhorred by everyone from the depths of his soul. We want to collaborate in German culture, on German soil, and [also] remain true to what we have inherited . . . from hundreds and thousands of years of Jewish history as the legitimate special character of our people [*Stamm*].[1]

The real question that separated Zionists and assimilationists was therefore not who was more assimilated, but whether assimilation, even of gigantic proportions, could secure Jewish integration into German society. Indeed, the question was whether there was any place at all for Jews as Jews in Germany. It was here that the Zionists parted company from their fellow Jews. The Jewish question, Zionism claimed, was an objective not a subjective matter. No Jew's subjective sense of belonging to the German people, no matter how intense or patently justified, could overcome the objective fact of his rejection by Christian Germany as an alien being. Thus no matter how much other Jews might want to regard anti-Semitism as an incidental aberration from tolerant, liberal norms, for the Zionists its apparent ineradicability was just one indication of the objective nature of the Jewish question. As long as the Zionists remained in Germany, their lives were played out against the tension between the theoretical conviction that there was no place for them there and the practical necessity of finding the place whose very existence their theory denied.

The Limits of Assimilationism

The ideology of assimilationism presumed that acculturation would find its reward in social and political integration in a Germany that was conceived of primarily in secular and liberal terms. The strategy had its flaws, and assimilationists had to overlook both the intrinsic limitations on the process of acculturation and the essential hostility of German society and politics to Jewish aspirations. To the extent that assimilationists were aware of these difficulties but ignored them, they did so in the expectation that in the end their optimism would justify itself. There was, however, much to overlook, for the awkward reality was that the Jews' desire for acceptance generally exceeded the welcome that they were accorded by non-Jewish society. Nevertheless, this rejection never appeared to be so decisive as to warrant the abandonment of assimilationism altogether. Rather, it only seemed to spur German Jewry on to renewed efforts at acculturation and repeated affirmations of devotion to Germany and German culture.

The avowal of the neo-Kantian philosopher Hermann Cohen, a reigning figure in the German Jewish intellectual pantheon, was typical:

We love our Germanness [*Deutschtum*], not only because we love our homeland as a bird loves its nest, [but because] . . . we have drawn our intellectual culture . . . from the treasures and mines of the German spirit, . . . the spirit of classical humanity and of true cosmopolitanism. What [other] people has a Kant? . . . And what people has this spiritual unity of poetic heroes such as have enlivened our spiritual history through Lessing and Herder, through Schiller and Goethe? What people has ever had this unity of classical poetry and philosophy! The German intellectuals are all of them prophets of humanity. It is really natural that we German Jews feel ourselves integrated as Jews and as Germans. . . . I read *Faust* not only as a beautiful poem, but my love goes out to it as to a German epiphany. I feel the same way about Luther . . . Mozart and Beethoven and . . . [Freiherr vom] Stein and Bismarck.

Doubtless it was sentiments such as these that prompted the remark that "if there were a Nobel Prize for German sentiment, the Jews would win it."[2]

The striking thing about Cohen's panegyric was his highly selective depiction of the German spirit as being identical with the German classical humanist tradition of the Enlightenment. This philosophical preference, which was broadly shared by German Jewry, was understandable given the fact that it was precisely this tolerant humanism that was potentially most receptive toward assimilationist aspirations. It was surely questionable, however, whether this tradition was as dominant in the German intellectual heritage as assimilationist Jews like Cohen liked to believe. Whether it had any real influence as political ideology was, as will be seen, more doubtful still.

Cohen may perhaps be excused an error of historical judgment, but as a philosopher he should have been aware of faulty logic. He tried to establish the identity of Jews as Germans through the intermediate term of German culture, but the Jews' subjective devotion to German humanism carried no necessary implications for substantive Jewish integration. In his *Religion of Reason from the Sources of Judaism* (1919) Cohen had devoted considerable energy to demonstrating that liberal Judaism and neo-Kantian philosophy were compatible, but that did not draw Germany any closer to the Jews. Nor, for that matter, did Lessing's popularity among German Jews or their exaggerated admiration for Goethe.[3]

Like the Jewish students in "parity" fraternities or the wealthy Jews of Berlin West, assimilationists lived intellectually in a Germany of their own making that was never as close to the external reality as they imagined. To some extent this behavior may simply have reflected the human inclination to see only what is most favorable to one's wishes, though harsher Zionist critics would call it an act of self-deception pure and simple. It may also have been a case of what one historian has described as a "displacement of courtship: people can reject and spurn; books and music cannot."[4]

Not only did the Jews' devotion to German culture prove unavailing in securing integration, but their very enthusiasm, bred perhaps of overcompensation for feelings of insecurity and rejection, could itself excite a negative response. No matter how assimilated, the Jew was still regarded as inescapably alien. Therefore his active and visible participation in German culture, besides doing nothing to confirm his claim to Germanness, allegedly threatened German culture with being "Judaized." Adolf Friedemann conceded that there was some truth to the anti-Semitic accusation that German theater and literature were indeed "Judaized," insofar as

the impressionistic, analytic, impractical [elements] that crowd today's market of intellectual production lie quite far from the authentic German, [who is] energetic and industrious. Our [German] literature is produced for the most part *by* Jews of German culture . . . *for* Jews of German culture, without however corresponding to the German character at all.

Moritz Goldstein, the editor of a series of German classics, feared that we are now faced with the problem that we Jews administer the spiritual possessions of a people that denies us the right and ability to do so. . . . Depending on one's viewpoint, it is either comical or tragic to look over the members of the "German" seminars of our universities. . . . Every guardian of German art knows to his ire how many Jews . . . there are among the "German poets."[5]

While Germans might reject the contribution of Jews to their culture, for the assimilated Jewish writer there was no escape. Goldstein acknowledged that

despite persecution, derision, and disdain, Judaism has become so tangled with Germanness in the course of over a thousand years of association that they can no longer be disentangled from one another.

As much as German Jews might want to withdraw from a culture that regarded their collaboration as "Jewish obtrusiveness," they "could no sooner become Hebrew poets," said Goldstein, skeptical of Zionism's promise of liberation, than they "could emigrate to Palestine." The plight of the German Jew was that of a hapless suitor. "Our relationship to Germany is that of an unlucky love. We should finally be manly enough to wrench our beloved from our heart with firm decisiveness, instead of endlessly pining away in misery—and for all that she sticks in our heart."[6] To describe German Jewish history as a long tragedy of unrequited love is not to deny the confessions of devotion that that passion spawned. But the shadow of a tragic misperception overlay the pathos of admiration and attachment.

Adversaries and Allies

Besides the unavailing nature of acculturation there was a second impediment to integration: the attitudes of German society itself. The fulfillment of assimilationist aspirations required a society that was both liberal and pluralistic, that is, one in which individuals would be judged on their own merits and in which residual differences, such as religion, would be of only secondary importance. Thus by restricting areas of diversity, and either minimizing their importance or seeking the mutual toleration of what differences remained, the Jews sought harmonious coexistence within the broad, shared realms that they thought were left. This was the theoretical foundation for the "neutral society" of the Berlin Haskalah, and it was the basis for the claim of "German citizens of the Jewish faith" to full inclusion in German civil society.

The problem was that their desire for integration made the Jews overlook the fact that this view was not widely enough shared for them to achieve their goal. Nor was there enough toleration of those diversities that were really ineradicable if Jews were to continue as Jews in any sense at all. Thus while the Jews' dual goals of social integration and retention of a narrowly conceived religious identity were not intrinsically mutually contradictory, the force of Christian opinion in Germany operated to make them so.

To be sure, the ideology of assimilationism could not have been entirely a self-deceptive fabrication of hopeful wishes. There was always enough acceptance and integration to suggest to Jews that their strivings would not go unrecognized. Nevertheless, closer examination reveals that beginning with the period of the Haskalah itself, the major premise of assimilationism was more often denied than accepted, even by Christian advocates of Jewish emancipation, who expected that eventually Jews would find their way to the Christian faith. This was true throughout the nineteenth century as well, and by the time of the German Empire (1871–1918) Jews faced what amounted to a constellation of ideological resistance to assimilationism. Uriel Tal has demonstrated in his recent survey of Christian attitudes in this period that Jewish integration in Germany proved to be problematic precisely to the extent that Jews insisted on retaining some measure of their own distinctive identity.

The real issue, then, was Jewish particularism, not integration itself (though to the extent that Jews sought integration as Jews the two issues remained intertwined). Ultimately the question was whether any kind of pluralistic framework could be defined that would offer political and social equality to the Jews at the same time that it allowed them the freedom to define themselves as they chose. Tal's conclusion is essentially the negative one that no such solution was forthcoming, and he portrays a range of anti-Jewish resistance that stemmed not only from conservatives and racists, but also from political liberals, intellectuals, and liberal Protestants, from whom such views might be less expected.[7]

The conservative and racist positions were relatively straight-forward. Conservatives held that Germany was fundamentally a Christian state, in which there were no grounds for equality for anyone refusing to recognize that fact. Jewish persistence could be maintained, but only at the price of social and political disadvantage. Conversely, integration could be had at the cost of abandoning Judaism—but this fact raised the suspicion that religious conversion was an opportunistic deception, undertaken in bad faith. Anti-Semites were opposed to the presence of Jews under any circumstances, though there was (at least in

Unsere Zukunft liegt auf dem Wasser.

Reform

Taufwasser

Ein Zuschauer: O Gott, o Gott, ich hab' immer so Angst, daß er mal 'neinplumst.

Zionist Views of Assimilation

Our Future Lies over the Water. *(A "modern" rabbi—note the preacher's garb—is walking the difficult tightrope of religious reform, which is suspended over a pool of baptismal water.)* "An onlooker: O God, O God, I'm always so afraid that one of these days he's going to fall in" (Der Schlemiel 1, no. 2 [1.12.1903]: 11

Nach der Taufe *Zeichnung von Ludwig Wronkow*

"Ich möchte ein neues Testament haben, ich hab mein altes verloren."

After Baptism. *"I'd like to buy a New Testament; I've lost my old one"* (Der Schlemiel n.s., no. 20 [1920]: back cover)

Darwinism. *"How the Hanukkah menorah of COHN the leather dealer . . . evolves into the Christmas tree of Commercial Councilor CONRAD . . ."* (Der Schlemiel 2, no. 1 [1.1.1904]: 3)

Christmas Presents. *("Assimilated" Jewish parents are offering a Christmas gift to their child, a member of the Zionist youth movement.) "And because you're in the Blau-Weiss, Santa brought you a menorah"* (Der Schlemiel n. s., no. 12 [1919]: back cover)

»*Sobald in Jerusalem ein Spielklub errichtet wird, werde ich Zionistin.*«

The Pleasure of Exile. *She to him:· "As soon as they build a card club in Jerusalem, I'll become a Zionist"* (Der Schlemiel *n. s., no. 5 [1919]: 75)*

An Appropriate Conversion. *"Are you a Lutheran now, Herr Marcuse?"* *"No, Greek-Orthodox—with due regard for my nose"* (Der Schlemiel *n. s., no. 4 [1919]: 51*)

rhetoric) a difference between those who regarded the offend-
ing Jewishness as a taint that could be erased and those who
held that it was an ineradicable matter of race.[8]

For liberal intellectual Christians the problem of Jewish
integration was especially vexing, since they recognized the
ethical and natural right of autonomous self-definition in theory at the same time that they required that Jews assimilate
totally and repudiate any specific Jewish identification. This
demand derived in part from the peculiar notion that the
political unity of Germany required a corresponding unity of
the German spirit, which was threatened by the Jews' maintaining their own religious identity. This insistence on self-
abnegation before the unified state derived in turn from the
German liberal solution to the problem of political authority.
Though liberals denied the state the right to impose its will on
the individual, they were able to preserve the ethical autonomy
of the individual will only by requiring that it identify itself
completely with the will of the state; thus any possibility of
conflict was precluded. This view of authority was what en-
abled the liberals to accept German national unification as
Bismarck delivered it to them, through wholly illiberal means.
The consequence of this position, as Tal described it, was that

the intellectual was required to forego his individual critical attitude
in the interests of national unity and state power, just as the Jew was
required to surrender his separatist position in the interests of that
same national unity. [Thus] the intellectual class in Germany, whose
influence extended far beyond its numerical representation in the
general population, . . . the class on which the Jews pinned their
hopes for achieving full integration, . . . was also the one from which
they suffered their deepest disappointment.[9]

Liberal Protestants, given their opposition to the Christian state and to the power of the Catholic Church, also might have been potential allies in the Jewish cause. But like the political liberals they proved to be antipathetic, for a complex set of reasons deriving largely from their claim that liberal Christianity was theologically superior to liberal Judaism. Although liberal Protestants might oppose in their own behalf conservative arguments for a formally Christian state, they joined conservatives in affirming "the exclusively Christian character of German society, nationality, and culture."[10]

Altogether, then, the tolerant religious pluralism that Jewish efforts at integration presumed seems to have been more imagined than real. Whereas German Christians understood Jewish emancipation as "the removal of barriers that had hitherto prevented Jews from completely assimilating to their environment," Jews took it to be "an incentive to continue to cultivate Jewish uniqueness." In retrospect, what is striking is that so few Jews shared the perception of one Jewish writer, who recognized in 1880 that even in the camp of liberal intellectuals the view prevailed that "the desire of the Jews to be German was . . . unrealistic as long as Judaism was not absorbed in its German-Christian environment by complete assimilation and dissolution by means of miscegenation." In the end Jewish integration apparently depended not on any Jewish definition of what was an acceptable version of German identity, no matter how deeply imbued with devotion to things German, but rather on a Christian definition that effectively barred any Jewish dimension at all.[11]

Apart from political ideology, what sources of actual organized political support were available to the Jews? The answer is that on the whole these were limited, and indeed one reflection of the weakness of the Jews' position in Germany was their difficulty in finding strong and reliable political allies.[12] Between 1867 and 1878 Jews gave their support to the National Liberal party, the party of German unification and consequent Jewish emancipation. Here Jews had the welcome opportunity of supporting both the regime and liberalism together, with no need to go into opposition in behalf of Jewish interests. This alliance lasted only until the late 1870s, when the party began to fall from power and also turned against Jewish interests, as was evident in the anti-Jewish utterances of the National Liberal historian Heinrich von Treitschke in 1879 and in the National Liberal support of anti-Semitic candidates during the 1880s.

Jewish support turned to the succession of progressive parties that formed and regrouped during the empire, with the unfortunate consequence that to the extent that these openly opposed anti-Semitism they were branded as the "Jewish guard" *(Judenschutztruppe)*. Perhaps nothing indicates the precariousness of the Jewish situation in Germany more than the fact that the espousal of the Jewish cause resulted less in any benefit for the Jews than in disadvantage for the party that attempted it. Jewish support was a liability for the party that received it—and this proved to be just as true later during the republic as it was during the empire.

Religious considerations prevented Jews from belonging to the Catholic Center party, and ideological considerations kept them out of the Social Democratic party, given the largely bourgeois composition of German Jewry (although some socialist tendencies could be found among the Jewish proletariat of Berlin and the industrial cities of eastern Germany). And so the Jewish voter was effectively left in a shaky alliance with the progressives—despite their increasingly ambiguous position on anti-Semitism, which was reflected in their open association with anti-Semitic candidates in the decade before World War I. The situation during the Weimar Republic was similar, as the Social Democrats' open opposition to anti-Semitism failed to win extensive Jewish support, which remained conditioned by the Jews' middle-class position and interests, and which went primarily to the German Democratic party, at least until its own turn to the right in 1930.[13]

One alternative to political alliances was the Centralverein's program of legal self-defense against anti-Semitism through reliance on established juridical procedures, such as prosecutions under the laws prohibiting libel and religious defamation. This approach represented the Centralverein's rejection of any specially protected status for the Jews and its conviction that "German citizens of the Jewish faith . . . need and demand no other protection than the duly constituted system of justice."[14] But the limited success of this strategy during the empire would seem to have provided ample grounds for questioning this conviction, as prosecutors declined to act against anti-Semitic offenders and judges refrained from imposing deterrent sentences. The resurgent anti-Semitism of the Weimar period, despite the republic's stronger legal guaranties of religious freedom and civil equality, seem to offer additional proof that legal restraint was not effective.

And yet it would not do to paint too bleak a picture of Jewish life in Germany. After all, there had been measurable progress under the empire, including the attainment of legal emancipation itself, and there was every expectation that it would continue. It is true that the empire also saw the emergence of anti-Semitism as an organized political force, its success made visible by the representation it won in the Reichstag. It is also true that now a racial dimension was added to the already-entrenched anti-Semitism based on religious, cultural, and economic arguments. But these were developments that German Jews hoped would be overwhelmed by the triumphant progress of liberalism. After World War I the Weimar Republic did bring real advances of its own, including the possibility for the first time of Jews' full participation in public life, and there was real substance to the Jews' subjective perception of an improvement in their situation. Assimilationists took heart, while Zionists continued to stress the theoretical weakness of the Jewish position in a Christian world—though to be sure they did not always apply the implications of this stance to their own situation in Germany.

These divergent reactions were to be expected. Given their conviction that the Jew's place in Germany would ultimately be assured, assimilationists could proceed only as they did. Even if anti-Semitism persisted, if the Jew's status at times seemed called into doubt, there was every reason for the assimilationists to believe, or at least to hope, that their stance would in the end prove to be justified. After all, liberalism and justice were on their side—theoretically.

Seen from this vantage, the great danger was not that obstacles would be overcome only with difficulty, but that Zionism's position of radical despair and its prediction of ultimate failure would prove to be self-fulfilling. Thus Hermann Cohen objected bitterly that

the loyal Jew—who wishes to remain in the German fatherland with his children and who hopes with his entire religious and patriotic soul, [and] with historical[ly conditioned] idealism and optimism for an improvement of political and social practices in accordance with the fundamental principle of modern culture, the principle of freedom of consciousness and mutual religious respect . . .—this dreamer is despised and scorned [by the Zionists]. He is [said to be] simply a coward and a hypocrite, for he only exploits his patriotism while he [supposedly] feels no other fatherland in his heart of hearts than the promised land, in which the cultivation of milk and honey is now being provided for. All of non-Zionist Jewry is thus accused of inner duplicity, to the malicious glee of every anti-Semite.[15]

By 1928 the Centralverein once more felt itself called upon to repudiate the Zionist position openly, this time in terms more hostile and direct than those of its 1913 resolution. The new resolution warned that

the propaganda that the Zionists have been carrying on in public has brought it about that the division between "Germans" and "Jews" that heretofore has been voiced in public . . . only by anti-Semites is more and more gaining ground. The notion is continually spreading that the Jews belong not to the German people, but rather . . . to a Jewish people that is dispersed across the earth [but] whose [real] abode is Palestine. This situation brings the achievements of a more than century long emancipation into the greatest danger. [Therefore] the Centralverein must more actively than before counter the Zionist view of Judaism as the national and cultural community [Volks- und Kulturgemeinschaft] of all Jews, with Palestine as its national and cultural center. In opposition to the Zionists, those Jews who share the Centralverein's perspective see in Judaism their religion. The Jewish people [Volk], which the Zionists either assert or strive for, is not theirs, for they belong both in culture and nationality exclusively to the German people.[16]

Here was the same note that Eugen Fuchs of the Centralverein had struck in 1913, when he insisted that ultimately "the question of whether [or not] I am German depends on whether or not I choose to be German." For the assimilationists, German identity was a matter of subjective affiliation, while for the Zionists the persistence and apparent irreducibility of anti-Semitism confirmed the objective nature of the Jewish question. Indeed, by failing to persuade, the very reasonableness and logic of the Centralverein's antidefamatory, "enlightening" propaganda proved that the roots of anti-Semitism lay beyond the reach of rational argument. Thus Blumenfeld contended that "only when you have succeeded in refuting all grounds for anti-Semitism have you really proven that the hatred of the Jews is genuine. Hate and love do not obey reason."[17]

Where the Centralverein saw isolated acts of anti-Semitism that could be combated through legal measures, Zionism saw a pattern of widely supported anti-Jewish resistance. One typically sweeping Zionist view, from a 1920 tract, reported that

the anti-Semitic movement in Germany is stronger than ever. It must be clear to anyone who has eyes to see what the trends among the German people are, that even here the danger of an explosion is fully within the realm of possibility. It would be false [but] exceedingly comfortable to ascribe this wave of anti-Semitism to the instigation of some few irresponsible manipulators. Even with all the energy of the reactionary elements the anti-Semitic wave in Germany could never have become so strong were it not for the presence of a latent readiness on the part of the German people. . . . Whoever would combat anti-Semitism must reduce the [hostile] frontiers and the areas of friction [between Jews and non-Jews]; he must gather the Jews on their own territory.[18]

Like anyone with an overall world view, the Zionists seemed to be especially aware of those things that confirmed their vision. Doubtless there was some inclination to look for the bad and to see the worst, and perhaps to exaggerate for the sake of effective propaganda. Nevertheless, continuing anti-Semitism provided ample corroboration of the Zionist vision.

At least in its rhetoric, Zionism recognized that modern anti-Semitism potentially threatened even the Jews of Germany, despite their momentary apparent security. After the Kishinev pogrom in 1903, Heinrich Loewe wrote that the Jews of Germany were themselves sitting on a volcano, even if for the moment it did not appear to be alive. "The same scenes as in Kishinev could take place in Germany," he warned, "and are impossible only because the Prussian state strictly maintains order."[19]

In November 1923 the volcano seemed to erupt when severe financial crisis, unemployment, and hunger sparked riots that turned against Jews and Jewish property in Beuthen (Upper Silesia), Munich, and finally in Berlin, where a Jewish bystander was killed. The apparent approval of the Christian public at large, the active encouragement of the rightist press, and the tardiness and hesitancy of police intervention made it seem that

the structure of the German constitutional state [*Rechtsstaat*] is finally collapsing, and with it the last barriers that have restrained the unbridled instincts [of the mob]. Germany has become a land of pogroms [*Deutschland ist ein Pogromland geworden*].

The picture painted on this occasion in the *Jüdische Rundschau* was even grimmer, expressing fears for the future that would unhappily not long go unrealized. In a lead article entitled GERMAN JEWRY'S HOUR OF FATE it proclaimed that

a pogrom has taken place in the streets of Berlin. Berlin has been the scene of sad and shameful events such as have heretofore been characteristic only of less cultivated states. The fruit of the seed that has been systematically sown for five years is now ripe. Anti-Semitism . . . has now demanded its victim in Berlin. . . . The conscience of the civilized world is stupefied. In the heart of Europe, in the German culture-state, we have experienced what no one would have thought possible ten years ago. The German Jews, who . . . have heard of the pogroms in Russia, would have never believed that such experiences were in store for them. . . . The Jews in Germany are no longer secure in their persons or their lives. Equality, which has always been extolled as the foundation of Jewish existence, is shaken. . . . The fruits of emancipation are called into doubt. The policy of assimilation, the policy of the systematic abrogation and dissolution of Judaism has suffered shipwreck. German Jewry today stands before the fact that its policy of the last hundred years is completely bankrupt.[20]

As gruesomely prophetic as the *Rundschau*'s warning appears in retrospect, for the moment the immediate anti-Jewish threat subsided. Concerned lest the real nature and extent of the danger to German Jewry be underestimated, Kurt Blumenfeld made the gravity of the situation the subject of a stark review of events. What is striking is how even for Blumenfeld the sense of immediacy waned, so that by the end of the article he is once again speaking the language of the party organizer:

How shall Zionism . . . react? There would be a very cheap and effective kind of reaction, and we . . . decisively reject it. One could incite deep anxiety among German Jewry. One could use the excitement to enlist the vacillating. *One could represent Palestine and Zionism as a refuge for the homeless. We do not wish to do that.* We do not wish to carry off by demagoguery those who have stood apart from Jewish life out of indifference. But we wish to make clear to them through [our] sincere conviction where the basic error of Jewish galuth existence lies. We wish to awaken their national self-awareness. We wish to direct their longing for the Jewish future and through patient and earnest educational work prepare them to participate in the upbuilding of Palestine with their complete personal devotion.[21]

Except for the anti-Semitic outbreaks of 1923, the *Jüdische Rundschau* did not begin to take systematic, detailed notice of anti-Jewish agitation and violence until 1931, a year whose outrages included an attack by Nazi toughs on Berlin Jews returning from Rosh Hashanah services along the Kurfürsten-damm. Earlier in the year the *Rundschau* had remarked, concerning Nazi-inspired anti-Semitic activity and the apparent impunity of those responsible, that "it is astounding that we have not yet experienced pogroms on the scale of those . . . in czarist Russia."[22] But once again the gap between Zionist rhetoric and action made its appearance. If the Zionists had actually realized that the situation was as bad as their rhetoric depicted it, they could have been expected to remain in Germany no longer than absolutely necessary. It appears, however, that Zionism's very overview of anti-Semitism operated to mute the specific awareness of particular events, whose implications could easily be fit to theory. In any case, no large-scale emigration, even by Zionists, came until 1933.

German Citizens of the Jewish *Volk*

Given the fact that the Zionists remained in Germany for as long as they did, it is not surprising that they developed a rationale for remaining more substantive than the notions that they were just about to depart, that the time was not yet ripe, or that further preparation was necessary. This rationale, remarkably enough, seemed to assume that a nationally assertive Jewry could find a place in Germany, at least temporarily, on the basis of some kind of *nationalist* pluralism.

The Zionists had criticized the Centralverein for assuming the separability of religious and political affiliation, a distinction not generally recognized by Germans. It followed from this, the Zionists argued, that there was no possibility of Jews finding acceptance as German citizens of the Jewish faith. But there was a strand in German Zionist thought from its very beginning that made an even stronger assumption—namely, that state and nation were separable. (This distinction appears more sharply in the contrast between the very specific German terms *Staat* and *Volk* than between the English terms "state" and "nation," which are sometimes used synonymously.) Accordingly, this view held that the Jew's self-affirmation in terms of a Jewish nation in no way prejudiced his political standing.

One of the first broadsides of the National-jüdische Vereinigung declared in 1897 that "a state can unite in itself a good number of nationalities [*Nationalitäten*], and neither nationality nor religious denomination can diminish or prejudice love of fatherland." It recommended therefore that Jews openly acknowledge themselves as "German citizens . . . of Jewish nationality." A 1910 pamphlet devoted entirely to the question of "Zionism and Citizenship" asserted that Zionism in no way conflicted with patriotism, except for the "hurrah patriotism" that was only an "empty echo of what was dictated from above." "State" and "nationality" were not identical, it said, and patriotism involved only the former. Furthermore, it argued, the state was not the exclusive domain of any single nation—a claim that would have been more fitting for Austria-Hungary than for the unified German Reich.

This general position was confirmed after World War I, and in 1919 the *Jüdische Rundschau* announced that

we Jews . . . belong among the groups . . . for whom state and nation are separate. . . . If a larger part of German Jewry has been and still is of the opinion that its citizenship forbids it to acknowledge Jewish nationality [*Volkstum*], this is a result of the identification of state and nation heretofore. The elimination of this view in the new Germany will . . . teach German Jewry that belonging to the German state does not prevent belonging to the Jewish *Volk*.

Not only did Zionism deny the Centralverein's allegations of a conflict between Zionism and German patriotism, it went so far as to make the astonishing suggestion that the Zionist's nationalistic consciousness itself actually made him a more valuable German citizen than the assimilationist, because the Zionist stood closer to an understanding of "the national sensitivities of the soul of the German Volk."[23]

The entire Zionist argument on this point is telling, for it betrayed a serious self-contradiction. The unified German identity was no more likely to tolerate differences of *Volk* than it was to tolerate religious particularisms. To speak of Germans of the Jewish *Volk* finding a place, even a temporary one, in a Germany defined in *völkisch* terms may have been psychologically reassuring, but it appears to have ignored the realities of the situation—not as seen by Jews, but as established by Germans. The Zionists rightly criticized as self-deluding the assimilationists' sense of the importance of their subjective feelings of belonging in Germany. But were not the Zionists' affirmations of their own subjective patriotism similarly irrelevant? The implications of the Zionists' version of nationalist pluralism were at least as unacceptable as the assimilationists' dream of religious pluralism, possibly more so. It was fortunate, reflected Richard Lichtheim, that the whole matter remained a largely academic one, a debate that was possible

only at a time when a liberal conception of the state could tolerate such intellectual radicalism without drawing the consequences that would have been certain to endanger the existence of the Jews as citizens.[24]

In effect, then, the Zionist analysis of the Jewish situation in Germany was little better than the assimilationist one. While it discerned the shortcomings of the latter, it nevertheless succumbed to weaknesses of the very sort that it had criticized. If there was no place in Germany for the Jews of the Centralverein, neither was there one for the Zionists.

8

THE POWER OF CONTEXT

It has been said that Jews are exactly like the people of the country in which they live—only more so. Certainly this was true of German Jewry, both Zionists and assimilationists. With the important exception of German Zionism's views on nationalist politics (the subject of the next chapter), the striking feature of the movement is just how very German it was, both in its organization and in its modes of thought and expression. As has been pointed out, the peculiarity of German Jewry's situation was not the extent to which it was acculturated but the absence of any commensurate degree of integration. The Germanness of German Zionism is notable not only because it strikes the modern observer as curious, but also because it distinguished German Zionism within the world movement.

One aspect of this Germanness was a penchant—perhaps even a passion—for order. While order and discipline are unquestionably useful in the organized pursuit of any goal, there is a characteristically German inclination to exaggerate

these ancillary values so that they assume a primary importance. Much of the ZVfD's energies were directed toward the
ongoing tasks of the organization: membership building and
fund raising and all the associated activities that these efforts
involved. It was with some justice that a Zionist fund-raising
circular claimed for the ZVfD "the honor of being the best
organized national unit in the Zionist movement. . . . In the
recognition that money means power we have endeavored to
provide the organization with the means for the attainment of
its goals—[and] not without success." Indeed, the ZVfD con-
sistently stood high on the list of contributors to the two
principal financial campaigns for development in Palestine, the
Keren Kayemeth (Jewish National Fund) and the Keren Hayesod (Palestine Foundation Fund).

Apart from this specifically directed activity, however, it was
also possible for the organization as such to become something
of an end in itself. This tendency was evident in an address on
"Organization," delivered to the ZVfD's 1903 *Delegiertentag*,
which insisted that

the Zionists have no more pressing duty than to subordinate themselves to the organization that they themselves have created. . . . It
is the greatest sin against our idea when individuals or groups are
unable or unwilling to fit into the framework of our organization. The
most important part of our current work that we are in a position to
achieve is to discipline and subordinate ourselves, thereby making us
capable of later organizing and administering the Jewish community,
[the goal] for which we are striving. . . . The hope for the success of
our great idea rises and falls with the preservation or the abandonment of our organizational institutions.[1]

The preservation of the formal unity of the ZVfD also
became an independent value, and issues that might disturb it
were avoided as far as possible. In practice this did not mean

that the German Zionists abstained from joining the great political debates and alignments that developed within the Zionist movement, but that such controversy was deferred to the arena of the World Zionist Organization and its congresses. Within the ZVfD itself something of a civil truce was observed, and it was a matter of great pride among German Zionists that the ZVfD, alone among national Zionist organizations, united within itself Zionists of every faction. (Originally the world movement had been organized entirely on the basis of territorial constituencies, but it was not long before interests and orientations that cut across national boundaries led to the organization of parties of an international scale *[Fraktionen]* within the movement. The first of these, the Mizrachi, representing religiously Orthodox Zionists, was organized in 1902.) Thus while representation at the ZVfD's *Delegiertentage* was apportioned to some extent according to the relative support won by various party lists of candidates (generally aligned with the world Zionist factions), the significant phenomenon was that all these delegates sat in a single national convention.[2]

The one serious challenge to this unity came from the Binjan Haarez group, founded in 1921 to represent a pragmatic, nonideological approach to Zionist development in Palestine, similar to that advocated by Louis Brandeis in the United States. But its attempt to constitute itself as an independent faction was beaten back by a coalition of the major groupings within the ZVfD. (The Revisionist group's secession from the ZVfD in 1932 was part of a major split within the world movement as a whole. This ended with the withdrawal of the Revisionists, under the leadership of Vladimir Jabotinsky, who sought a revision of Chaim Weizmann's conciliatory stance toward Britain, the holder of the Mandate for Palestine, and demanded a more militant policy toward the Arabs.)[3]

The order and discipline on which the ZVfD's unity depended was not, however, an unmixed virtue, in that it could lead to a typically German "unpolitical" approach to politics. This attitude assumed that conflict could be adjudicated by impartial reference to abstract principles of right, rather than being resolved by hard political bargaining among power blocs and interest groups. Germans tended to look to officials and bureaucrats for guidance, instead of taking an active, independent role in attempting to shape policy. In this regard Richard Lichtheim conceded that "the manners of the surrounding population . . . left a certain stamp on German Zionism . . . from which the world movement drew great advantage" in that it "made the German Zionists the loyal support of the Zionist leadership." But he added that the same attitude also

led to a renunciation of the critical attitude and independence of judgment that are necessary in political life—a genuine German fault. The majority of the German Zionists were therefore always inclined to submit to the leadership, whether the president was Herzl or Wolffsohn or Weizmann.

It is not surprising, therefore, to discover Weizmann, in the midst of the 1929 controversy over his conciliatory attitudes toward the British and Arabs, urging Blumenfeld "if at all possible, to use your influence to maintain discipline. Once the Germans break ranks we may as well pack up."[4]

German Zionism was also an unmistakably German product in terms of its overall intellectual orientations. In a general sense this is understandable, given the deep roots of German Zionists in German culture. Franz Oppenheimer, the opponent of the Posen Resolution, described himself as "ninety-nine percent Kant and Goethe and only one percent Old

Testament"—and even that was mediated by Luther's translation and Spinoza's criticism. Hugo Bergmann, who later served as professor of philosophy at the Hebrew University, confessed that "only because we had a Fichte [the prophet of German nationalism] could we find our way to the corresponding currents of Jewish culture."[5]

Rather more remarkable, however, was the extent to which German Zionism shared the rhetoric and assumptions of the distinctively German *völkisch* ideology. This was a system of ideas, and more often of feelings, that looked to the German *Volk* of the pagan Teutonic tribes as the true basis for German culture and society, rather than to any supposedly foreign notions of modern Western civilization or secular political citizenship, such as were represented by the Enlightenment. The *völkisch* ideology was a nostalgic response to modern society, and in outlook it embraced opposition to modernism in all its forms, attacking industrialization, liberalism, and—since they stood as an easy target for all that was hated in this new order from which they had visibly benefited—the Jews.[6]

This anti-Semitic component was not necessarily always present, however, and the *völkisch* ideology had a partial Jewish counterpart in German Zionism's exposition of Jewish identity in terms of a Jewish *Volk*. In fact, the common vocabulary that Jewish and German *völkisch* orientations shared was doubtless one source for the Zionist assumption that the assertion of Jewish nationalism would stabilize, rather than weaken, the Jewish position in Germany. For if Jewish and German nationalisms were but different species of the same common type, there might be reason to hope that anti-Semitic antagonism would be dampened by the recognition that the Jews were an equally "valid," if on that account inescapably alien, *Volk*. Thus notions characteristic of *völkisch* ideology, such as the organic, collective, spiritual, and even mystical nature of the *Volk*, easily found a place in Zionist utterances. Richard Lichtheim, for example, denied that Zionism was a mere "colonization association," insisting that it was rather

a movement to arouse the spirits and revivify the energies of Judaism. We join in the colonization of Palestine not to liberate a number of Jews from the ghetto, but to pave the way for the recovery of the organism of the people [*Volksorganismus*] to which we ourselves belong.

Theodor Zlocisti, one of the proposers of the Posen Resolution, described Zionism as a merging of the individual into the collective whole of the Jewish people:

Whoever has experienced Zionism redeems his individuality in his Jewish peoplehood [*Volkstum*]. I become you, and you become me. For there can be no "unfortunate brethren." You are the unfortunate brother. It can no more be a matter of a homeland for the wretched. For you are the wretched one who seeks the tabernacle of his good fortune. You are the one, who neither can nor will assimilate.

And Salman Schocken, the chairman of the ZVfD's Committee for Jewish Cultural Work, saw in the common task of the Zionist effort a "community of action" *(Werkgemeinschaft)* that would bind individuals together and counter the atomization of modern society:

The *Werkgemeinschaft* is the noblest form of the union of man. It exalts the unison of souls and crushes the human tendencies toward atomization [*Absplitterung*] and eccentricity. The more we join in our *Werkgemeinschaft* and the more common effort fills our day, the more unity, love, and joy we experience. We should give our thanks for the fate that has set us . . . such a great challenge.[7]

(It was only another indication of how far reality could diverge from rhetoric that in fact Schocken could be a fierce individualist.)

Of course certain other aspects of *völkisch* ideology were foreclosed to Zionism, such as its antiliberal orientation and its typical nostalgic yearning for the corporate religious society of the Christian Middle Ages. To the extent that Zionism recalled a golden age it was found in the past periods of independent Jewish political nationhood in Palestine. The holiday of Hanukkah and the exploits of the Maccabees, for example, were much celebrated. But on the whole Zionism was almost necessarily forward-looking, as is clear in the picture of the Jewish homeland that Herzl painted in his utopian novel *Altneuland,* and there was no place for the antimodernist element that was characteristic of *völkisch* ideology generally. The cultural program adopted by the second Zionist Congress, for example, stressed that Zionism sought the spiritual, economic, and political rebirth of the Jewish *Volk* "on the foundation of modern culture, whose achievements it embraces."[8]

Possibly the best-known instance of a *völkisch* manifesto in the history of Zionism was Martin Buber's celebration of "blood" as the paramount essence of Jewish identity. In his 1909 address "Judaism and the Jew" Buber argued that the Western Jew is rootless and is confronted with a land, a language, customs, and thoughts alien to his essential being—that are not part of the "community of his blood [*Gemeinschaft seines Blutes*] but belong to a different community." Despite that, the Jew's origin "can become a reality" because it means more than

the mere continuity with the past. [It] has deposited something in us that can never leave us in any hour of our life, that determines every tone and hue of our lives, whatever we do and whatever befalls us—namely blood, the deepest, [most] potent level of the soul.

Although the lectures of which this address was the first were originally delivered to the Zionist Bar Kochba fraternity in Prague, in their printed form they enjoyed an immense response among German Zionists, both at the time and long afterward. Prague-born Robert Weltsch, one of Buber's original audience, recalled that

we few young Western Zionists had no spiritual orientation, no inner confidence in Zionism. . . . [Buber] formulated the question that had tormented us, and gave an answer. The affirmation of Jewish nationality . . . of "blood" as the formative power of our experience, gave us a new orientation in time and space. It indicated to us our historical place.[9]

Perhaps the most curious and fascinating manifestations of the Germanness of German Zionism were the Zionist student organizations and the Zionist youth movement. The Zionist student movement was the outgrowth of groups such as the already-mentioned Berlin Verein jüdischer Studenten, which was joined within five years of its founding by similar fraternities in Leipzig, Breslau, and Munich. In 1901 these four formed the Bund jüdischer Corporationen, which, while not openly Zionist, adopted a platform intended to imply a general Zionist inclination. This described the BJC as "the rallying point for all Jewish students who consciously feel themselves to be Jews, and who want to work together for the development of a living Judaism." What this actually came to mean, it was later explained, was that while "not every member has to be a Zionist . . . it is certainly true that anyone who in the long run is working *against* the Jewish national movement has no place in the BJC." Between 1900 and 1914 nine more Vereine jüdischer Studenten were added to the Bund, although by the outbreak of the war one had already been dissolved and one had been dropped from the Bund.[10]

Meanwhile, in 1902 an explicitly Zionist fraternity, the Hasmonaea, had been established in Berlin to propagate Zionism directly, in contrast with the fraternities of the BJC. This was joined in 1905 by a similar fraternity in Munich, and together the two formed the Kartell zionistischer Verbindungen (Federation of Zionist Fraternities) in 1906. By 1914 two other fraternities were added. But as the implicit Zionism of the BJC became more and more outright there was ample cause to reconsider the formal rivalry that had separated it from the KZV. In July 1914 the two federations resolved on fusion into a Kartell jüdischer Verbindungen (Federation of Jewish Fraternities), which, despite the absence of Zionism in its title, adopted a specifically Zionist platform:

The KJV seeks to educate its members to be men who in the consciousness of the national unity of the Jewish community are decided to engage in the renewal of a Jewish nationality [*Volkstum*] worthy of the Jewish past.[11]

These Zionist student groups were particularly significant for the ZVfD because of the contribution that their members later made to the parent organization. They provided the backbone of the ZVfD—the bulk of its reliable active membership, the bulk of leadership on the local chapter level, and the officers in the most important posts in the ZVfD's central leadership and administration. Of the eight presidents of the ZVfD, for example, all but one (Alfred Landsberg, who served for only a year) had passed through the Zionist student movement. "We regarded our fraternities," recalled Richard Licht-heim, "as training grounds [*Kadettenanstalten*] for the move-ment, and aimed to provide its officers; in many cases we succeeded." It was no exaggeration to say, as Lichtheim did, that German Zionism was the creation of the alumni of these Zionist fraternities.[12]

Although the initial impulse for the formation of Jewish student fraternities was the barring of Jews from the German student *Corps* and *Burschenschaften*, this exclusion did not engender any corresponding rejection by the Jews of the singu-lar customs and ceremonies of German fraternity life. This was true of the assimilationist Kartell-Convent, but no less so of the BJC and the KZV, despite the presumably greater critical awareness that had brought the members of the latter two groups to their Zionist outlook. To be sure, specific Zionist content was not absent from these Zionist fraternities. Pledges were put through courses in the history of Judaism, of Zionism, and of the student movement itself, and the clubhouses rang with Zionist songs of recent composition. But more traditional German drinking songs had perhaps the larger role, and drink-ing and dueling held their customary places at the center of German fraternity life. Though a refusal on the part of many non-Jewish students to duel with Jews made fencing at times more a matter of physical exercise than combat for Jewish honor, this did not prevent matches at which Zionist students too could obtain the dueling scars that were the obligatory decorations of a German university student. Zionist fraternity brothers, like their Christian counterparts, undertook to quaff large steins of beer on command, but their total consumption lagged somewhat behind that of the more committed, authen-tic Teutonic guzzlers. Blumenfeld recalled a *Corps* student's humorous remark that the real contribution of the Jews to

German culture lay in their invention of the small glass of beer.[13]

While the Germanness of the Zionist student movement was largely a matter of form, for the Zionist youth movement it was a matter of substance as well. The Wanderbund Blau-Weiss, one of the larger of these youth groups, was indistinguishable in most regards from the German *Wandervogel* (youth movement) of which it was the Zionist counterpart, sharing its program of outdoor rambling, its glorification of nature, and its rejection of urban culture and bourgeois adult values. (*Blau* and *Weiss*, blue and white, were adopted from the tallith as the Jewish national colors and were incorporated in the Zionist, and later Israeli, flag.) According to an official Blau-Weiss statement, the Jewish *Wanderbewegung* (hiking movement) was founded

solely out of the necessity of working for the physical, spiritual, and moral training and toughening of Jewish youth. A relatively great part of our youth suffers under the harmful influences of big city life. We regard it as our task to take them away from the influence of the movie theater and of cheap literature; away from the company of materialistic . . . adults, of skeptical, joyless men, alienated from nature; away from the atmosphere of Jewish humor and Jewish self-derision. . . . The Blau-Weiss *Wanderbünde* [hiking leagues] seek to lead the young man to nature, [and] within nature to achieve his spiritual and moral rehabilitation and the awakening of an idealistic view of life.[14]

Unlike the KJV, however, the Blau-Weiss never achieved a position of central importance within the ZVfD. This was due as much to its systematic insistence on a separation between itself and the world of adult politics, including the sponsoring ZVfD, as to the fact that there was never really time between the founding of the Blau-Weiss in 1912 and 1933 for the

school-age membership to assume a role in the ZVfD comparable to the KJV's.

With parties and party politics [insisted one member], we have nothing to do. We are not . . . Zionist, as our ill-wishers say of us. We
are Jewish. For us that says more. And [we are also] a youth movement. As such we stand above parties. Nothing Jewish is foreign to
us. We even venture to use words like "freedom," "Palestine," "Shalom," and sing Jewish freedom songs. But nothing would be so foolish
as to deliver up the Jewish youth to a [political] party.[15]

Indeed, this militant sense of independence was one source of
Blau-Weiss's attraction for Jewish youth, who were rebelling
partly against assimilation but mostly against the bourgeois
liberalism of their parents.

Perhaps the most striking development in the Blau-Weiss
was its turn toward militaristic authoritarianism in the early
1920s, a stark contrast with the casual organization of its first
years, now deemed no longer adequate. The new constitution
promulgated in 1922 declared that

the grand tasks [of the Blau-Weiss] require a leader and armies—a
leader to command and an army to serve, together a tightly ordered
organization. The first epoch of carefree existence [*ungebundenes
Sichausleben*] is past. . . . The hope for the fulfillment of life through
the triumph of freedom will be replaced by the stern faith in the
triumph of might. . . . Membership in the Blau-Weiss imposes
. . . obligations that encompass the whole realm of life. . . . The orders
of the leadership or its deputies demand unconditional obedience.
. . . Personal interests are secondary to the demands of the Bund.

This attempted authoritarian reorientation of the Blau-Weiss
(denounced by the *Jüdische Rundschau* as "fascist") led to
sharp divisions within the Bund (and played a part in its eventual dissolution, which was also brought on by the failure, for

a combination of economic, political, and personal reasons, of a small Blau-Weiss engineering and construction cooperative that had been established in Palestine in 1924).[16] Nevertheless, it demonstrates, if in an extreme way, how like their German counterparts some Jews could become, even to the point of adopting values and attitudes that would in the end, under different circumstances and direction, bring about their own destruction.

9

JEWISH AND ARAB
NATIONALISM IN PALESTINE

The Conflict of National Aspirations

As thoroughly German as the German Zionists were in all other regards, in the area of nationalist politics they shunned the German example. Zionism must not succumb, they insisted, to the lure of aggressive, chauvinistic, expansionist nationalism. The matter was one of considerable practical significance, since at the same time that Zionism undertook to build a homeland for the Jews, it had to cope with the reality of the Arab population of Palestine. To this demographic fact was added the more formidable challenge of an Arab nationalist movement whose origins were scarcely more recent than Zionism's own.[2]

Zionism responded to this situation optimistically: by denying that any insurmountable conflict existed—either between

Jew and Arab or between Jewish and Arab nationalist aspirations. Imbued with the humanitarianism of their cause and ignorant of the physical realities of Palestine, the Zionists tended to minimize what difficulties they did perceive and to assume that mutual goodwill would bring their resolution. Any Arab resistance that might possibly arise would be easily allayed, they thought, by the patent benefit that Jewish settlement would bring to the land and to all its people, through soil reclamation, agricultural improvement, and the improvement of the standard of living and the level of public health.[3]

This Zionist optimism about an Arab-Jewish rapprochement received a welcome early confirmation—which proved however to be an isolated one—in the amicable contacts at the time of the Versailles Conference between Chaim Weizmann, representing the Zionist movement, and Emir Faisal, representing Arab nationalism. At the end of 1918 Faisal stated that

the two main branches of the Semitic family, Arabs and Jews, understand one another, and I hope that as a result of the interchange of ideas at the Peace Conference, which will be guided by ideals of self-determination and nationality, each nation will make definite progress towards the realization of its aspirations. Arabs are not jealous of Zionist Jews, and intend to give them fair play; and the Zionist Jews have assured the Nationalist Arabs of their intention to see that they too have fair play in their respective areas.

Shortly thereafter Faisal added, even more explicitly, that "the Jewish Movement is national and not imperialist. Our Movement is national and not imperialist, and there is room in Syria for us both. Indeed, I think, that neither can be a real success without the other."[4]

Unfortunately, partly as a result of Arab disappointment with the final outcome of the peace conference, these views were not generally adopted by the Arab side. Nevertheless, it was in this spirit of cooperation and mutual advantage that the Zionists presented their program for the development and colonization of Palestine—an approach that was dictated, as a ZVfD pamphlet of 1920 explained, by ethical as well as practical considerations:

For us [Zionists] who . . . despite our nationalist orientation reject any chauvinism or imperialism, it is a matter not only of political good sense but, *above all* a moral obligation, to establish amicable relations with the Arabs. . . . Even if all the Arabs remain in the land, no hostility could exist between nations so closely related in language and descent as ours. The land has place and productive capabilities for both. All the more so if the Arabs—whose agriculture and labor . . . stand at an outdated, extensive stage—will increasingly shift to intensive agriculture, spurred on by the example of Jewish colonists. Both groups will live together in harmony. For the Jews, contact with the Arabs can only help them to overcome their European hypercivilization. The Arabs [in turn] will benefit from the treasures of genuinely worthwhile European culture that the Jews will transmit—[for example, accomplishments in the field of medicine]. . . . The Arab question is certainly difficult, but with mutual goodwill it is surmountable.[5]

Even after serious anti-Zionist rioting in Palestine in May 1921, the twelfth Zionist Congress, the first full congress since World War I, reaffirmed the Zionist attitude of conciliation and cooperation at its meeting in September 1921:

The hostile conduct of a part of the Arab population of Palestine, instigated by unscrupulous elements, which has erupted in bloody violence, can weaken neither our resolve to establish the Jewish national home nor our will to live with the Arab nation in a relationship of harmony and mutual respect; and in league with it to make [our] common home [*Wohnstätte*] into a flourishing commonwealth [*Gemeinwesen*], whose achievement assures to each of its nations an undisturbed national development. The two great Semitic nations, who have already been joined by the bond of shared cultural creativity, will also understand how to unite their essential interests into a joint enterprise in the hour of their national rebirth. . . . Jewish colonization activity will not encroach upon the rights and needs of the working Arab nation.[6]

Lest the subsequent failure of an Arab-Zionist accord appear to be simply the consequence of misunderstanding or ill will, it is necessary to point out some of the genuine conflicts of interests and outlook that separated the two sides. The foremost was the extent to which a policy of national self-determination would be reflected in the distribution of power, and ultimately of political sovereignty. Conceivably such matters as political representation and the administration of the autonomous affairs of each national community in Palestine could have been regulated in the presence of a mediating Mandatory power that enjoyed the confidence of both sides. Faisal had suggested the possibility, for example, in his declaration that, while in principle Jews and Arabs were

absolutely at one, nevertheless the Arabs cannot assume the responsibility of holding level the scales in the clash of races and religions that have, in this one province, so often involved the world in difficulties. They would wish for the effective super-position of a great trustee, so long as a representative local administration commended itself by actively promoting the material prosperity of the country.[7]

But such a coexistence presumed the compatibility of Arab and Zionist interests. Beyond a certain point conflicting aspirations regarding possession and settlement of the land, as well as ultimate political sovereignty, created a situation where Britain could satisfy neither side.

The focus of contention was basically the question of whether there was sufficient room in Palestine for the creation of a Jewish national home without, in the words of the Balfour Declaration, prejudicing "the civil and religious rights of existing non-Jewish communities in Palestine." For without the possibility of sizable Jewish immigration and settlement, limited only by the land's "absorptive capacity"—which was the subject of sharp debate—Palestine had only symbolic significance for Zionism. To the Arab assertion that there was not enough space, the Zionists replied that the adoption of modern intensive methods of agriculture would make increased Jewish immigration feasible.

The matter was not that simple, however. In hoping for an easy technological solution to the problem of conflicting claims to the land, the Zionists overlooked the possibility of Arab resistance to the sweeping social changes that modernization of agriculture was likely to bring. Furthermore, the hard fact was that Jewish settlement did involve the displacement of Arab agricultural labor. This was the unfortunate consequence of a Zionist policy that seemed otherwise entirely laudable—namely, the policy of "Jewish labor," which maintained that a Jewish Palestine should be built up entirely by the work of Jewish hands. It was at once a rejection of the established imperialistic practice of exploiting native populations and an embracing of the conviction that only a return to the soil would "normalize" the skewed pattern of Jewish occupational distribution, which still reflected the medieval exclusion of Jews from agriculture. Furthermore, without some artificial discrimination in favor of Jewish labor, successful competition with cheaper Arab labor, which subsisted at a lower standard of living, would have been extremely difficult. So while the Zionists argued that the policy of "building up Palestine on the foundation of Jewish labor in no way implied any hostility against the Arab population,"[8] to the individual Arab worker it might appear that the opposite was true.

Though the clash between Arab nationalism and Zionism

centered on the dispute over immigration and settlement policies, there was an additional point of conflict that was more
substantial than the Zionists realized—namely, the confrontation between the two very different cultures of the Palestinian
Arab and the European Zionist. This was minimized to some
extent by the expectation that the Jew would be re-"oriented"
once he was restored to his Middle Eastern homeland and the
hope that the reunited Semitic brothers would embrace each
other fraternally. Robert Weltsch portrayed the Jewish people
as rejoining the family of oriental nations, after centuries of
sojourn in the West, in order to cooperate in the cultural and
spiritual reconstruction of the East. Hugo Bergmann, a close
friend of Weltsch's from his days in the Prague Bar Kochba
group, explained the matter:

One of the most important causes of suspicion between Jews and
Arabs is the Western mentality—the overwhelming of religion and
spirit by politics—which has taken possession of both peoples. [They
should both withdraw] from the influence of the West and return
again to the original spirit of the East—perhaps still more to the spirit
of the Far East. Although the Jews are a people which, having lived
for two thousand years in the West, has without doubt acquired
much of the Western restlessness, yet there is in the Zionist movement a strong current which, flowing toward Zion, hopes to carry
with it the peace of the East.[9]

Despite this optimism, the expectation that Arab nationalism and Zionism would find grounds for accord on the basis
of Judaism's "Eastern" roots seems to have rested either on
simple confusion or on a deeper ambivalence about the modern
culture of the West. As has been indicated, not only did Zionism not intend to renounce the advances of Western civilization, but it also proclaimed these very advantages to be among
the benefits that Zionist settlement would bring to Palestine.

The Ethics of Nation Building

In the face of all these difficulties, the Zionists persisted in their hope that an accommodation with the Arabs in Palestine could be reached on terms that were acceptable to both parties. What these terms were depended, of course, on which of the many factions within the Zionist movement was formulating them. They ranged from the maximalist territorial and political demands of the Revisionists at one extreme to the minimalism of those willing to accept an essentially symbolic Jewish presence in Palestine at the other. The representative German Zionist position, which advocated a large measure of moderation and self-restraint in advancing Zionist interests in Palestine, lay closer to the latter. This version of Zionism, which was by no means the exclusive property of the ZVfD—though German Zionists were its most consistent and strongest supporters—owed its articulation especially to Robert Weltsch, from 1919 the editor of the ZVfD organ, the *Jüdische Rundschau*.[10]

Essentially, Weltsch's ideal was that of a humanistic, tolerant nationalism that would avoid the chauvinist excesses commonly evident in other nationalist movements. Weltsch's premise was that the Jews, who had known ill treatment at the hands of other nations, were particularly obligated not to indulge in the kind of behavior from which they themselves had suffered:

Intolerant brutal egotistic nationalism would be unacceptable to Jews who had learned to know what it means. The Jewish people . . . would be sympathetic to other peoples in similar conditions who are striving to recover their national freedom, and from this attitude a mutual understanding could arise which would enable different nationalities to live together and to cooperate for the sake of the well-being of all.[11]

The specific political form that Weltsch supported for accommodation with the Arabs in Palestine was that of a binational federation, backed by international guaranties, in which both Jews and Arabs would participate as sovereign nations *(Staatsnationen)*. Palestine was to become what Weltsch called an "oriental Switzerland." Unfortunately this proposal did not so much solve the political question as avoid it—especially the sensitive issue of the flow of settlers into Palestine. Weltsch declaimed strongly against those who campaigned simply for a Jewish majority in Palestine, as if Zionism were entirely a matter of establishing political sovereignty over the land, rather than "bringing as many Jews as possible for the sake of [their] creative activity, entirely independent of how many Arabs are there."

But this vague formulation did not eliminate the fact that numbers were indeed a problem: any Jewish settlement that would be small enough to escape Arab resistance (given Arab opposition to the very notion of a Jewish national home in Palestine) was unlikely to be large enough to satisfy Zionist aspirations. A binational solution, Weltsch admitted, seemed to preclude a Jewish majority. But as long as the Jews were in a minority there was no reason for the Arabs to accept any binational solution as a compromise parity formulation. Indeed, Weltsch himself realized that Arab assent to a binational constitution would involve an immense renunciation on their part. Not surprisingly, proposals for binationalism in Palestine never found any significant response from the Arab side.[12]

However, the inherent weaknesses of binationalism did not lose for it the backing of German Zionists, with Weltsch at their head. This was reflected, for example, in their identification with and support of the work of the Brith Shalom, a small but influential group founded in Palestine in 1925 to foster a binationalist accord with the Arabs. (A German branch was constituted under the name of the Arbeitsgemeinschaft für zionistische Realpolitik.) The object of the Brith Shalom, its statutes explained, was

to arrive at an understanding between Jews and Arabs as to the form of their mutual social relations in Palestine on the basis of absolute political equality of two culturally autonomous peoples, and to determine the lines of their cooperation for the development of the country.

This program assumed that the source of friction with the Arabs lay not in any objection to the creation of a Jewish national home, but rather in their fears of Jewish political statehood in Palestine. The two goals, insisted Brith Shalom, were separate ones, with the first in no way entailing the second:

The political aim of the Zionist movement, as laid down in its official programs and as recognized by the Government and in the Balfour Declaration and by the League of Nations in the Mandate of Palestine, is to constitute a National Home in Palestine for the Jewish People. In accordance with these fundamental principles of the National Home, we recognize that Palestine must be neither a Jewish State nor an Arab State, but a Bi-national State in which Jews and Arabs shall enjoy equal civil, political, and national rights, without distinction between majority and minority.[13]

This formulation came no closer to grappling with the real problems that a Jewish national home posed than Weltsch had. Rather, it represented the conviction that continuing goodwill and cooperation would be adequate for resolving a conflict whose enormousness was therefore best minimized.

Weltsch's efforts for Arab-Zionist rapprochement were heavily influenced by a moralistic and spiritual approach to

Zionism whose principle sources were Ahad Haam and Martin Buber. Weltsch argued that Zionism was to be no mere political enterprise for Jewish settlement in Palestine, but rather involved the spiritual regeneration of the entire Jewish people. From Ahad Haam, the advocate of Zion as a spiritual center for world Jewry, Weltsch drew the lesson that since "quantitatively speaking, political Zionism can solve only a tiny fraction of the Jewish question . . . it is the quality of the Jewish settlement that will constitute its significance for the Jewish collectivity." But underneath this rather practical-sounding consideration lay Weltsch's ethical notion, derived from Ahad Haam, that

the principle of Jewish history is the constantly self-renewing, relentless striving for justice, which can never be realized, however, in the mortal world of impulse and selfishness. And nevertheless this world can survive only as long as the attempt is constantly made anew.

It was this goal that Weltsch set for the "true Jewish community in Zion."[14]

From Buber, Weltsch drew the conclusion that

embracing the [Jewish] *Volk*, which is only a beginning, poses not only a life work that is national, but also one that is moral. . . . Jewish nationalism has thus become a great ethical force, and is clearly distinct from the national self-righteousness and self-satisfaction [that is noticeable] in nationalists of other nations, and even in a certain primitive Zionism, which we have rejected. . . . For we have recognized that it is a matter of nothing less than the renewal of a people and of its spirit [*Geist*]. We have realized that we need more than a mere party organization . . . but rather the conjuring up of vital energies, in order that we might again create a reality, with all the sorrows and all the grandeur and tragedy [involved] in such an act of creation. *The spiritual movement* [*geistige Bewegung*] that has always been the precursor, the companion, and the completing force in political transformations was (and is) also in Zionism *the decisive factor.*[15]

Clearly these considerations were, to the extent that the two spheres are separate, more ethical and spiritual than realistically political. Indeed, Weltsch was inclined to make a rather sharp distinction between the two realms, though a distinction of a peculiar sort. For there are two types of idealism: a moral idealism that stands opposed to unethical action, and an idealism of world view in which the ideal stands opposed to the real. Weltsch tended to confuse these two and to accuse persons who did not share his moral aversion to the realities of political conflict of acting unethically out of sheer hunger for power; hence his insistence on the ethical superiority of his own position that an amicable Arab-Jewish accommodation was possible. That real conflicts of interest might exist, which despite abundant goodwill could in the end be resolved only by force, Weltsch discounted entirely. Thus he could easily accuse those who opposed the Churchill white paper (a 1922 British statement of Mandatory policy that restricted Zionist development) of actually opposing the principle of parity that it set out. They did so, he suggested, because they could conceive of Zionism only in terms of territorial domination. Weltsch feared the moral and spiritual implications of this position, because its advocates appeared to be succumbing to the temptation of imitating other nations in trying to gain the upper hand. This, Weltsch charged, was not what was meant by Zionism, at least not by what Ahad Haam regarded as the true love of Zion.[16]

Weltsch's concern reflected one of the very deepest paradoxes of Zionism, which sought to "normalize" Jewish existence by reconstituting the Jewish nation and assuring it the security of political statehood. But to the extent that the Jews might then become like all the other nations and lose any distinctive Jewish qualities, Zionism would have succeeded only in achieving an assimilation grander and more complete than the assimilationists could have hoped for. To escape this dilemma, Weltsch's spiritual Zionism sought to evade the responsibilities of political power by renouncing, if necessary, Zionism's claim to a Jewish state, as opposed to a more vaguely defined "Jewish national home." Weltsch's fear of the potential dangers of real political involvement seemed to justify a reproach that Richard Lichtheim had leveled in 1926 in behalf of the Revisionist group:

The Jews are an unpolitical people, and they suffer from always setting up axioms and representing basic principles. For that is simpler than dealing with specific matters. Our editors and speakers are continually inclined to operate on a general plane of thought. Herr Dr. Weltsch is a clever man, but he is typically unpolitical. He cares more for his axioms, feelings, and principles, and while he always sees the reality, he strives to subordinate it to his principles.[17]

Although Lichtheim saw in Weltsch's unpolitical attitude a typical Jewish failing, it would be equally fair to call it a characteristically German one. While in one sense Weltsch's opposition to aggressive nationalism indicated a conscious rejection of German influence, his confusion of the ethical and the political demonstrated that in another sense his German background still prevailed.

Accommodation and Appeasement

As long as relative peace prevailed between Arabs and Jewish settlers, the proposition that mutual goodwill would provide a basis for accord could easily seem plausible to its formulators. Such was the long period of relative quiet following the Arab riots of May 1921. The real test for Weltsch's policy, however, came in the form of the brutal anti-Jewish attacks that erupted in Palestine in August 1929. The immediate pretext was a dispute that had been simmering for almost a year over the question of conflicting Jewish and Arab rights at the Western, or "Wailing," Wall in Jerusalem.[18] On the western side of this section of massive masonry, which once formed part of the western wall of the court of the Jewish Second Temple and is its only vestige, there was a traditional site for Jewish prayer in a small courtyard. The wall also served as the western boundary of the large compound of the Haram al-Sharif, which includes the Dome of the Rock mosque and, along with Mecca and Medina, figures as a principal holy site in the Muslim religion. A series of incidents in 1929—including interference with Jewish arrangements for worship at the wall as well as a provocative demonstration by the Revisionist youth group—resulted in a serious heightening of tensions by the third week in August.

During the few days preceding Friday, 23 August 1929, it became widely known in the Arab community that that day would bring a climax to these events. On the morning of August 23 multitudes of armed Arabs gathered in Jerusalem in the Haram area, from which they erupted after noon to attack first the Mea Shearim quarter, populated by extremely traditional Orthodox Jews, and then other Jewish sections of the city. British police and military forces proved wholly inadequate to protect the Jewish populace or to contain the attacks, which the next day spread throughout the country. The worst slaughters took place in Hebron and Safed, which were not recent Zionist settlements but traditional centers of Jewish piety long inhabited by Orthodox Jews. On Saturday, August 24, 60 Jews were murdered and 50 wounded in Hebron, a toll that included casualties inflicted when the Hebron Talmudical Academy was overrun. An attack on the Jewish quarter of Safed on August 28 left 45 Jews killed or wounded. The final toll was 133 Jews killed and 339 wounded, 116 Arabs killed and 232 wounded. The parliamentary report on the disturbances, the source for these figures, noted that "many of the Arab casualties and possibly some of the Jewish casualties" were inflicted by police or military forces.[19]

Weltsch's public response in the *Jüdische Rundschau* was the only one possible under the circumstances. He demanded the restoration of order, sought the protection of life and property, and accused the Mandatory government of criminal negligence in ignoring the clear warning signs of an outbreak of violence and of gross ineptitude in its entire handling of the Wailing Wall affair.[20] Despite all this, there was still no call to abandon a policy of accommodation of a decade's standing, Weltsch indicated. While condemning the murders and British mishandling of the situation, he added that Jews still had to take into consideration the national aspirations of the Arab people and to work for a modus vivendi. He accused the Zionist organization of insufficient effort in this regard and demanded that it restrain any irresponsible extremist claims from the Jewish side (referring to the militant Revisionists), which only served the cause of Arab agitators.

The balance in Weltsch's private reaction was rather different from that in his public stance. He emphasized what he regarded to be the ultimate Zionist responsibility for the conflict with the Arabs and urged greater self-restraint in pursuing Zionist aims. To be sure, there was no evading the enormity of the Arab excesses. But while voicing indignation and outrage, Weltsch counseled concession and appeasement. Writing to his close friend Hugo Bergmann, then the director of the Hebrew University library, Weltsch said he regretted that an editorial he had written condemning the Revisionist demonstration, which he had suppressed in view of the events of the twenty-third, had not appeared. In it he had assigned to the Zionists the responsibility for preventing the development of a hate psychology—since they were the outsiders and maintaining peace was so much in their interest that it was worth suffering some injustice in the Wailing Wall matter. Weltsch realized that such a position would strike many Zionists as treasonous, despite what he regarded as its decisive moral import. He did concede that in the light of recent events survival itself seemed to be at issue, and he approved of Jewish efforts at self-defense. Still he insisted that the Zionist Executive do nothing to provoke the Arabs, since the Zionists could not impose Jewish immigration by force of arms and ultimately would have to make peace with them.[21]

Whatever its actual tactical value may have been—something that was sharply challenged—Weltsch's willingness to make concessions in the hope of an ultimate settlement presents a striking parallel to the assimilationist position regarding the relationship between Jew and German. Here was the same optimism that it was in the Jew's power to compel acceptance from a reluctant negotiating partner, whether Arab or German, the same self-castigation for failure, the same assumption that the absence of initial success indicated not any difficulty in the objective situation, but rather an insufficient effort on the part of the Jew, which required even greater concessions —in the one case at the expense of Zionist aspirations and in the other at the expense of Jewish identity. For the Zionist of Weltsch's orientation, appeasement was the functional analogue of assimilation, with the dream of international brotherhood substituting for the myth of religious pluralism.

Weltsch's second great concern in the wake of the August pogrom was that the moral position of Zionism not be compromised, that Zionism not succumb, even under attack, to the lure of self-righteous aggressiveness. Thus in his letter to Rosenblüth, Weltsch denounced the danger of a war hysteria reminiscent of 1914 and the tendency for every nation to proclaim values and standards to which it did not itself adhere. He feared that the Zionists would simply cast themselves in the role of the innocent victims. To Hans Kohn, another alumnus of the Bar Kochba group, Weltsch wrote that preserving Zionism's ethical position was the most important thing.[22]

Not surprisingly, Weltsch's views on Arab-Zionist accommodation, which had always had their critics, drew especially heavy fire after the events in Palestine. From Palestine came the voice of Moses Calvary, a German Zionist who had actually taken the step of *aliyah*, charging Weltsch with shying away from the hard realities of the situation in Palestine in the name of an ethereal, imaginary transnationalism:

We [German Zionists] have a deep mistrust of everything that has to do with the masses, with power, with force. . . . What was the aim of Ahad Haam's philosophy? A spiritual center. How free of the taint of power that sounds. One creates for himself his own bloodless "Ahad Haamism," which he then takes as an ideal to contrast with a "chauvinistic" Herzlean Zionism. . . . There are men who are attached to their own nation, but nevertheless have the greatness to put themselves, in a conflict between nation and mankind, on the

side of mankind. . . . [But] I suspect that some German Jews declare
so lightly for a peace between nations at any price because for over
a century the fate of our nationality has not been our ultimate
concern. We have an inclination to be, not international, but trans-
national. These people [Weltsch and the German Zionists in Ger-
many] refuse to see how difficult our problem is and that logically it
is *insoluble*. A Jewish Palestine can be built up only with as much
use of Jewish labor as possible. This means, however, a de facto
boycott against Arab labor. The moral difficulty [involved] in this
choice has for years troubled the [Jewish] labor organizations just as
much as it has troubled national-minded individuals of bourgeois
circles. It is easy to strike a compromise at the expense of the nation
—for those whose national instinct is broken; but to do so is impossible for anyone who cares as earnestly for his nation as he does for
mankind.[23]

Even more telling than Calvary's personal critique was a
statement drawn up by a group of leading German Zionists in
Palestine at a meeting held in Tel Aviv at the end of October
1929. The declaration, which bore among its fifty-two signa-
tures the names of Theodor Zlocisti, a mover of the Posen
Resolution, and Ernst Simon, a leading member of Brith Shalom, condemned Weltsch's constant casting of the Zionists in
the aggressor's role, and accused him of political naïveté and
defeatism:

The continually repeated demands of the *Jüdische Rundschau* directed to the Zionist public that peace be concluded with the Arabs
creates the impression that some Palestinian Jews or the Zionist
Organization had until now made war on the Arabs, that some Jews
did not want peace. At the same time these demands show a remarkable ignorance of the Arab and English mentality. When the blood
of the Jewish murdered still goes unexpiated, when the courts have
not yet delivered their verdicts, when those officials responsible for
the revolt have not yet been punished, the Arab will see in such
declarations only a confession of our uncertainty and our hopeless-
ness. He will be confirmed in his belief that a repetition of pogroms

will increasingly force us in the end to renounce our political demands.

It is striking that even Chaim Weizmann, who was to lose his office as president of the World Zionist Organization in 1931 for seeming to be willing to make concessions in the face of Arab and British resistance, remarked in a letter to Blumenfeld that

if we proclaim to the Arabs (who are brilliant carpet traders!) that we are ready to revise everything, then we put ourselves entirely at their mercy. Another little pogrom and we will run away [*Noch ein Pogrömchen und wir werden davon laufen*]—that is how the Arabs will interpret our advances.[24]

Under these circumstances the question of whether Weltsch's position enjoyed the support of the ZVfD membership became particularly urgent and figured as a principal issue at the *Delegiertentag* held in Jena at the end of December 1929. Here Weltsch spoke openly of his optimism for a binational settlement to the problem of Arab-Jewish coexistence in Palestine, "not in such a form that Palestine will be a Jewish state, but rather in a form that will establish a Jewish national home in Palestine alongside the already existing Arab commonwealth . . . that will likewise continue to develop."

Despite a sharp attack on Weltsch's treatment of the Arab question, a resolution of no confidence in the editorial policy of the *Rundschau* was defeated by a vote of ninety-four to forty-seven. The *Delegiertentag* furthermore confirmed, in terms similar to those of the twelfth Zionist Congress's resolution on the Arab question, the wish of the Zionist movement to live together with the Arab nation in harmony and mutual respect, and together with it to transform [our] common homeland [*die gemeinsame Heimat*] into a flourishing commonwealth [*Gemeinwesen*], whose upbuilding assures to all sectors of the population an undisturbed national development.

At the same time Blumenfeld was reelected to the ZVfD presidency, after surviving an eighty-four to fifty-four vote of confidence on his support of the *Rundschau*'s position. Thus Weltsch's conviction that he spoke in the name of the ZVfD appears to have been justified.[25]

Writing thirty years later about the apparent failure of his program for Arab-Zionist accord, Weltsch remained the optimist in insisting first, that he had been betrayed, rather than disproved, by events, and second, that the Zionists shared partial responsibility for the failure by their lack of persistence in pursuing a policy of accommodation. A binational state under British auspices, Weltsch conceded, simply became impossible as the world, Palestine and the Jews with it, was engulfed in events of unprecedented horror. Not Arab nationalism, but German nationalism grown wild, was the source of failure:

The ideas that typified German Zionism . . . foundered on reality. Those who, like myself, believed in a kind of stability on the part of the great world powers and in their adhering to moral principles were mistaken. The idea that a Jewish state under the flag of the British Empire could reach an accommodation with its neighbors . . . was confounded. We did not suspect that the British Empire stood on the eve of its own dissolution. That a constructive nationalism did not absolutely have to turn into an aggressive one, that the idea of spiritual renaissance, moral renewal, personal human worth, and national creative energy could also—in reality could only—be realized in peaceful coexistence with the other free nations, was an illusion. World history took a different turn. Armageddon triumphed. The

Jewish people was caught in an unimaginable catastrophe. A nationalism of diabolical origins unchained evil and tore the world to pieces.
Brutal force alone seemed to reign.[26]

As for the charge of inconstancy on the part of the Zionists,
Weltsch continued to insist, despite his partial admission of
defeat on the first count, that it had indeed been in the Zionists' power to achieve an amicable settlement with the Arabs
and that the Zionists had failed to exert themselves sufficiently.
In his introduction to a collection of Buber's writings published
in 1963 Weltsch regretted that

Buber's exhortation that [the Jews] . . . pursue a rapprochement with
the new emerging Orient through . . . building a common, all-
inclusive Palestinian society and economy died away unheard, and
with it the last chance for a timely basis of cooperation with the
Arabs. Without this, an inescapable rivalry and hostility was bound
to develop. The attempt to establish a Jewish settlement without at
the same time acquiring an irreconcilable . . . foe was not undertaken.[27]

In one sense Weltsch's contention is incontrovertible, insofar as it can always be argued that a greater effort might have
produced better results. But Weltsch's prescription for Zionist
conduct made sense only if it evoked a reciprocal response from
the Arab side. In the face of Arab intransigence, goodwill was
irrelevant, and the readiness to make concessions would in the
long run produce not gains but losses. Weltsch's approach to
the problem of an Arab-Zionist accommodation would have
seemed more balanced had he recalled his own strictures
against the unresponsiveness of Arab nationalism to Jewish
needs that he had leveled in 1928:

The national will to live is not by itself moral, but only that national will [is moral] which at the same time bears in itself the goal of justice. Justice, however, is an idea that applies to everyone equally. . . . It is the approach of European nationalism to say "justice" and to mean one's own advantage. Unfortunately, as far as we have observed, Arab nationalism has not kept itself free from the poor example of European [nationalism], either in its spirit or its methods. And we have heard from its camp no voice raised to counter [that trend], representing in politics the humanism appropriate to the spirit of the Orient.

In Jewish nationalism such voices have become loud and, although it is naturally difficult to determine, we believe that at the decisive moment it will be this orientation in Jewish thinking that will predominate. . . . During past years the view has gained greater currency within Zionist circles of the necessity of coexistence between these two peoples. The proposition that Palestine must be a binational state, in which in some form *both* nations must live in freedom, becomes all the more self-evident in Jewish circles the more one speaks of it. . . . From the Arab side [however] the national needs of the Jewish people have still not been appreciated. Even a sympathizer with the Arab cause must recognize that the national *center* of the Arabs does not lie in Palestine and that the Arab [nationalist] renaissance movement will not be diminished either in its goals or in its possibilities for development if hand in hand with it the Jewish national movement creates its center in Palestine, the only land with which the Jews are closely bound both by spirit and history and whose connection with the Jewish people the whole world recognizes.[28]

Nevertheless, to the end Weltsch remained optimistic that Zionist self-restraint and accommodation could provide a basis for an amicable accord with Arab nationalism and preserve the moral, nonaggressive virtue of Jewish nationalism. Zionists had been quick to point out to the assimilationists that good intentions by themselves were unavailing. It was a lesson that the Zionists themselves might have taken into account.

10

CONCLUSION

The establishment of the Nazi regime in Germany in 1933 effectively marked the close of the epoch in modern German Jewish history that had begun with the eighteenth-century Haskalah. Social integration was undone and, with the Nuremberg Laws of 1935, emancipation was rescinded. The Jews were again excluded from the society in which they lived, though now the basis for their exclusion was racial rather than religious. With the deterioration of the Jewish situation in Germany, a great many Jews, Zionists and assimilationists alike, found that the time for emigration had come. Here the ZVfD was able to provide considerable guidance and leadership, even as individual Zionists who tarried in Germany worked to maintain the cultural and social institutions of the community in its time of crisis.[1]

Of the Zionists who have appeared in this study, a number continued to play leading roles in Jewish life both in Palestine —later Israel—and elsewhere. Richard Lichtheim, who settled in Palestine in 1933, later served as the representative of the Jewish Agency in Geneva during World War II. Arthur Hantke, the president of the ZVfD from 1910 to 1920, moved to Palestine in 1926, where he served as president of the Keren Hayesod until shortly before his death in 1955. Felix Rosen-blüth (later Pinchas Rosen), who succeeded Hantke as ZVfD president, settled in Palestine in 1931. He later helped found the Organization of Immigrants from Germany (afterward the Organization of Immigrants from Central Europe) and from 1941 to 1948 served as the president of Aliyah Hadasha, the political party that grew out of it. After 1948 he continued his political activity as leader of the Progressive (later Liberal) party. Rosen served as the first minister of justice in the new state of Israel, a post that he held until 1961. Kurt Blumenfeld, who settled in Palestine in 1933, joined the board of the Keren Hayesod and, after wartime service for that organization in the United States, was active in the Organization of Immigrants from Germany. Siegfried Moses, who succeeded Blumenfeld as president of the ZVfD, from 1933 until his own emigration in 1937, later served as the first state comptroller of Israel, from 1949 to 1961. Moses was president of the Organization of Immigrants from Central Europe and was later chosen as presi-dent of the Leo Baeck Institute, an international association of Jews from Germany, whose Jerusalem branch he headed. Robert Weltsch immigrated to Palestine in 1938, where he joined the staff of the prestigious Hebrew daily *Haaretz.* After the war he moved to London, where he directed the Leo Baeck Institute's London branch, also editing the Institute's *Year Book.*[2]

Zionism and the Nazi Challenge

At least initially, Zionism's response to Nazism and its hypertrophied version of German nationalism was conditioned by the same idealism and optimism that were evident in its view of Arab nationalism. After the Nazis were in power, utterances assumed an Aesopian character that makes interpretation difficult, but before 1933 the matter was somewhat clearer. In brief, Zionists were unanimous in condemning Nazi brutality and racism; concerning other aspects of Nazism, however, there was a range of opinion. Some Zionists thought that there might be respectable and moderate elements within the Nazi movement who would serve to restrain it from within. (This view was shared by many others both inside and outside Germany.) These elements might serve as suitable negotiating partners for reaching some kind of German-Jewish accommodation. There was serious division over this possibility, with Weltsch, for example, arguing in its behalf and Blumenfeld sharply opposing it. What is striking is the undaunted inclination of some Zionists to persist in seeking an admittedly short-term basis for continued Jewish life in Germany, even when the Zionist doctrine of the necessity of emigration seemed increasingly urgent.[3]

The official viewpoint of the ZVfD was expressed by the resolution adopted at the *Delegiertentag* in September 1932, which declared that

the Jews in Germany are fighting for their legal position and [their very] existence. . . . Zionism condemns a nationalism whose foundations include the conviction of the inferiority of other national groups. Against this nationalism, which would use the power of the state to deny freedom and the possibility of existence to men who happen to be of a different sort [*Art*] or a different opinion, Zionism

—as the movement of national renewal for the Jewish people—sets
. . . the true national idea: constructive effort and the development
of the creative energies of a nation, not a battle of different groups
of men against one another. Guided by this conception of the national idea the Zionist movement struggles for the [equal] legal status
of the Jews in Germany. Just as it recognizes the significance of
nationality for the life of other nations, so does it also demand respect
for Jewish nationality. . . . From the state of which we are a part by
right and by fate we demand the protection of full equality and
freedom, and of the development of our own nature [*unsere eigene
Art*].[4]

The remarkable aspect of this declaration is not the Zionists'
insistence on full civil equality, which they had never ceased
to claim despite their theoretical intention to depart from
Germany eventually, but rather their persistence in maintaining their own ideals of benign nationalism and nationalist pluralism, and their optimism in holding these ideals up to the
Nazis in the expectation that the Nazis would be bound by
them.

Unfortunately there was another parallel between German-
Zionist relations and Arab-Zionist relations: in both cases
Zionist expectations were disappointed. On 1 April 1933 the
new Nazi regime launched its first large-scale anti-Jewish action with an organized one-day boycott of Jewish business,
during which Jewish stores were branded with paint and posters. The psychological blow that this visible ostracism dealt to
German Jewry was staggering. Assimilationists were wholly
unprepared for this turn of events, which seemed to confound
their established world view. The Zionists were rather better
prepared—in theory, at least—and the Zionist response to the
boycott, voiced by Weltsch in the *Rundschau*, demonstrated
at once both the strengths and weaknesses of the Zionist position. In a front-page editorial immediately following the boy-

cott, Weltsch urged German Jewry to bear the "yellow badge" of Nazi-assigned Jewishness with pride:

The first of April can be a day of Jewish awakening and rebirth—*if the Jews themselves will make it so;* if they possess the maturity and inner greatness necessary; if the Jews are *not* as their enemies have depicted them. . . . The directors of the boycott have ordered that the boycotted businesses be marked by posters "with a yellow patch on a field of black" [to recall the medieval Jew's badge]. . . . This measure is meant as a stigma, as a sign of contempt. *We take up this symbol and make of it thereby a badge of honor.* Many Jews had a severe shock on Saturday. Suddenly they stood as Jews—not out of inner avowal, not out of loyalty to their own community, not out of pride for a glorious past and great human achievement, but rather through the stamp of the red placard and the yellow patch. . . . The Star of David was supposed to be a [sign of] dishonor. *Jews: accept it, this Shield of David, and bear it with pride.* . . . If the Shield of David is today stained, it is not our enemies alone who are responsible; [for] there were many Jews who could not do enough to deride themselves. . . . The greatest danger that threatens Jewry is the corruption and crippling of its character. The Nazis declare in their speeches and proclamations that more than anything else it is the lack of character that they despise. . . . If this is the way things are . . . then Nazism must prefer as a Jewish partner a Jewry that maintains its honor. . . .

On April 1 every Jew in Germany was affixed with the stamp "Jew." . . . It is known who is a Jew. There is no longer [the possibility of] evasion or concealment. The Jewish answer is clear. It is the short sentence that Moses spoke to the Egyptians: I am a Jew. Yes, a Jew. To affirm being Jewish—that is the moral sense of the present events. The times are too excited to debate with [rational] arguments. We hope that a calmer time will follow and that a movement that takes pride in being the vanguard of a national renaissance [i.e., the Nazi movement] will not find pleasure in dishonoring others, even those it feels it must combat. But we Jews can defend our honor. We are mindful of all those who for five thousand years have been called Jews, who have been stigmatized as Jews. We are reminded that we are Jews. We say "Yes" and we bear it with pride.[5]

Here, at the twilight of Zionism's free development in Germany, the themes that had informed it from the beginning were restated: the affirmation of Jewish identity as a source of individual psychological well-being; the assumption that it was in the Jew's power to modify the attitudes of anti-Semites and the corollary that self-affirmation and self-respect would evoke respect in others; and finally the unshakable desire to remain in Germany, coexisting with the German *Volk* on the basis of a tolerant *völkisch* pluralism. Tragically for German Jewry, Weltsch's vision of benign nationalism proved to be groundless, in Germany as well as in Palestine. German Zionism, which had begun as a movement to build a refuge for East European Jewry, found in 1933 that the need for a refuge had become its own.

Nationalism and Identity

One could say that the history of Zionism in Germany represents the failure of an ideology—a failure to gain the support of a significant proportion of German Jewry and a failure to move even its nominal adherents to act as the movement demanded. This charge is incontestable. As the German Zionists themselves acknowledged, their movement was decidedly a minority one. And despite the impassioned dispute that surrounded the adoption of the Posen Resolution, the "radical" formulation of Zionism seems to have been limited to rhetoric.

From a different standpoint, however, German Zionist ideology proved to be a distinct success: it offered its adherents a version of Jewish identity that at the same time seemed to be particularly suited to their situation in Germany. This ideology of national distinctiveness and even separatism paradoxically provided the Zionists with a rationalization of their lives in Germany. Being about to depart apparently made one all the more comfortable in remaining. Zionism offered an escape from the demeaning pressure of anti-Semitism, an antidote to self-denial and self-disdain, and a solution to the dilemma of Jewish existence in a Germany that seemed to deny the Jew the right to a full life of his own.

On the other hand, the Centralverein's version of Jewish identity seems to have functioned just as well for those who espoused it as the Zionist one did for its adherents. It may be true that people see only what they want to, but the important thing psychologically is for them to comprehend the "reality" they observe. From a purely subjective point of view, one integrated world view seems to be as good as any other and any identity is better than none. In this regard the Centralverein's and Zionism's versions of reality evidently served equally well. And if the Jew's pretension to membership in German society as a German citizen of the Jewish faith now seems ill founded, the Zionist alternative was in its own way equally inappropriate.

Indeed, the ZVfD and the Centralverein appear to have been much closer than either would have liked to think. Both shared the assumption that had characterized Jewish efforts for acceptance in Germany from the time of the Haskalah—namely, that German resistance to the Jews could be traced to some objective defect in the Jews themselves and that self-improvement would have to precede, but would assuredly bring, emancipation and subsequent integration. While the assimilationists sought their remedy in an increased measure of acculturation, the Zionists imagined that the enhancement of Jewish pride and self-respect would be sufficient to elicit respect and acceptance from others. Both groups were perhaps too self-effacing in their willingness to make concessions in seeking their ultimate goals—the assimilationists in the matter of acculturation and the Zionists in their appeasement of Arab nationalism. And both groups had the same basically liberal, tolerant, humanitarian outlook, manifested in their respective pluralist visions, an outlook that would become increasingly anachronistic in the German context.

German Jews were optimists—understandably, since pessimism meant envisioning their own downfall. Throughout the modern period the assimilationists maintained their hope that, as German citizens of the Jewish faith, they could find a place in the German society that was, after all, theirs. The Zionists too were optimists, necessarily so since they faced a task of national restoration of unprecedented difficulty. They had an even greater hope: that the principle of nationality at the heart of their doctrine would everywhere prove to be as benign as they themselves intended. Concerning Jewish life in Germany, however, they were pessimists, and their pessimism would calamitously prove to be as correct as their optimism about a benevolent nationalism was mistaken.

To be sure, there is the danger of seeing what happened as inevitable or singling out only those factors that explain what occurred. That anti-Semitism ultimately triumphed in Germany—both in gaining ideological currency and in providing a program for action—does not mean that there were not many Germans who were either opposed or indifferent, or that its ascendance was irreversible. Even during the first years of the Nazi regime some Germans were willing to dissociate themselves, if only privately, from anti-Semitic developments, and this of course reinforced any remaining Jewish optimism. But the statement that the Jews in Germany faced strong enemies with the support of weak friends is more than an expression of our retrospective knowledge that in the end their enemies were *too* strong and their friends *too* weak for them to survive. Rather, it is a judgment that could have fairly been made by contemporary observers, as in fact it was.

The Zionists should not, however, be given more than their due. Although ultimately the Zionist analysis seemed to have been justified, this does not necessarily mean that it was always as valid as it eventually proved to be. The course of history is complex, and the successful prediction of an outcome does not imply the discovery of the laws of historical motion. The Zionists' conviction that the Jewish question was both objective and insoluble derived after all from their own subjective perception of the German situation, a perception not shared by most German Jews. Nevertheless, it is clear in retrospect—and here retrospect can validly intervene—that the Zionist analysis of the situation of the Jews in Germany was not simply a matter of fortuitous prescience, but was based on a correct identification of the issues that would later prove to be decisive.

To be sure, the Zionist theory had its flaws, such as the peculiar notion that some kind of nationalist pluralism was possible. But its virtue was that it integrated and rationalized what the Zionists perceived to be the reality of Jewish life in Germany. Indeed, this was its real function. Thus the absence of any large emigration to Palestine did not reflect simply the German Zionists' failure to act on their convictions. For them to have sacrificed present comfort for some possible future advantage would have required an immense faith in theory in addition to integrity and courage. In the end the Zionists proved to be right, but they were more right than they ever realized.

Thesen der National-jüdischen Vereinigung, Köln (1897)

I.

Durch gemeinsame Abstammung und Geschichte verbunden, bilden die Juden aller Länder eine nationale Gemeinschaft. Die Betätigung patriotischer Besinnung und Erfüllung der staatsbürgerlichen Pflichten seitens der Juden, insbesondere der deutschen Juden für ihr deutsches Vaterland wird durch diese Überzeugung in keiner Weise beeinträchtigt.

II.

Die staatsbürgerliche Emanzipation der Juden innerhalb der anderen Völker hat, wie die Geschichte zeigt, nicht genügt, um die soziale und kulturelle Zukunft des jüdischen Stammes zu sichern, daher kann die endgültige Lösung der Judenfrage nur in der Bildung eines jüdischen Staates bestehen; denn nur dieser ist in der Lage, die Juden als solche völkerrechtlich zu vertreten und diejenigen Juden aufzunehmen, die in ihrem Heimatland nicht bleiben können oder wollen. Der natürliche Mittelpunkt für diesen auf legalem Wege zu schaffenden Staat ist der historisch geweihte Boden Palästinas.

III.

Dieses Endziel muss sowohl durch die Hebung des jüdischen Selbstbewusstseins als durch zielbewusste praktische Tätigkeit vorbereitet werden. Als Mittel hierzu dienen:

    a) die Förderung der jüdischen Kolonien in Syrien und Palästina;

    b) die Pflege jüdischen Wissens und jüdischer Sitte (Literatur, Geschichte und hebräische Sprache);

    c) die Verbesserung der sozialen und kulturellen Lage der Juden.

Source: Henriette Hannah Bodenheimer, ed., *Im Anfang der zionistischen Bewegung* (Frankfort on the Main: Europäische Verlagsanstalt, 1965), pp. 22–24, and Richard Lichtheim, *Die Geschichte des deutschen Zionismus* (Jerusalem: R. Mass, 1954), following p. 120, and pp. 134–35.

Theses of the National-Jewish Association, Cologne (1897)

I.
Bound together by common descent and history, the Jews of all lands constitute a national community. The manifestation of patriotic consciousness and the fulfillment of civil duties by the Jews, especially by the German Jews for their German fatherland, is in no way prejudiced by this conviction.

II.
The civil emancipation of the Jews within the other nations has not sufficed, as history shows, to assure the social and cultural future of the Jewish people. Therefore the final resolution of the Jewish question can consist only in the creation of a Jewish state; for only such a state will be in the position to represent the Jews as such in international law, as well as to receive those Jews who cannot or will not remain in their homeland. The natural focus for this state, to be created by legal means, is the historically consecrated soil of Palestine.

III.
This final goal must be prepared for by the heightening of Jewish self-consciousness as well as by purposeful practical activity. Serving as means to this end are:
   a) the promotion of Jewish colonies in Syria and Palestine;
   b) the cultivation of Jewish knowledge and Jewish customs (literature, history, and Hebrew language);
   c) the improvement of the social and cultural situation of the Jews.

Das Baseler Programm (1897)

Der Zionismus erstrebt für das jüdische Volk die Schaffung einer öffentlich-rechtlich gesicherten Heimstätte in Palästina.

Zur Erreichung dieses Zieles nimmt der Congress folgende Mittel in Aussicht:

1. die zweckdienliche Förderung der Besiedlung Palästinas mit jüdischen Ackerbauern, Handwerkern und Gewerbetriebenden;

2. die Gliederung und Zusammenfassung der gesamten Judenschaft durch geeignete örtliche und allgemeine Veranstaltungen nach den Landesgesetzen;

3. die Stärkung des jüdischen Volksgefühles und Volksbewusstseins;

4. vorbereitende Schritte zur Erlangung der Regierungszustimmungen, die nötig sind, um das Ziel des Zionismus zu erreichen.

Source: *Stenográphisches Protokoll der Verhandlungen des I. Zionisten-Congresses* (1897), pp. 114, 119.

The Basel Program (1897)

Zionism endeavors to create for the Jewish people a homeland in Palestine secured by public law.

For the attainment of this goal the Congress envisions the following means:

1. the purposeful promotion of the settlement of Palestine with Jewish farmers, artisans, and tradesmen;

2. the organization and unification of world Jewry, in accordance with the law, through appropriate local and general institutions;

3. the strengthening of Jewish national feeling and national consciousness;

4. preparatory steps toward securing the governmental assent necessary for achieving the goal of Zionism.

Table 1   *Jewish Population of Germany (territory of Reich at time of census)*

Year	Total Population[1]	Jewish Population[1]	% of Total Population	Foreign-born Jews[2]	% of Jewish Population[2]
1871	41,058,641	512,158[a]	1.25	—	—
1880	42,234,061	561,612	1.33	15,000	2.7
1890	49,428,470	567,884	1.15	22,000	3.9
1900	56,367,178	586,833	1.04	41,113	7.0
1910	64,925,993	615,021	.95	78,746	12.8
1925	62,410,619[b]	564,379[b]	.93	107,747[b]	19.1
1933	65,218,461[c]	499,682[c]	.80	98,747[c]	19.8

Remarks
—   = not available
a   cited in comparative tables in subsequent volumes of *Statistik des Deutschen Reichs* as 512,153.
b   excluding the Saar.
c   excluding the Saar (see *Statistik des Deutschen Reichs*, vol. 451, part 4, p. 9).

Sources
[1]*Statistik des Deutschen Reichs* (new series). Jewish population as defined by religion ("*Israeliten*").
Data for:
1871	vol. 2, part 2, section 1, p. 122 (total population).
1871	ibid., p. 188d (Jewish population).
1880	vol. 57, part 1, p. iv (total population).
1880	ibid., part 2, p. lxxxiv (Jewish population).
1890	vol. 68, p. 75*.
1900	vol. 150, p. 185.
1910	vol. 240, part 1, p. 135.
1925[b]	vol. 401, part 2, p. 596.
1933[c]	vol. 451, part 3, p. 28.

[2]Schalom Adler-Rudel, *Ostjuden in Deutschland* (Tübingen: J.C.B. Mohr, 1959), Tables B, C, pp. 164–65, "Anteil der ausländischen Juden an der jüdischen Gesamtbevölkerung im Reich. . . ."

Table 2 *Jewish Population of Germany (corrected for German boundaries of 1934, including the Saar)*

Year	Total Population	Jewish Population	% of Total Population
1871	36,323,000	383,000	1.05
1880	40,218,000	437,000	1.09
1890	44,230,000	465,000	1.05
1900	50,626,000	497,000	.98
1910	58,451,000	539,000	.92
1925	63,181,000	568,000	.90
1933	66,029,000	503,000	.76

Source
Statistik des Deutschen Reichs, vol. 451, part 5, p. 7, "Die Glaubensjuden in Deutschen Reich 1816 bis 1933" ("Gebietsstand 1934 einschl. Saarland").

Table 3 *Membership of Zionistische Vereinigung für Deutschland, Annual Totals*

Year[1]	German Zionists	Total Zionists	% of Total Zionists
1897	100	—	—
1901	2,200	—	—
1903	4,500	—	—
1904	6,000	—	—
1905/06 (5666)	5,308	67,295	7.9
1906/07 (5667)	5,960	97,038	6.1
1907/08 (5668)	4,500	76,584	5.9
1908/09 (5669)	6,239	106,224	5.9
1909/10 (5670)	4,791	71,530	6.7
1910/11 (5671)	7,836	104,364	7.5
1911/12 (5672)	7,442	87,871	8.5
1912/13 (5673)	8,964	129,414	6.9
1920/21 (5681)	20,000	778,487	2.6
1921/22 (5682)	18,145	373,217	4.9
1922/23 (5683)	33,339	584,765	5.7
1923/24 (5684)	20,847	300,267	6.9

Table 3   *(continued)*

Year[1]		German Zionists	Total Zionists	% of Total Zionists
1924/25	(5685)	21,910	638,017	3.4
1925/26	(5686)	13,826	214,384	6.4
1926/27	(5687)	20,686	416,767	5.0
1927/28	(5688)	10,816	217,550	5.0
1928/29	(5689)	15,559	387,106	4.0
1929/30	(5690)	9,539	201,250	4.7
1930/31	(5691)	17,548	425,987	4.1
1931/32	(5692)	7,546	152,214	5.0
1932/33	(5693)	—	691,393	—
1933/34	(5694)	43,661	239,901	18.2
1934/35	(5695)	57,202	978,033	5.8

Remarks
— = not available
[1]Note that shekel sales were regularly higher in years during which a Zionist Congress was held. In view of this fact the representation at the Congress, distributed proportionately according to shekel sales, was based after the tenth Zionist Congress (1911) on sales averaged over the two-year Congress period. See Adolf Böhm, *Die zionistische Bewegung* (Tel Aviv: Hozaah Ivrith, 1935, 1937), 1:601.

Sources
1897   Bodenheimer to Herzl (14.7.1897) in Henriette Hannah Bodenheimer, ed., *Im Anfang der zionistischen Bewegung: Eine Dokumentation auf der Grundlage des Briefwechsels zwischen Theodor Herzl und Max Bodenheimer von 1896 bis 1905* (Frankfort on the Main: Europäische Verlagsanstalt, 1965), p. 45.
1901   *Israelitische Rundschau* 7, no. 21 (23.5.1902): 4.
1903   ZVfD, *Zionistisches A-B-C Buch* (Berlin: ZVfD, 1908), pp. 285–90.
1904   *Jüdische Rundschau* 9, no. 21 (27.5.1904): 222.
1905 et seq. *Stenographisches Protokoll der Verhandlungen des XIX. Zionisten-Kongresses* (1935), "Schekelstatistik für die Jahre 5659–5695," pp. 16–19. (The figures for 5659–5665, 5674–5680 are not broken down by country.)

Table 4   *Sales of Shekalim by Cities, 1921–27*

	1921	1923	1925	1926	1927
Berlin	4,308	5,500	5,223	1,557	4,311
Beuthen	—	—	354	181	321
Breslau	595	508	1,191	599	1,100
Chemnitz	330	503	465		381
Cologne	494	—	761	347	379
Danzig	311	—	—	—	—
Dresden	109	—	315	124	—
Frankfort on the Main	969	380	1,224	357	800
Hamburg	942	1,269	1,446	839	1,150
Hanover	183	494	322	—	178
Königsberg	463	225	702	226	415
Leipzig	1,570	2,328	1,331	130	1,050
Munich	653	410	351	355	430
Nuremberg	490	383	750	336	390

Remarks
Sales of over 300 shekalim. The shekel was the token Zionist membership fee, named after a biblical coin and assessed in Germany at one mark.
—   = not available.

Sources
1921   *JR* 27, no. 78/79 (6.10.22): 528.
1923   *JR* 28, no. 50 (22.6.1923): 316; data incomplete, to 20.6.1923.
1925   *JR* 31, no. 65 (20.8.1926): 474.
1926   ibid.; data incomplete, to 12.7.1926.
1927   *JR* 32, no. 51 (28.6.1927): 366; data incomplete, to 26.6.1927.

Table 5   *Zionistische Vereinigung für Deutschland Delegiertentage
(Delegates' Meetings)*

1	11 July 1897	Bingen
2	31 October 1897	Frankfort on the Main
3	26 December 1898	Berlin
4	19–20 March 1899	Cologne
5	30 April–1 May 1901	Berlin
6	19–21 May 1902	Mannheim
7	20 August 1903	St. Ludwig
8	23–24 May 1904	Hamburg
9	25–26 July 1905	Basel
10	4–5 June 1906	Hanover
11	8–9 June 1908	Breslau
12	11–12 September 1910	Frankfort on the Main
13	27–28 May 1912	Posen

Ausserordentliche Tagung (concerning the Centralverein anti-Zionist resolution)

	1 May 1913	Berlin
14	14–15 June 1914	Leipzig

Ausserordentlicher Delegiertentag

	24–26 December 1916	Berlin
15	25–27 December 1918	Berlin
16	20–25 June 1920	Berlin
17	13–16 May 1921	Hanover
18	11–12 September 1922	Kassel
19	25–27 June 1923	Dresden
20	28–31 December 1924	Wiesbaden
21	22–24 August 1926	Erfurt
22	27–29 May 1928	Breslau
23	29–30 December 1929	Jena
24	11–12 September 1932	Frankfort on the Main
25	2–4 February 1936	Berlin

A meeting of representatives of the ZVfD held on 28 August 1897 during the Zionist Congress is sometimes regarded as a *Delegiertentag*, without affecting the series numbering of the later *Delegiertentage*.

Table 6 *Presidents of the Zionistische Vereinigung für Deutschland*

1897–1910	Max Isidor Bodenheimer
1910–1920	Arthur Hantke
1920–1921	Felix Rosenblüth (joint presidency) Alfred Klee
1921–1923	Felix Rosenblüth
1923–1924	Alfred Landsberg
1924–1933	Kurt Blumenfeld
1933–1937	Siegfried Moses

Table 7 *Jewish Immigration to Palestine*

Year[1]	Total Jewish Immigration from Germany	Immigrants from Germany with Non-German Citizenship (included in total)[2]	German Percentage of Total Jewish Immigration[3]	Total Jewish Immigration[4]	Total Jewish Emigration[5]
1919	—	—	—	806	—
1920	175	—	2.1	8,223	—
1921	185	—	2.2	8,294	—
1922	38	—	0.4	8,685	—
1923	71	—	0.9	8,175	—
1924	180	—	1.3	13,892	2,037
1925	630	—	1.8	34,386	2,151
1926	242	—	1.7	13,855	7,365
1927[6]	33	—	1.1	3,034	5,071
1928	12	—	0.6	2,178	2,168
1929	152	—	2.9	5,249	1,746
1930	103	56	2.1	4,944	1,679
1931	72	30	1.8	4,074	666
1932	155	2	1.6	9,553	—
1933	6,803	1,053	22.4	30,327	—
1934	8,497	1,771	20.1	42,359	—
Total 1920–32	2,048		1.6	124,542	

Table 7 *(continued)*

— = no data given

Remarks and Sources

[1]There is little information on *aliyah* before World War I since the Jewish community regarded publicity in this matter to be undesirable, in view of the fact that such immigration was carried on partly in opposition to the policy of the Turkish regime. See David Gurevich, "Fifteen Years of Immigration to Palestine" (Hebrew), *Aliyah: Kovetz le-Inyane ha-Aliyah* 2, (1935):45–46.

[2]Ibid., Table 26, "Immigration from Germany during 1920–1934 (Jewish Agency Records of Jewish Immigration)," p. xxxviii.

[3]I have calculated these figures myself from the data given in the tables cited in notes 2 and 4. I cannot account for the discrepancy between these results and the figures given in column 3 of the table cited in note 2.

[4]Gurevich, "Immigration," Table 8, p. xii (Jewish Agency Records), and Table 10, pp. xiv–xv. It should be noted that these figures are generally somewhat higher than those given in official records of the British Mandatory government. See [Zionist Organization] Palestine Zionist Executive, Immigration Department, *Ten Years of Jewish Immigration into Palestine, 1919–1929* (Jerusalem, 1929), Table 15, "Annual Immigration and Emigration (Government Records)," p. 23. I have preferred the Jewish Agency statistics, however, in order to maintain consistency with the data for German immigration.

[5]David Gurevich, Aaron Gertz, Roberto Bachi, *The Jewish Population of Palestine: Immigration, Demographic Structure, and Natural Growth* (Hebrew; Jerusalem: Jewish Agency for Palestine, Statistical Department, 1944), p. 24.

[6]During 1927 Palestine suffered a serious economic depression, a fact that is reflected in the net surplus of emigration over immigration that year.

Table 8 *German Contributions to the Keren Kayemeth (Jewish National Fund)*

Year	German Contribution[1]		Total Contributions		Germany's Rank among Countries in Total Amount Collected[2]
1903	RM	7,200			
1910	RM	55,000			
1913	RM	107,000			
1914	RM	62,300	Fr 77,800	Fr 744,700	3
1915	RM	61,000	Fr 76,300	Fr 636,800	3
1916	RM	130,900	Fr 163,500	Fr 933,100	3
1917	RM	149,400	Fr 169,900	Fr 1,753,700	3
1918	RM	273,300	Fr 192,000	Fr 2,243,200	4
1919	RM	1,001,000	Fr 418,700	Fr 5,551,000	3
1920	RM	1,705,200	Fr 494,400	Fr 9,637,000	5
1921	RM	2,007,200	£ 5,465	£ 128,899	4
1922	RM	4,272,602	£ 1,533	£ 72,609	10
1922/23 (5683)			£ 1,684	£ 114,150	4
			E	E	
1923/24 (5684)			£ 13,813	£ 167,664	2
			E	E	
1924/25 (5685)			£ 21,617	£ 260,336	3
			E	E	
1925/26 (5686)			£ 12,081	£ 281,451	5
			E	E	
1926/27 (5687)			£ 11,958	£ 281,005	6
			E	E	
1927/28 (5688)			£P 13,623	£P 263,112	6

Remarks

[1]Figures in German currency are also presented by the sources in the currency in which Total Contributions are given for the sake of comparison (RM = Reichsmark, Fr = franc, £ = pound sterling, £E = Egyptian pound, £P = Palestinian pound). Note the dramatic effect of the German inflation in 1922.

[2]First place was held by North America (except for 1924/25 when it fell to second place). Either England or Poland was usually in second place. This ranking is based on absolute amounts collected. Per capita ranking was different, with Germany falling much lower. For example in 1925/26 Germany ranked twenty-fifth on a per capita basis, behind such countries as Finland, New Zealand, and China, which had far smaller Jewish populations.

Sources

1903, 1910, 1913: Richard Lichtheim, *Die Geschichte des deutschen Zionismus* (Jerusalem: R. Mass, 1954), p. 152.

1914–28: *Report of the Head Office of the Keren Kayemeth Leisrael to the . . . Zionist Congress* (title varies slightly; London and Jerusalem, biannual). There is no breakdown by country for the figures in the reports of 1931 and 1933.

Table 9 *German Contributions to the Keren Hayesod (Palestine Foundation Fund)*

Year[1]	German Contributions	Total Contributions	Germany's Rank among Countries in Total Amount Collected[2]
1920/21	£13,127	£177,449	3
1921/22	14,724	411,134	4
1922/23	4,383	379,216	10
1923/24	15,302	463,074	3
1924/25	30,213	494,859	3
1925/26 1926/27	48,723	1,143,850	5
1927/28	27,719	440,624	3
1928/29	31,274	417,454	3
1929/30	29,829	389,148	3
1930/31	20,989	258,028	4

Remarks

[1]The fiscal year ran from April to March, except for the first year, when it closed in August.

[2]First and second place were held most frequently by the United States and South Africa, respectively.

Source

Keren Hayesod, *Bericht des Hauptbüros des Keren Hajessod an den . . . Zionisten-Kongress* (title varies slightly; London and Jerusalem, biannual).

Centralverein	Centralverein deutscher Staatsbürger jüdischen Glaubens (Central Association of German Citizens of the Jewish Faith)
CZA	Central Zionist Archives, Jerusalem (for identification of archive series, see Bibliography)
IsrR	*Israelitische Rundschau*
JNUL	Jewish National and University Library, Jerusalem
JR	*Jüdische Rundschau*
LBI	Leo Baeck Institute
LBIYB	*Leo Baeck Institute Year Book*
ZVfD	Zionistische Vereinigung für Deutschland (German Zionist Federation)

I have adopted the German convention in the matter of dates to avoid confusion: 31.12.1897

NOTES

Preface

1. See the lists of early German settlers in Palestine in Richard Lichtheim, *Die Geschichte des deutschen Zionismus* (Jerusalem: R. Mass, 1954), pp. 142–44, 267–69.

2. Yonathan Shapiro, *Leadership of the American Zionist Organization: 1897–1930* (Urbana: University of Illinois Press, 1971), p. 5. Melvin Urofsky's history of Zionism in the United States develops the important issue of the influence of the American context and stresses the extent to which the movement has "not only been Zionist, but American as well." *American Zionism from Herzl to the Holocaust* (Garden City: Anchor Press, Doubleday, 1975), p. 2. The history of the Dutch Zionist movement is presented in a series of articles by L. A. M. Giebels, "Het onstaan van eew zionistische Beweging in Nederland . . . [The Rise of the Zionist Movement in the Netherlands . . .]," *Studia Rosenthaliana* 7, no. 1 (January 1973): 90–115; 8, no. 1 (January 1974): 64–106; 8, no. 2 (July 1974): 214–67; and 9, no. 1 (January 1975): 103–52. An English summary appears in vol. 9, no. 1: 148–52. The Lichtheim volume is cited in note 1 above. A study devoted to the conflict between the assimilationist Centralverein deutscher Staatsbürger jüdischen Glaubens and the ZVfD has recently appeared: Jehuda Reinharz, *Fatherland or Promised Land: The Dilemma of the*

German Jew, 1893–1914 (Ann Arbor: University of Michigan Press, 1975). For other works touching on Zionism in general, the Zionist movements in other countries, and German Zionism, see the Bibliography.

3. Although a complete basis for such comparative analysis has yet to be established, Henry Feingold has offered some interesting suggestions for the comparison of various Zionist movements in terms of their specific national characteristics in his comments in Melvin I. Urofsky et al., "Zionism: An American Experience," *American Jewish Historical Quarterly* 63, no. 3 (March 1974): 232–34.

4. These questions are considered in detail, though for the earlier period of the pre-Weimar Reich, by Peter Gay, "Encounter with Modernism: German Jews in German Culture, 1888–1914," *Midstream* 21, no. 2 (February 1975): 23–65.

5. *JR* 19, no. 1 (1.1.1914):1; emphasis in the original (for an explanation of the German date style and the abbreviations used, see the List of Abbreviations). The information on the fate of the ZVfD archive was provided by the staff of the Bundesarchiv, Koblenz.

1. Introduction

1. For a fuller description of the traditional Jewish community and its relations with the Christian world, see Jacob Katz, *Tradition and Crisis: Jewish Society at the End of the Middle Ages* (New York: Free Press, 1961), and idem, *Exclusiveness and Tolerance: Studies in Jewish-Gentile Relations in Medieval and Modern Times* (London: Oxford University Press, 1961). A vivid picture of the medieval Jewish community is portrayed by the documents collected in Jacob R. Marcus, *The Jew in the Medieval World* (New York: Meridian; Philadelphia: Jewish Publication Society, 1960).

2. See Salo Baron, "Newer Approaches to Jewish Emancipation," *Diogenes*, no. 29 (Spring 1960): 68–69, n. 12.

3. See Jacob Katz, "The Term 'Jewish Emancipation': Its Origin and Historical Impact," in Alexander Altmann, ed., *Studies in Nineteenth-Century Jewish Intellectual History* (Cambridge, Mass.: Harvard University Press, 1964), pp. 1–25.

4. See Baron, "Newer Approaches," especially pp. 57, 65, as well as his earlier "Ghetto and Emancipation: Shall We Revise the Traditional View?" *Menorah Journal* 14, no. 6 (June 1928): 524. The polemical animus of Baron's argument is that emancipation was imposed on the Jews and that it is historically incorrect to cast them in the role of the suppliant. This did not prevent contemporaries from regarding the process in these terms, however.

5. Arthur Hertzberg, *The French Enlightenment and the Jews* (New York: Columbia University Press, 1968), ch. 9, "The Men of the Enlightenment."

6. Meeting of the National Assembly, 23 December 1789, in *Réimpression de L'Ancien Moniteur (Gazette Nationale ou le Moniteur Universel)* (Paris: Henri Plon, 1859), 2:456.

7. Gotthold Ephraim Lessing, *Nathan der Weise*, act 2, scene 5. Mendelssohn's remark appears at the end of his introduction to the German translation of Manasseh ben Israel's *Vindiciae Judaeorum*, which appeared in 1782 and was reprinted in Moses Mendelssohn, *Gesammelte Schriften* (Leipzig, 1843–45), 3:202. The best general works on German Jewry in this period are Michael A. Meyer, *The Origins of the Modern Jew: Jewish Identity and European Culture in Germany, 1749–1824* (Detroit: Wayne State University Press, 1967), and Jacob Katz, *Out of the Ghetto: The Social Background of Jewish Emancipation, 1770–1870* (Cambridge, Mass.: Harvard University Press, 1973). Further bibliographical references may be found there. A recent comprehensive biography of Mendelssohn has been published by Alexander Altmann, *Moses Mendelssohn: A Biographical Study* (University, Alabama: University of Alabama Press; Philadelphia: Jewish Publication Society, 1973).

8. Quoted in Meyer, *Origins of the Modern Jew*, p. 17.

9. Naphtali Herz Wessely, *Divre Shalom ve-Emet* [Words of Peace and Truth], 4 parts (Berlin: Die jüdische Freischule, 1782–85), pt. 1, ch. 1. Concerning Mendelssohn's motivations in translating the Torah, see his introduction to his translation, *Netivot ha-Shalom*, 1st ed. (Berlin, 1780–83). See also his letter to Avigdor Levi (25.5.1774) in *Gesammelte Schriften: Jubiläumsausgabe* (Berlin, Breslau, 1929–32, 1938), 16:252. Landau's criticism of the Mendelssohn translation is quoted in *Hameassef* 3:143.

10. Christian Wilhelm [von] Dohm, *Über die bürgerliche Verbesserung der Juden* [On the Civil Improvement of the Jews], 2 vols. (Berlin: Friedrich Nicolai, 1781, 1783). An excellent analysis of the work may be found in Katz, "The Term 'Jewish Emancipation.'"

11. See Katz, *Tradition and Crisis*, ch. 23, "The Emergence of the Neutral Society." In recognition of the limitations of the neutral society, Katz has modified the term in his most recent book to "semineutral society." See *Out of the Ghetto*, ch. 4, and Katz's essay, "The German-Jewish Utopia of Social Emancipation," reprinted in Jacob Katz, *Emancipation and Assimilation: Studies in Modern Jewish History* (Westmead: Gregg International, 1972), pp. 91–110. Concerning the Haskalah's attack on the national elements within Judaism, see Isaac E. Barzilay, "National and Anti-National Trends in the Berlin Haskalah," *Jewish Social Studies* 21, no. 3 (July 1959): 165–92.

12. Concerning Zionist usage of the term "assimilation," and Blumenfeld's

concept of "postassimilation," see Robert Weltsch, "Siegfried Moses: End of an Epoch," *LBIYB* 19 (1974): viii. See also Helga Krohn, *Die Juden in Hamburg, 1800–1850: Ihre soziale, kulturelle und politische Entwicklung während der Emanzipationszeit* (Frankfort on the Main: Europäische Verlagsanstalt, 1967), p. 5 and note. I have found very helpful the typology of integration and assimilation developed by Walter B. Simon, "The Jewish Vote in Austria," *LBIYB* 16 (1971): 98–103. A good general discussion of assimilation, including reference to additional theoretical material, is presented by Milton Gordon, *Assimilation in American Life: The Role of Race, Religion, and National Origins* (New York: Oxford University Press, 1964).

13. Concerning the duration of this debate and the consequences of delay, see Reinhard Rürup, "Kontinuität und Diskontinuität der 'Judenfrage' im 19. Jahrhundert: Zur Entstehung des modernen Antisemitismus," in Hans-Ulrich Wehler, ed., *Sozialgeschichte Heute: Festschrift für Hans Rosenberg* (Göttingen: Vandenhoeck und Ruprecht, 1974), pp. 388–415. A lively discussion of Germany's halting political modernization may be found in Ralf Dahrendorf, *Society and Democracy in Germany* (Garden City: Doubleday, 1967).

14. Ismar Elbogen and Eleonore Sterling, *Die Geschichte der Juden in Deutschland: Eine Einführung* (Frankfort on the Main: Europäische Verlagsanstalt, 1966) is the best general introduction to German Jewish history. The specific subject of Jewish emancipation is treated in detail in Ernest Hamburger, "One Hundred Years of Emancipation," *LBIYB* 14 (1969): 3–66. The "productivization" of German Jewry is the subject of two recent works by Jacob Toury: *Kavim le-ḥeker kenisath ha-yehudim la-ḥayim ha-ezraḥiyim be-germanyah* [Prolegomena to the Entrance of Jews into German Citizenry] (Hebrew; 1972); and *Der Eintritt der Juden ins deutsche Bürgertum: Eine Dokumentation* (1972), both published by the Diaspora Research Institute of the University of Tel Aviv. On the matter of military careers, see Werner T. Angress, "Prussia's Army and the Jewish Reserve Officer Controversy before World War I," *LBIYB* 17 (1972): 19–42.

15. Concerning Jewish emancipation and its relationship to general political development and to Jewish assimilation see, respectively, Reinhard Rürup, "Jewish Emancipation and Bourgeois Society," *LBIYB* 14 (1969): 67–91; and Stephen Poppel, "New Views on Jewish Integration in Germany," *Central European History*, forthcoming.

16. The standard work on the precursors of the modern Zionist movement is N. M. Gelber, *Zur Vorgeschichte des Zionismus* (Vienna: Phaidon, 1927). Jacob Katz analyzes the notion of "precursors of Zionism" in his article "Toward the Clarification of the Concept 'Precursors of Zionism,'" *Shivat Zion* (Hebrew) 1 (1949/50): 91–105. The pre-Zionist German settlers in Palestine are the subject of Mordechai Eliav, *Love*

of Zion and Men of "HOD": German Jewry and the Settlement of
Eretz-Israel in the Nineteenth Century (Hebrew; Tel Aviv: University
of Tel Aviv, Hakibbutz Hameuchad, 1970). For general works on Zionism, see the Bibliography.

17. See Henry J. Cohn, "Theodor Herzl's Conversion to Zionism," *Jewish
Social Studies* 32, no. 2 (April 1970): 101–10; and Peter Loewenberg,
"Theodor Herzl: A Psychoanalytic Study in Charismatic Political Leadership," in Benjamin B. Wolman, ed., *The Psychoanalytic Interpretation
of History* (New York: Basic Books, 1971), pp. 150–91. The most recent
biography is Amos Elon, *Herzl* (New York: Holt, Rinehart and Winston, 1975).

18. *Der Judenstaat: Versuch einer modernen Lösung der Judenfrage*, 1st ed.
(Vienna, 1896); reprinted in Theodor Herzl, *Zionistische Schriften*, 3d
ed., rev. and enl. (Tel Aviv: Hozaah Ivrith, 1934), pp. 19, 25–26.

19. *"Der Zionismus ist die Heimkehr zum Judentum noch vor der Rückkehr
ins Judenland,"* in "Eröffnungsrede zum ersten Kongress," reprinted in
Herzl, *Zionistische Schriften*, 3d ed., p. 176.

2. Two Zions

1. Concerning the Bingen conference, see Lichtheim, *Geschichte des
deutschen Zionismus*, pp. 135–36, and Bodenheimer's memoir, printed
in Henriette Hannah Bodenheimer, ed., *Im Anfang der zionistischen
Bewegung: Eine Dokumentation auf der Grundlage des Briefwechsels
zwischen Theodor Herzl und Max Bodenheimer von 1896 bis 1905*
(Frankfort on the Main: Europäische Verlagsanstalt, 1965), p. 372. The
accounts diverge slightly with regard to the number of participants, and
I have followed Lichtheim's, which is better documented. Max Isidor
Bodenheimer, *Wohin mit den russischen Juden? Syrien ein Zufluchtsort
der russischen Juden* (Hamburg: Die Menorah, 1891). Bodenheimer's
Kölner Verein zur Förderung von Ackerbau und Handwerk in Palästina
was intended as a parallel organization to the Odessa Society for the
Support of Jewish Farmers and Craftsmen in Syria and Palestine,
founded in 1890 and associated with the Hovevei Zion movement. See
Lichtheim, *Geschichte des deutschen Zionismus*, p. 112. On Boden-
heimer's meeting with Wolffsohn at the Cologne Verein für jüdische
Geschichte und Literatur, see Bodenheimer, ed., *Im Anfang*, pp. 17–
18. The naming of the ZVfD is reported in the *Protokoll des III.
Delegiertentages der deutschen Zionisten am 31. Oktober 1897 zu
Frankfurt am Main*, p. 1. (A copy may be found in CZA: DD 2/7/10/1
National-jüdische Vereinigung, Köln. DD = *Ossef divre d'fus* [Miscel-
laneous printed matter].) A number of earlier German Jewish efforts to

organize support for Russian Jewish settlement in Palestine are described in Mordechai Eliav, "Zur Vorgeschichte der jüdischen Nationalbewegung in Deutschland," *LBI Bulletin* 12, no. 48 (1969): 282–314. Since these groups did not share the nationalist premise of modern Zionism, and since there was no real continuity between them and the organized movement that later emerged—as Eliav himself admits (pp. 304, 312)—I have excluded them from this account.

2. Information on the early history of the student Zionist movement is drawn from Lichtheim, *Geschichte des deutschen Zionismus*, pp. 112–22; Max Jungmann, *Erinnerungen eines Zionisten* (Jerusalem: R. Mass, 1959), pp. 34–41; Adolf Friedemann, Diary in CZA: A8/2(7), entries for 1893–95; Paul Graetz, "Daten zur Geschichte der zionistischen Studentenbewegung in Deutschland," in "Kartell jüdischer Verbindungen: Aktenverzeichnis," CZA: A231; and Walter Gross, "The Zionist Students' Movement," *LBIYB* 4 (1959): 143–64. Concerning the Kartell-Convent, see Adolph Asch and Johanna Philippson, "Self-Defence at the Turn of the Century: The Emergence of the K. C.," *LBIYB* 3 (1958): 122–39, especially pp. 134, 136; and Adolph Asch, *Geschichte des K.C. (Kartellverband jüdischer Studenten) im Lichte der deutschen kulturellen und politischen Entwicklung* (London: privately printed, 1964). For a biography of Loewe, see Jehuda Louis Weinberg, *Aus der Frühzeit des Zionismus: Heinrich Loewe* (Jerusalem: R. Mass, 1946).

3. The later development of the student Zionist movement is treated in chapter 8 below.

4. Friedemann's diary is preserved in the Central Zionist Archives, CZA: A8/2(6), with a typescript, A8/2(7).

5. CZA: A8/2(7), entries for 25.12.1893; 5.1.1894; 20.2.1894; 9.4.1894.

6. The full text of the Basel Program is reprinted in Appendix B. For the discussion and adoption of this program, see the debate as recorded in *Stenographisches Protokoll der Verhandlungen des I. Zionisten-Congresses* (1897), pp. 114–19. The phrase about those who "could not or would not assimilate" appeared in Herzl's *Programm* for the organ of the world Zionist movement, *Die Welt* 1, no. 1 (4.6.1897), and was echoed in Herzl's "Eröffnungsrede zum ersten Kongress," reprinted in Herzl, *Zionistische Schriften*, p. 180. It soon became one of the clichés of Zionist rhetoric. Bodenheimer's Theses may be found in Bodenheimer, ed., *Im Anfang*, pp. 22–24, and in Lichtheim, *Geschichte des deutschen Zionismus*, plate following p. 120, and pp. 134–35. Bodenheimer had already sent a copy to Herzl on 28 May 1896 (*Im Anfang*, p. 21). The full text is reprinted in Appendix A.

7. ZVfD, *Was will der Zionismus?* (Berlin: Jüdische Rundschau, 1903), p. 17. For the attribution of this anonymous pamphlet to Adolf Friedemann, see *Zeitschrift für hebräische Bibliographie* 18, no. 4/6 (July/December 1915): 99, item no. 376.

8. Richard Lichtheim, *Das Programm des Zionismus* [The Program of Zionism] (Berlin: ZVfD, 1911), pp. 41–42 (= 2d rev. ed. [1913], p. 37). For Lichtheim's amusing account of his authorship of this pamphlet, see his memoirs, *Rückkehr: Lebenserinnerungen aus der Frühzeit des deutschen Zionismus* (Stuttgart: Deutsche Verlags-Anstalt, 1970), p. 143. Friedemann, in ZVfD, *Was will der Zionismus?* p. 18; emphasis in the original.

9. National-jüdische Vereinigung, *Der Zionismus* (Cologne, c. 1896), p. 10. Friedemann, in ZVfD, *Was will der Zionismus?* pp. 16–17. ZVfD, "Unser Programm," *Flugblatt Nr. 4* (Cologne, c. 1898), p. 3; copy in CZA: DD 2/7/10/1 National-jüdische Vereinigung, Köln.

10. Lichtheim, *Das Programm des Zionismus*, 2d rev. ed., pp. 23–24. (This passage does not appear in the 1st ed., 1911.)

11. ZVfD, "Unser Programm," p. 1.

12. Quoted from Ludwig Holländer, *Deutsch-jüdische Probleme der Gegenwart* (Berlin: Philo, 1929), p. 13, by Ruth Louise Pierson, "German Jewish Identity in the Weimar Republic" (Ph.D. diss., Yale University, 1970), p. 135. For an example of the Zionist attitude toward conversion, see Lichtheim, *Rückkehr*, pp. 50–60. Concerning the Centralverein's attack on conversion, see Ismar Schorsch, *Jewish Reactions to German Anti-Semitism, 1870–1914* (New York: Columbia University Press; Philadelphia: Jewish Publication Society, 1972), pp. 139ff.

13. Concerning the conflict between the Centralverein and the ZVfD, see chapter 4 below and the works cited there.

14. For an early Zionist accusation of the weakness of the religious convictions of members of the Centralverein, see "Der Nationaljude als Staatsbürger," National-jüdische Vereinigung, *Flugblatt Nr. 2* (Cologne, 1897), pp. 1–2; copy in CZA: DD 2/7/10/1 National-jüdische Vereinigung, Köln.

3. Building the Movement

1. See the data in Tables 1 and 2, "Jewish Population of Germany," and 3, "Membership of Zionistische Vereinigung für Deutschland, Annual Totals." Concerning standards for membership see Sammy Gronemann, "Der Schekel," *JR* 9, no. 21 (27.5.1904): 225–28, and his remarks in his memoirs, *Zichronot shel Yekeh* (Hebrew; Tel Aviv: Am Oved, 1946), p. 123. Estimates of active participants are taken from Lichtheim, *Rückkehr*, p. 132, and president's report to the seventeenth *Delegiertentag*, 1921, printed in *JR* 26, no. 38 (13.5.1921): 267. Lichtheim's figure of six thousand shekel-payers in 1909 is, however, exaggerated.

2. Data taken from Arnold Paucker, *Der jüdische Abwehrkampf gegen Antisemitismus und Nationalsozialismus in den letzten Jahren der Weimarer Republik,* 2d rev. ed. (Hamburg: Leibniz, 1969), pp. 27, 246; and Schorsch, *Jewish Reactions to German Anti-Semitism,* p. 119. Lichtheim's statement (*Rückkehr,* p. 132) that in 1909 the Centralverein included sixty thousand individual members seems to confuse postwar with prewar levels.

3. Lichtheim, *Geschichte des deutschen Zionismus,* p. 107. Kurt Blumenfeld, "Ursprünge und Art einer zionistischen Bewegung," *LBI Bulletin,* no. 4 (July 1958), p. 131.

4. Lichtheim, *Geschichte des deutschen Zionismus,* p. 110. On early Zionist propaganda, see Artur Ruppin, "An die deutschen Zionisten: Rede auf dem Delegiertentag der Zionistischen Vereinigung für Deutschland (1932)," in Ruppin, *Dreissig Jahre Aufbau in Palästina: Reden und Schriften* (Berlin: Schocken, 1937), p. 287. For Bodenheimer's criticism of Loewe, see CZA: A15/I8e, Bodenheimer to Loewe (29.6.1908), and ibid., Bodenheimer to Centralbureau der ZVfD: Hantke (29.6.1908). The *Jüdische Rundschau,* originally the *Israelitische Rundschau,* was adopted by the ZVfD as its official organ in 1901, but was managed by an interim publication committee until Loewe assumed the editorship in 1902. See *Jüdisches Lexikon,* s.v. "Zionistische Vereinigung für Deutschland," vol. 5, cols. 1623–24. Bodenheimer also disapproved of what he regarded as Friedemann's rhetorical and tactical excesses. See Marjorie Lamberti, "The Attempt to Form a Jewish Bloc: Jewish Notables and Politics in Wilhelmian Germany," *Central European History* 3, no. 1/2 (May/June 1970): 83–84.

5. Lichtheim, *Geschichte des deutschen Zionismus,* pp. 162–64, and *Rückkehr,* p. 113. Aron Sandler, "Memoirs" (Israel, 1950), 1:8–9. Copies in LBI, New York, archives, C/347, and CZA: A69/2. Kurt Blumenfeld, *Erlebte Judenfrage: Ein Vierteljahrhundert deutscher Zionismus* (Stuttgart: Deutsche Verlags-Anstalt, 1962), p. 49. For a representative sample of leading Zionists, see the listing of the ZVfD Central Committee of 1914 in Lichtheim, *Geschichte des deutschen Zionismus,* pp. 156–59, which includes short biographies and the following list of the birth and death dates for some of the major German Zionists (pp. 160–63): Kurt Blumenfeld (1884–1963), Max Bodenheimer (1865–1940), Adolf Friedemann (1871–1932), Sammy Gronemann (1875–1952), Arthur Hantke (1874–1955), Alfred Klee (1875–1943), Richard Lichtheim (1885–1963), Heinrich Loewe (1869–1951), Franz Oppenheimer (1864–1943), Felix Rosenblüth (b. 1887), and Robert Weltsch (b. 1891). Another interesting example of the association between wealth and ZVfD activity, and one that throws light on a certain stratum of German Jewry, is that of Eduard Leszynsky, a successful Berlin lawyer. Leszynsky's father was the director of Viktoria Lebensver-

sicherung in Berlin, and had built for himself a large home in Berlin's exclusive Grünewald, which—in a way that typified the accommodation between things German and things Jewish—he had equipped with both a small private synagogue and a *Weinstube* (interview with Dr. Hannah E. Leszynsky-Steinfeldt, Jerusalem, 23.3.1971).

6. Lichtheim, *Rückkehr,* p. 131. Data for 1907 from "Ein Beitrag zur Statistik des B.J.C.," *Der jüdische Student* 4, no. 8 (November 1907): 207; for 1932, from Eli Rothschild, ed., *Meilensteine: Vom Wege des Kartells Jüdischer Verbindungen (K.J.V.) in der zionistischen Bewegung: Eine Sammelschrift* (Tel Aviv: Präsidium des KJV, 1972), p. 401. For a fuller treatment of the student Zionist organizations, see chapter 8. For geographical distribution, see Table 4, "Sales of Shekalim by Cities, 1921–27," and table of Jewish population of German cities with over 100,000 inhabitants in *Jüdisches Lexikon,* s.v. "Statistik der Juden," vol. 5, col. 639. By 1899 there were *Ortsgruppen* in the following cities: Berlin (2), Breslau, Cologne (2), Darmstadt, Dortmund, Dresden, Frankfort on the Main, Giessen, Hamburg, Hanover, Heidelberg, Kattowitz, Königsberg, Leipzig, Mülhausen, Munich. See Bodenheimer, ed., *Im Anfang,* p. 137. Concerning the central office and Bodenheimer's difficulties, see "Bericht des Zentralbureaus der ZVfD über das erste Geschäftsjahr," *JR* 10, no. 29 (21.7.1905): 347–50; and drafts of letters from Bodenheimer to Hantke, Vorsitzender des geschäftsführenden Ausschusses, Berlin, April–May 1910, in CZA: A15/I8e. Also see Bodenheimer's critical remarks in his "Eröffnungsrede des Präsidenten" (tenth *Delegiertentag,* 1906) in *JR* 11, no. 23 (8.6.1906): 2.

7. Blumenfeld, *Erlebte Judenfrage,* p. 115. Data on *Ostjuden* from Schalom Adler-Rudel, *Ostjuden in Deutschland, 1880–1940* (Tübingen: J.C.B. Mohr, 1959), pp. 164–65. See Tables 1 and 2, "Jewish Population of Germany."

8. Sandler, "Memoirs," 1:10. Blumenfeld regretted the loss in World War I of Germany's eastern provinces, from which "a larger part of the German Zionists came"; Blumenfeld et al., *Beiträge zur Frage unserer Propaganda: Ein Briefwechsel zwischen Max Jacobsohn und Kurt Blumenfeld . . .* (Berlin: ZVfD, 1928), p. 13; copy in Schocken Archive 531/4. In Hanover, as was doubtless the case elsewhere, "for the settled members of the community, Zionist and *Ostjude* were identical terms. None was *gesellschaftsfähig* [socially acceptable]"; quoted in Herbert Strauss, "The Jugendverband: A Social and Intellectual History," *LBIYB* 6 (1961): 212. Nevertheless, Adler-Rudel's statement—"Until the outbreak of the First World War not a single foreign Jew could have been active in the leadership of the ZVfD. The function of the foreign Jews seemed to have consisted of filling up Zionist gatherings and serving as the public . . . for the young Zionist speakers."—is exag-

gerated; Adler-Rudel, *Ostjuden in Deutschland*, p. 26. For examples of some leading German Zionists of foreign birth, see Lichtheim, *Geschichte des deutschen Zionismus*, pp. 156ff., 162. With regard to the reception of East European Jewish immigrants by the Jewish communities in the West, see Michael R. Marrus, *The Politics of Assimilation: A Study of the French Jewish Community at the Time of the Dreyfus Affair* (Oxford: Oxford University Press, 1971), pp. 161ff., and passim for the case of France; for that of England, see Lloyd P. Gartner, *The Jewish Immigrant in England, 1870–1914* (London: Allen and Unwin, 1960), "Native Jewry and Immigration," pp. 49–56; and for that of the United States, see Moses Rischin, *The Promised City: New York's Jews, 1870–1914* (Cambridge, Mass.: Harvard University Press, 1962), ch. 6, "Germans versus Russians," pp. 95ff.

9. The Jüdische Volkspartei was active only in the internal politics of the Jewish community. Founded in 1919, it represented a coalition of Zionists, *Ostjuden*, and conservative religious elements. Its growing strength was reflected by the election in 1928 of Georg Kareski, one of its founders, as president of the Berlin Jewish *Gemeinde*. See Raphael Patai, ed., *Encyclopedia of Zionism and Israel* (New York: Herzl Press, 1971), s.v. "Germany, Zionism in," 1:390. On the alliance between the Zionists and *Ostjuden* in internal Jewish politics, see Naomi Katzenberger, "Dokumente zur Frage des Wahlrechts ausländischer Juden in den preussischen Synagogengemeinden," in Shlomo Simonsohn and Jacob Toury, eds., *Michael: On the History of the Jews in the Diaspora* (Tel Aviv: University of Tel Aviv, 1973), 2: 194, 195, 201. For official statements of Zionist policy concerning the *Ostjuden*, see the Theses on activity in the *Gemeinden* adopted at the 1908 *Delegiertentag*, which included a statement defending the rights of the *Ostjuden*, quoted in Max Kollenscher, *Jüdische Gemeindepolitik* (Berlin: Zionistisches Zentralbureau, 1909), pp. 5–6; also the resolution adopted at the 1922 *Delegiertentag* affirming the right of the *Ostjuden* to participate in the elections of the *Gemeinden* (*JR* 27, no. 73 [15.9.1922]:494). Concerning Zionist involvement in social work among the *Ostjuden*, see Adler-Rudel, *Ostjuden in Deutschland*.

10. The Theses are reprinted in Appendix A. Bodenheimer's remarks appeared in "Rückblicke auf dem [II.] Kongress," in *ZVfD Correspondenz, Nr. 10* (December 1898), pp. 1–2; copy in CZA: DD 2/7/10/1, National-jüdische Vereinigung, Köln. See also Adolf Böhm, *Die zionistische Bewegung* (Tel Aviv: Hozaah Ivrith, 1935, 1937), 1:206.

11. Demokratisch-zionistische Fraktion, *Programm und Organisations-Statut* (Berlin, 1902), paras. 32–34. Also see Israel Klausner, *Opositsia le-Herzl* (Jerusalem: Achiever, 1960). The account of the *"Kulturdebatte"* at the 1901 congress is recorded in *Stenographisches Protokoll der Verhandlungen des V. Zionisten-Kongresses*, pp. 389–402, 412–13,

417–31. The founding circle of the Jüdischer Verlag included Buber, Berthold Feiwel, E. M. Lilien, Leo Motzkin, Alfred Nossig, Davis Trietsch, and Chaim Weizmann, all of whom were eminent figures in the world Zionist movement. For Buber's personal account of the founding of the press, see Jüdischer Verlag Berlin, *Almanach, 1902–1964* (Berlin: Jüdischer Verlag, 1964), p. 9. The *Almanach* also includes a history of the press and its book lists (following p. 66, and pp. 159–67). A prospectus for the Jüdischer Verlag is printed in *IsrR* 7, no. 12 (21.3.1902): 7. The Jüdischer Verlag went through several reorganizations in which it was associated with the Zionist organization in a variety of legal relationships.

12. Schocken's address is printed in *JR* 12, no. 1 (5.1.1917):2–4. For a fuller description of the committee's publications and an account of Schocken's publishing activities and of the Schocken Verlag, see my article "Salman Schocken and the Schocken Verlag: A Jewish Publisher in Weimar and Nazi Germany," *Harvard Library Bulletin* 21, no. 1 (January 1973): 20–49; also *LBIYB* 17 (1972): 93–113.

4. The Radical Reorientation of German Zionism

1. See Blumenfeld's memoirs, *Erlebte Judenfrage.* The childhood incidents are reported on pp. 27–28.

2. *Erlebte Judenfrage*, p. 39. Blumenfeld's early activity in the Zionist student movement is described in Gross, "Zionist Students' Movement," pp. 148–49.

3. Lichtheim's contention that Blumenfeld's radicalism was "not a matter of the well-known zeal of the converted" seems contradicted by his own account. See Lichtheim, *Rückkehr*, pp. 127–28. In 1917 Victor Jacobson, then a member of the Zionist Executive, judged Blumenfeld to be "one of the most valuable, if not *the* most valuable [Zionist] among the younger upcoming generation" (CZA: Z3/727, Jacobson to Julius Berger [3.1.1917], p. 3).

4. Kurt Blumenfeld, "Referat über zionistische Agitationsmethoden," *JR* 15, no. 37 (16.9.1910):442; idem, *Erlebte Judenfrage*, pp. 59–60; Maarabi [Kurt Blumenfeld], "Deutscher Zionismus," *JR* 15, no. 35 (2.9.1910):414. Identification of author from reprint of article in Kurt Blumenfeld, *Zionistische Betrachtungen: Fünf Aufsätze* (Berlin: VJSt Maccabaea–Altherrn Bund, 1916).

5. The original text of the resolution read: "In Konsequenz der überragenden Bedeutung der Palästina-Arbeit für die Befreiung der Einzelpersönlichkeit, sowie als Mittel zur Erreichung unseres Endziels, erklärt es der Delegiertentag für die Pflicht jedes Zionisten—in erster Reihe der

wirtschaftlich Unabhängigen—die Uebersiedlung nach Palästina in ihr Lebensprogramm aufzunehmen. In jedem Falle sollte jeder Zionist für sich *persönliche Interessen* in Palästina schaffen"; *JR* 17, no. 23 (7.6.1912):205; the resolution's adoption is reported in ibid. For confirmation that the phrase "personal interests" referred primarily to economic investment, see Lichtheim, *Geschichte des deutschen Zionismus*, p. 146.

6. For the account of the proceedings of the *Delegiertentag*, see *JR* 17, no. 22 (31.5.1912), and *JR* 17, no. 23 (7.6.1912). The passage of the resolution was also reported, without comment, in the account of the Posen *Delegiertentag* that appeared in *Die Welt*, the German-language organ of the World Zionist Organization; *Die Welt*, 16, no. 22 (31.5.1912):657.

A somewhat milder version of the Posen Resolution was presented to the eleventh World Zionist Congress in 1913: "Considering the overwhelming importance of the principle of [the centrality of] Palestine [*Palästinaprinzip*] in the Zionist movement, the congress declares it the obligation of every Zionist—primarily those who are in a financial position to do so—to become acquainted with Palestine through his own [direct] observation, to establish personal economic interests there and to incorporate emigration to Palestine in his life program"; *Stenographisches Protokoll der Verhandlungen des XI. Zionisten-Kongresses* (1913), pp. 346, 348. For lack of time this resolution was "referred for [further] consideration or execution as far as possible," i.e., tabled.

Friedemann in *JR* 19, no. 25 (19.6.1914):267. Max Kollenscher, "Memoirs" (typescript in LBI, Jerusalem, archives), p. 83. I am grateful to Mr. Y. Ginat of the Jerusalem Leo Baeck Institute for providing me with this material.

It is interesting that two years earlier Blumenfeld seems to have attempted a similar gambit involving the Bund jüdischer Corporationen, though with less success. The BJC was a student organization that, while sympathetic to Zionism, was not officially Zionist. (This changed in 1914 when it joined with the Kartell zionistischer Verbindungen to form the Zionist Kartell jüdischer Verbindungen.) At the BJC's *Kartelltag* (annual meeting) in February 1910 a resolution altering the "neutral" position of the BJC to a more directly Zionist one was proposed by Blumenfeld and passed by the *Kartelltag*—evidently by a vote unrepresentative of the majority opinion of the organization. A storm of protest forced the retraction of the resolution, first by the *Präsidium* (governing board) and later by a special *Kartelltag*. For the account of the February *Kartelltag* in Breslau, see *Der jüdische Student* 6, no. 11/12 (24.3.1910):247. For the reaction against the resolution and the *Präsidium*'s retraction, see ibid. 7, no. 1 (27.4.1910). The action of the special *Kartelltag* in May is reported in ibid. 7, no. 2/3 (21.6.1910).

7. *JR* 17, no. 23 (7.6.1912):205, 208; Blumenfeld, *Erlebte Judenfrage*, p. 90; Felix Rosenblüth, "Unsere neue Programmschrift," *JR* 16, no. 30 (28.7.1911):344.
8. "Protokoll, Plenarsitzung des Zentralkomitees" (3.11.1912), pp. 7–8, 18–19; emphasis in original; in CZA: A15/VII25.
9. Ibid., pp. 13–14.
10. Ibid., p. 20.
11. *JR* 19, no. 25 (19.6.1914):267. Concerning Estermann, see CZA: Z3/727, Lichtheim (?) to Blumenfeld (10.5.1916), p. 2, in which Estermann is referred to as a "Palästinenser." Information on Zlocisti from *Jüdisches Lexikon*, s.v. "Zlocisti," vol. 5, col. 1631.
12. CZA: A15/I8e, Bodenheimer to Friedemann (29.5.1914).
13. Oppenheimer quoted in Alex Bein, "Franz Oppenheimer als Mensch und Zionist," *LBI Bulletin* 7, no. 25/28 (1964):9; Franz Oppenheimer, "Stammesbewusstsein und Volksbewusstsein," *JR* 15, no. 8 (25.2.1910):86–88.
14. Oppenheimer published a parallel article in *Die Welt* 14, no. 7 (18.2.1910):139–43. Friedemann seconded Oppenheimer's analysis in his anonymous ("Ad. Fr.") article "Westlicher Zionismus," *JR* 15, no. 13 (1.4.1910):147.
15. CZA: A15/I8e, Bodenheimer to Oppenheimer (13.5.1914).
16. This and the following quotations from Oppenheimer's address appear in *JR* 19, no. 25 (19.6.1914):269–70.
17. Adolf Friedemann, "Politisierung des deutschen Judentums," *Neue jüdische Monatshefte* 1, no. 8 (25.1.1916):213; Kurt Blumenfeld, "Innere Politik: Zur jüdischen Entwicklung in Deutschland," *Der Jude* 1, no. 11 (1916/1917):715.
18. "Warum nicht auch Berliner Wohnbewusstsein? und englisches Parlamentsbewusstsein? und französisches Malereigefühl?"; Richard Lichtheim, "Das Märchen vom Radikalismus: Offener Brief an Herrn Dr. Franz Oppenheimer," *JR* 19, no. 27 (3.7.1914):289. Oppenheimer's final remarks paraphrased the much-quoted statement by Gabriel Riesser, a nineteenth-century advocate of Jewish emancipation, that "whoever contests my claim on my German fatherland denies me the right to my thoughts, my feelings, to the language I speak and the air that I breathe. Therefore I must defend myself against him as against a murderer"; Gabriel Riesser, *Gesammelte Schriften*, ed. M. Isler (Frankfort on the Main: Verlag der Riesser Stiftung, 1868), 4:320. See also Franz Oppenheimer, *Erlebtes, Erstrebtes, Erreichtes: Erinnerungen* (Berlin: Welt Verlag, 1931), p. 214.
19. *JR* 19, no. 25 (19.6.1914):271.
20. For an appreciation and critique of Blumenfeld's leadership of the ZVfD, see Lichtheim, *Geschichte des deutschen Zionismus*, pp. 226–29. On the precedence of practical work over ideological squabbling, see *JR* 25, no. 19 (17.6.1920):303.

21. Blumenfeld, *Erlebte Judenfrage*, p. 115. The general reorientation toward practical Zionism was confirmed by the respondents in the symposium "Zur Entwicklung des zionistischen Gedankens: Eine Rundfrage," *Die Welt* 16, no. 5 (2.2.1912):135–37, although they disagreed about the desirability of the shift.

22. The original German read: "Der Centralverein deutscher Staatsbürger jüdischen Glaubens E.V. bezweckt, die deutschen Staatsbürger jüdischen Glaubens ohne Unterschied der religiösen und politischen Richtung zu sammeln, um sie in der tatkräftigen Wahrung ihrer staatsbürgerlichen und gesellschaftlichen Gleichstellung sowie in der unbeirrbaren Pflege deutscher Gesinnung zu bestärken"; *Jüdisches Lexikon*, s.v. "Central-Verein," vol. 1, cols. 1289–90. The 1913 clash between the ZVfD and the Centralverein is discussed in Schorsch, *Jewish Reactions to German Anti-Semitism*, ch. 7, "Internal Discontent, 1897–1914," pp. 179–202. That the conflict greatly exercised both sides, as Schorsch's treatment clearly indicates, is incontestable. This has not, however, precluded my skepticism about the more permanent consequences of Blumenfeld's "radical" transformation of the ZVfD. For a fuller, more detailed account of the conflict between the ZVfD and Centralverein, see Reinharz, *Fatherland or Promised Land*, chapter 5.

23. *Im deutschen Reich* 19, no. 5/6 (May 1913):200; emphasis in original.

24. Report of the *Ausserordentliche Tagung* held 1 May 1913, in *JR* 18, no. 19 (9.5.1913):178, 187; Ludwig Holländer, "Zur Klarstellung," *Im deutschen Reich* 19, no. 5/6 (May 1913):196.

25. Quoted in Blumenfeld, *Erlebte Judenfrage*, p. 41. Concerning Blumenfeld's cooperation with non-Zionists, see Kurt Blumenfeld, "Zionistische Arbeit in Deutschland," *JR* 33, no. 42/43 (1.6.1928):302, and his remarks in *Beiträge zur Frage unserer Propaganda*, p. 7.

5. The Failure of *Aliyah*

1. See Table 7, "Jewish Immigration to Palestine."

2. Elias Auerbach, "K.J.V.-er in Palästina," in *30 Jahre V.J.St. Hasmonaea* (Berlin: VJSt Hasmonaea im Kartell jüdischer Verbindungen, 1932), pp. 34–35; Lichtheim, *Geschichte des deutschen Zionismus*, p. 143.

3. List in Brith Shalom archive, CZA: A187/2 (5.3.1928); "Liste der Bundesbrüder in Palästina," *Der jüdische Student* 26, Special Palestine Issue (March 1929):44–46.

4. Quoted in CZA: Z3/727, Lichtheim (?) to Blumenfeld (10.5.1916), p. 3.

5. Fritz Loewenstein, "Der deutsche Zionismus und Palästina," *JR* 29, no. 69 (29.8.1924):493; Felix Rosenblüth, "Verhältnis der deutschen Zionisten zu Palästina," *JR* 31, no. 69 (3.9.1926):497.

6. CZA: Z3/727, Jacobson to Blumenfeld (26.5.1916), p. 5. *Golus* is Yiddish for "exile," specifically the state of being exiled from Zion. For another discussion of the apparent inability of *aliyah* to put an end to Jewish rootlessness, even in Palestine, see Moses Calvary, "Deutsche Juden in Erez-Israel," *JR* 34, no. 83 (22.10.1929):556.

7. Interview with Dr. Siegfried Moses (president of the ZVfD from 1933 to 1937), Jerusalem, 14.6.1971.

8. Max Kollenscher, "Memoirs" (LBI, Jerusalem, archives), p. 83; Elias Auerbach, *Pionier der Verwirklichung: Ein Arzt aus Deutschland erzählt vom Beginn der zionistischen Bewegung und seiner Niederlassung in Palästina kurz nach der Jahrhundertwende* (Stuttgart: Deutsche Verlags-Anstalt, 1969), p. 318.

9. Davis Trietsch, quoted in Blumenfeld, *Erlebte Judenfrage*, p. 38; Gronemann, *Zichronot shel Yekeh*, 1:8.

10. The Zionist reaction to anti-Jewish outbreaks in 1923 might at first seem to constitute an exception to this generalization, but a closer examination indicates that this was not the case. See below, chapter 7.

11. Kurt Blumenfeld, "Wie gestalten wir unseren Nationalismus wesenhafter?" *Der jüdische Student* 12, War Issue no. 12 (27.11.1916):327. The phrase evidently appealed to Blumenfeld, for he repeated it at the 1916 *Delegiertentag* (*JR* 22, no. 1 [5.1.1917]:2). Lichtheim, "Das Märchen vom Radikalismus," *JR* 19, no. 27 (3.7.1914):289–90.

12. Blumenfeld's conclusion of the discussion of his address on "Erziehung zum Zionismus," *JR* 17, no. 23 (7.6.1912):207; Lichtheim, *Das Programm des Zionismus*, 1st ed., p. 40 (= 2d ed., p. 36); Salman Schocken, "Palästinaaufgaben des deutschen Zionismus," *JR* 27, no. 73 (15.9.1922):493.

13. Moritz Bileski, "Nach Palästina," *Der jüdische Student* 12, War Issue no. 8 (30.4.1916):163; "Deutsche Chaluziuth," *Der jüdische Student* 27, no. 5/6 (May/June 1930):4–5.

14. *JR* 25, no. 40 (23.6.1920):316.

15. Bileski, "Nach Palästina," p. 164.

16. "Vor dem Delegiertentag," *JR* 23, no. 54 (13.12.1918):417.

17. Adler-Rudel, *Ostjuden in Deutschland*, p. 50; letter of Franz Rosenzweig to his mother (23.5.1918), quoted in Nahum N. Glatzer, ed., *Franz Rosenzweig: His Life and Thought*, 2d rev. ed. (New York: Schocken, 1961), p. 74. See also the memoirs of Walter Preuss, *Ein Ring schliesst sich: Von der Assimilation zur Chaluziuth* (Tel Aviv: Martin Feuchtwanger, 1950), pp. 90, 95; and the account of the significance of contact with the *Ostjuden* given in *JR* 21, no. 49 (8.12.1916):405, "Vor dem Delegiertentag." Sammy Gronemann's memoir of his service on the eastern front provides an account that is at once humorous and illuminating: *Hawdoloh und Zapfenstreich: Erinnerungen an die ostjüdische Etappe, 1916–1918* (Berlin: Jüdischer Verlag, 1924).

18. Adler-Rudel, *Ostjuden in Deutschland;* Zosa Szajkowski, "The Komitee fuer den Osten and Zionism," *Herzl Year Book* 7 (1971):199–240; Egmont Zechlin, *Die deutsche Politik und die Juden im Ersten Weltkrieg* (Göttingen: Vandenhoeck & Ruprecht, 1969); David Yisraeli, *The Palestine Problem in German Politics, 1889–1945* (Hebrew; Ramat Gan: Bar Ilan University Press, 1974). The text of the German statement is printed in *JR* 23, no. 2 (11.1.1918):9, along with the enthusiastic response of the ZVfD.
19. See *Jüdisches Lexikon*, s.v., "Judenzählung im Weltkrieg," vol. 3, cols. 460–61; and the poignant memoir by Ernst Simon, "Unser Kriegserlebnis," published originally in *Jüdische Jugend* 1 (1919):39–45, reprinted in idem, *Brücken: Gesammelte Aufsätze* (Heidelberg: Lambert Schneider, 1965), pp. 17–23. On Jewish service in the Prussian officer corps, see Angress, "Prussia's Army," pp. 19–42.
20. CZA: A8/2(7), Friedemann diary, entry for 3.9.1914.
21. Hantke's opening address to the 1918 *Delegiertentag, JR* 23, no. 58 (31.12.1918):448.

6. Ideology and Identity: The Functions of German Zionism

1. The epigraphs are taken from Sigmund Freud, *New Introductory Lectures on Psychoanalysis*, trans. and ed. James Strachey (New York: Norton, 1965), lecture 35, "The Question of a *Weltanschauung,*" p. 158; and Erik H. Erikson, *Young Man Luther: A Study in Psychoanalysis and History* (New York: Norton, 1962), p. 22.
2. Moritz Goldstein, "Deutsch-jüdischer Parnass," *Der Kunstwart* 25, no. 11 (Erstes Märzheft, 1912):286; emphasis added; Kurt Blumenfeld, "Ursprünge und Art einer zionistischen Bewegung," *LBI Bulletin*, no. 4 (July 1958), p. 136; and Friedrich Rühs, *Die Rechte des Christentums und des deutschen Volkes. Verteidigt gegen die Ansprüche der Juden und ihrer Verfechter* (Berlin, 1816), p. 27, quoted in Zechlin, *Die deutsche Politik und die Juden*, p. 26.
3. Berthold Feiwel and Robert Stricker, *Zur Aufklärung über den Zionismus* (Brünn: Jüdisch-akademische Verbindung Zephirah, 1898), pp. 8–9.
4. Robert Weltsch, introduction to Martin Buber, *Der Jude und sein Judentum* (Cologne: Joseph Melzer Verlag, 1963), p. xv. Also see National-jüdische Vereinigung, "Der Nationaljude als Staatsbürger," *Flugblatt Nr. 2* (Cologne, 1897), pp. 1–2; copy in CZA: DD 2/7/10/1 National-jüdische Vereinigung, Köln.

5. National-jüdische Vereinigung, *Der Zionismus* (Cologne: n.d., [c. 1896]), p. 13; ZVfD, "Unser Programm," p. 3.
6. Lichtheim, *Rückkehr*, pp. 65, 66, 68; emphasis added.
7. Gershom Scholem, "With Gershom Scholem" (Hebrew), interview by Moki Zur, *Shdemot*, no. 55 (Winter 1974), p. 10. See also Dolf Michaelis, "Mein 'Blau-Weiss' Erlebnis," *LBI Bulletin* 5, no. 17 (1962):65; and Robert Weltsch, "Siegfried Moses: End of an Epoch," *LBIYB* 19 (1974):viii.
8. Max Isidor Bodenheimer, *So wurde Israel: Aus der Geschichte der zionistischen Bewegung: Erinnerungen von Dr. M. I. Bodenheimer*, ed. Henriette Hannah Bodenheimer (Frankfort on the Main: Europäische Verlagsanstalt, 1958), p. 44. The quotation is taken from the English translation, *Prelude to Israel: The Memoirs of M. I. Bodenheimer*, trans. Israel Cohen (New York: Yoseloff, 1963), pp. 60–61. See also the brief memoir by Bodenheimer reprinted in H. Bodenheimer, ed., *Im Anfang*, p. 368; and *So wurde Israel*, pp. 21–45 (=*Prelude to Israel*, pp. 29–61).
9. Blumenfeld, *Erlebte Judenfrage*, p. 39; Karl Hilb, "Die Wendung," in Rothschild, ed., *Meilensteine*, p. 35; and Walter Gottheil, "Mein Leben in Deutschland vor und nach dem 30. Januar 1933" (unpublished manuscript in Houghton Library, Harvard University, bMsGer91(81). This is included in the remarkable collection of entries in an autobiography contest on "My Life in Germany before and after January 30, 1933."

   The announcement of this contest, held in 1940, read: "For the purely scientific purpose of collecting materials which will be used to study the social and psychological effect of National Socialism on German society and on the German people, one thousand dollars has been made available to be offered as prizes for the best unpublished life histories (autobiographies) on the theme 'My Life in Germany before and after January 30, 1933.' The competition is being personally sponsored by the following members of the Faculty of Harvard University, who will serve as a Committee of Judges . . . : Gordon Willard Allport, Sidney Bradshaw Fay, Edward Yarnall Hartshorne."

   The contest drew over two hundred and fifty entries, mostly from German refugees, the bulk of whom were Jewish. A few had had some involvement with the Zionist movement.

   These substantial autobiographies, many of book length, are a mine of information about life in Germany and about personal reactions to the establishment of Nazi rule. Included with most of the entries is an analysis form on which readers of the entries noted various sociological data to be derived from the life history. These forms help to make the collection accessible to the interested researcher.

   Two articles were published on the basis of the entries to this contest:

G.W. Allport, J.S. Bruner, and E.M. Jandorf, "Personality under Social Catastrophe: Ninety Life-Histories of the Nazi Revolution," *Character and Personality* 10, no. 1 (September 1941):1–22; and Jerome Bruner and Katherine Bruner, "The Impact of Revolution," *The Saturday Review of Literature,* 24, no. 36 (27 December 1941):3–4, 20–21.

10. Robert Weltsch, "Entscheidungsjahr 1932," in W. E. Mosse, ed., *Entscheidungsjahr 1932: Zur Judenfrage in der Endphase der Weimarer Republik,* 2d ed., rev. and enl. (Tübingen: J.C.B. Mohr, 1966), p. 560.

11. Siegfried Kanowitz, "Vom post-assimilatorischen Zionismus zur post-zionistischen Assimilation," in [Kartell jüdischer Verbindung] Maccabaea (Königsberg), Verbindung jüdischer Studenten im K.J.V., *Rückblick und Besinnung: Aufsätze gesammelt aus Anlass des 50. Jahrestages der Gründung der Verbindung jüdischer Studenten "Maccabaea" im K.J.V. (Königsberg)* (Tel Aviv: Präsidium des KJV, 1954), p. 22.

12. Lichtheim, *Rückkehr,* p. 65; Bodenheimer in the passage describing the consequences of his conversion quoted above; Georg Herlitz, *Mein Weg nach Jerusalem: Erinnerungen eines zionistischen Beamten* (Jerusalem: R. Mass, 1964), p. 59; Jungmann, *Erinnerungen eines Zionisten,* p. 16.

13. Pinchas Rosen (Felix Rosenblüth), interview, 15.6.1971; concerning Bodenheimer, see Lichtheim, *Geschichte des deutschen Zionismus,* p. 165.

14. Hans Tramer, "Jüdischer Wanderbund Blau-Weiss: Ein Beitrag zu seiner äusseren Geschichte," *LBI Bulletin* 5, no. 17 (June 1962):26; Michaelis, "Mein 'Blau-Weiss' Erlebnis," pp. 51, 63–67; Strauss, "The Jugendverband," pp. 212–13; Scholem, "With Gershom Scholem," pp. 8–10. On adolescent identity crisis, see Erikson, *Young Man Luther,* ch. 1.

15. Blumenfeld, "Ursprünge und Art," p. 136. In this chapter I consider only the psychological benefits of Zionism. For a discussion of the political aspects of this problem and of the significance of the German context, see chapters 7 and 8 below.

16. Jakob Klatzkin, *Probleme des modernen Judentums,* 3d enl. ed. (Berlin: Lambert Schneider, 1930), p. 80. See also Böhm, *Die zionistische Bewegung,* 1:560–61. For parallel statements by Blumenfeld, see his address on "Zionist Work in Germany" at the 1928 *Delegiertentag, JR* 33, no. 42/43 (1.6.1928):302, and his remarks in *Beiträge zur Frage unserer Propaganda,* p. 36.

17. Ahad Haam [Asher Ginzberg], "The Negation of the Diaspora" (1909), in Arthur Hertzberg, ed., *The Zionist Idea: A Historical Analysis and Reader* (Cleveland: World, 1960), p. 270.

18. Lichtheim, *Das Programm des Zionismus* (1911), pp. 41–42; emphasis added. The passage was reprinted unchanged in the second edition in 1913, a year after the Posen Resolution, p. 37. Hermann Lelewer, *Was will der Zionismus?* (Berlin: ZVfD, 1920), p. 44.

19. Blumenfeld, "Ursprünge und Art," p. 137; "Dr. Sch.," in Blumenfeld, *Beiträge zur Frage unserer Propaganda*, p. 19.
20. Ismar Schorsch argues that the Centralverein was devoted to the strengthening of Jewish identity, *Jewish Reactions to German Anti-Semitism*, pp. 12–13, 117, 136, 139, 147. For a more critical view, see the review by Jehuda Reinharz in *Jewish Social Studies* 35, no. 3/4 (July/October 1973):298.
21. See Scholem, "With Gershom Scholem," pp. 8–10; and Michaelis, "Mein 'Blau-Weiss' Erlebnis," p. 64.

7. Zionism, Anti-Semitism, and German Politics

1. Eugen Fuchs, "Referat über die Stellung des Centralvereins zum Zionismus in der Delegierten-Versammlung vom 30. März 1913," in Eugen Fuchs, *Um Deutschtum und Judentum: Gesammelte Reden und Aufsätze (1894–1919)* (Frankfort on the Main: J. Kauffmann, 1919), p. 237.
2. Hermann Cohen, "Antwort auf das offene Schreiben des Herrn Dr. Martin Buber an Hermann Cohen" (1916), *Hermann Cohens Jüdische Schriften*, ed. Bruno Strauss (Berlin: C. A. Schwetschke und Sohn, 1924), 2:335–37. The quip on Jewish devotion to *deutsche Gesinnung* is attributed to Alfred Wiener by Paucker, *Der jüdische Abwehrkampf*, p. 67.
3. Concerning German Jewish preferences for the humanism of Kant and Goethe, see Jürgen Habermas, "Der deutsche Idealismus der jüdischen Philosophen," in Thilo Koch, ed., *Porträts deutsch-jüdischer Geistesgeschichte* (Cologne: DuMont Schauberg, 1961), pp. 106–7. A recent book by Sidney M. Bolkosky, *The Distorted Image: German Jewish Perceptions of Germans and Germany, 1918–1935* (New York: Elsevier, 1975) undertakes to explain the behavior and attitudes of German Jews in terms of their myth of German culture, which supposed that eighteenth-century classical humanism continued to determine German thought and action. The logical fallacy of Jews attempting to identify Jewishness with Germanness through some intermediate term such as Kantianism was pointed out by Ferdinand Ostertag, "Erziehungsreferat, gehalten auf dem Jugendtag," *Blau-Weiss-Blätter: Führerzeitung* 1, no. 6 (January 1919):107.
4. See Scholem, "With Gershom Scholem," pp. 8, 10; idem, "Jews and Germans," *Commentary* 42, no. 5 (November 1966):31–38; and idem, "Wider den Mythos vom deutsch-jüdischen Gespräch," *LBI Bulletin* 7, no. 27 (1964):278–81. I am indebted to D. S. Landes for his characterization of the courtship of German Jewry.

5. Ad[olf] Fr[iedemann], "Westlicher Zionismus," *JR* 15, no. 13 (1.4.1910):147–48; and Moritz Goldstein, "Deutsch-jüdischer Parnass," *Kunstwart* 25, no. 11 (Erstes Märzheft, 1912):283, 286. For Goldstein's own retrospective reflections on this article and his account of its writing, see "German Jewry's Dilemma: The Story of a Provocative Essay," *LBIYB* 2 (1957):236–54.

6. Goldstein, "Deutsch-jüdischer Parnass," pp. 291–92.

7. On the period of the Haskalah, see Katz, *Out of the Ghetto,* pp. 78–79, and the same author's essay "The German-Jewish Utopia of Social Emancipation," in idem, *Emancipation and Assimilation,* pp. 91–110. Two interesting examples of the expectation of Jewish conversion are reprinted in Toury, ed., *Der Eintritt der Juden ins deutsche Bürgertum,* pp. 33–36, 43–49. The situation during the German Empire is described in Uriel Tal, *Christians and Jews in Germany: Religion, Politics, and Ideology in the Second Reich, 1870–1914* (Ithaca: Cornell University Press, 1975).

8. Tal, *Christians and Jews,* chs. 3, 5.

9. Ibid., pp. 79, 31–32, and ch. 1, passim.

10. Ibid., p. 163, and ch. 4, passim.

11. Ibid., pp. 58, 32.

12. Concerning the overall subject of Jewish political orientations during the empire, see Jacob Toury, *Die politischen Orientierungen der Juden in Deutschland: Von Jena bis Weimar* (Tübingen: J. C. B. Mohr, 1966), especially pp. 110–229, and the criticism of Toury's account in Schorsch, *Jewish Reactions to German Anti-Semitism,* pp. 132–35. More lucid than Toury is the discussion of this subject in Ernest Hamburger, *Juden im öffentlichen Leben Deutschlands: Regierungsmitglieder, Beamte und Parlamentarier in der monarchischen Zeit, 1848–1918* (Tübingen: J. C. B. Mohr, 1968), ch. 2, "Die Juden als Wähler," pp. 120–69. Hamburger has extended the account of his book, which treats the period 1848–1918, through the Weimar period in "One Hundred Years of Emancipation," pp. 3–66. For a treatment of the period of the Weimar Republic from the specific viewpoint of the Centralverein's activities, see Paucker, *Der jüdische Abwehrkampf,* passim, especially pp. 90–96.

The subject of the Jews and the Left in Germany is treated in two recent studies: Hans-Hellmuth Knütter, *Die Juden und die deutsche Linke in der Weimarer Republik, 1918–1933* (Düsseldorf: Droste, 1971); and Donald L. Niewyk, *Socialist, Anti-Semite, and Jew: German Social Democracy Confronts the Problem of Anti-Semitism, 1918–1933* (Baton Rouge: Louisiana State University Press, 1971), which deals more with the Left's relationship to the Jewish question than with Jewish political alignments. See also George L. Mosse, "German Socialists and the Jewish Question in the Weimar Republic,"

LBIYB 16 (1971):123–51, and his remarks on Knütter and Niewyk, pp. 150–51.

13. Paucker, *Der jüdische Abwehrkampf,* p. 94; concerning the possibility of an alliance with the Social Democratic party, see especially p. 287, n. 3; Hamburger, "One Hundred Years of Emancipation," p. 42.

14. [Raphael Löwenfeld], *Schutzjuden oder Staatsbürger? Von einem jüdischen Staatsbürger,* 3d ed. (Berlin, 1893), p. 8, quoted in Schorsch, *Jewish Reactions to German Anti-Semitism,* p. 108. For a discussion of the legal activities of the Centralverein, see ibid., pp. 123–32 and Paucker, *Der jüdische Abwehrkampf,* passim.

15. Hermann Cohen, "Religion und Zionismus" (1916), in *Hermann Cohens Jüdische Schriften,* 2:320–21.

16. This resolution was passed by the Centralverein at a meeting of delegates in February 1928. Quoted in *JR* 33, no. 14 (17.2.1928):98. The chronology surprisingly refers to the period beginning with the Prussian emancipation edict of 1812, which was limited to begin with and was later further weakened. Hamburger, *Juden im öffentlichen Leben Deutschlands,* pp. 9–10, 12–15.

17. Fuchs, "Referat über die Stellung des Centralvereins zum Zionismus," p. 239; Blumenfeld, *Erlebte Judenfrage,* p. 54.

18. Lelewer, *Was will der Zionismus?,* pp. 26–28.

19. *JR* 8, no. 19 (8.5.1903):175.

20. "Deutschland als Pogromland," *Die B.Z.V.: Nachrichtenblatt der Berliner Zionistischen Vereinigung* 2, no. 30 (18.11.1923):1–2; "Die Schicksalsstunde des deutschen Judentums," *JR* 28, no. 96 (9.11.1923):557.

21. [Kurt] Bl[umenfeld], "Zur Lage," *Die B.Z.V.* 2, no. 31/32 (2.12.1923):1–2; emphasis added.

22. *JR* 36, no. 21 (17.3.1931):133. On the Rosh Hashanah attacks, see *JR* 36, no. 72 (15.9.1931) and subsequent issues. Also see Paucker, *Der jüdische Abwehrkampf,* pp. 133–35.

23. National-jüdische Vereinigung, "Der Nationaljude als Staatsbürger," pp. 1–2; Max Kollenscher, *Zionismus und Staatsbürgertum,* 2d ed. (Berlin: Zionistisches Zentralbureau, 1910), pp. 3–6; "Die Frechheit des Volkstums im neuen Deutschland," *JR* 24, no. 8 (31.1.1919):61; and Lichtheim, "Das Märchen vom Radikalismus," *JR* 19, no. 27 (3.7.1914):289.

24. Lichtheim, *Geschichte des deutschen Zionismus,* pp. 167–68.

8. The Power of Context

1. Letter from Central Committee of the ZVfD soliciting special *Jahres-beitrag,* November 1909, in CZA: A15/VII 22; Dr. J. Moses, "Referat über 'Organisation,'" *JR* 8, no. 41/42 (16.10.1903):444. Also see Table 8, "German Contributions to the Keren Kayemeth," and Table 9, "German Contributions to the Keren Hayesod."

2. On the value and preservation of unity, see the comments made at the 1928 *Delegiertentag,* reported in *JR* 33, no. 40/41 (23.5.1928):295–96; and *JR* 33, no. 42/43 (1.6.1928):306. Concerning the ZVfD's unique-ness in embracing all factions, see the remarks of Arthur Hantke at the 1925 *Delegiertentag, JR* 30, no. 3 (9.1.1925):3; and Georg Herlitz, *Der Zionismus und sein Werk* (Berlin: Jüdische Rundschau, 1933), pp. 19–20.

3. See Lichtheim, *Geschichte des deutschen Zionismus,* pp. 224–26. The program and origins of Binjan Haarez are described by Max Kollenscher, one of its founders, in *JR* 26, no. 25/26 (30.3.1921):173. Despite heavy opposition, Binjan Haarez won 10 percent of the German delegation to the 1921 World Zionist Congress. See *JR* 26, no. 58 (22.7.1921):416; 26, no. 59 (26.7.1921):420–21; and 26, no. 65 (16.8.1921):463. In view of these sources, Lichtheim's account seems slightly inaccurate in some specific details. Concerning the Revision-ist secession, see Lichtheim, *Geschichte des deutschen Zionismus,* pp. 241–42.

4. Lichtheim, *Geschichte des deutschen Zionismus,* pp. 9–10; Weizmann to Blumenfeld (13.11.1929), Weizmann Archive.

5. Oppenheimer, *Erlebtes, Erstrebtes, Erreichtes,* 1st ed., p. 214; Hugo Bergmann to Martin Buber, 11.5.1915, in Martin Buber, *Briefwechsel aus sieben Jahrzehnten* (Heidelberg: Lambert Schneider, 1972–), 1:389.

6. On the *völkisch* movement in Germany, see Fritz Stern, *The Politics of Cultural Despair: A Study in the Rise of the Germanic Ideology* (Berkeley: University of California Press, 1961); and George L. Mosse, *The Crisis of German Ideology: Intellectual Origins of the Third Reich* (New York: Grosset and Dunlap, 1964); and idem, *Germans and Jews: The Right, the Left, and the Search for a "Third Force" in Pre-Nazi Germany* (New York: Grosset and Dunlap, 1970).

7. *JR* 14, no. 42 (15.10.1909):461; *JR* 19, no. 26 (26.6.1914):278. Schock-en's remark comes from his address at the 1916 *Delegiertentag* on Zionist Cultural work, reported in *JR* 22, no. 1 (5.1.1917):2.

8. *Stenographisches Protokoll der Verhandlungen des II. Zionisten-Con-gresses* (1898), p. 222; see also Lichtheim, *Geschichte des deutschen Zionismus,* p. 109.

9. "Das Judentum und die Juden," from *Drei Reden über das Judentum* (Frankfort on the Main: Rütten und Loening, 1911), reprinted in Martin Buber, *Der Jude und sein Judentum: Gesammelte Aufsätze und Reden* (Cologne: Melzer, 1963), p. 14; Robert Weltsch, "Was wir Buber danken," *JR* 33, no. 11 (7.2.1928):76.

   The vagueness and obscurity of Buber's utterances were legendary. One reviewer confessed that "there are many of us who venerate Buber's personality without always being able to understand or follow his statements" (Hugo Bergmann's review of Buber's *Die jüdische Bewegung* in *JR* 21, no. 32 [11.8.1916]:265). Another Zionist despaired that Buber's "formulation about politics as the art of the impossible [at the 1916 *Delegiertentag*] . . . was only a specimen of the possibilities for the future" (Victor Jacobson to Julius Berger [3.1.1917], p. 2, in CZA: Z3/727). But Sammy Gronemann probably had the last word when he quipped that after Buber's emigration to Palestine Buber already spoke "enough Hebrew to make himself understood, but not enough to make himself incapable of being understood" (interview with Dr. Pinchas Rosen, 15.6.1971).

10. On the history of the Zionist student movement, see the literature cited in chapter 2, note 2. The BJC platform is quoted from *Der jüdische Student* 1 (1904), verso of title page; interpretation from Leopold Ambrunn, "Der Zionismus im B.J.C.," *Der jüdische Student* 4, no. 4 (July 1907):105; emphasis in original.

11. KJV platform quoted from *Der jüdische Student* 11, no. 5 (1.11.1914), inside front cover. Aside from the newly formulated Zionist *Tendenzparagraph*, the remaining four articles of the KJV's program were identical with that of the BJC. On the amalgamation of the BJC and the KZV, see *Der jüdische Student* 11, no. 5 (1.11.1914):91; and Gerhard Holdheim, "Das K.J.V.: Seine Tendenzen, seine Erziehungsmethoden und seine Gemeinschaftsformen," *Der jüdische Wille* 1, no. 4 (1918/1919):222–24.

12. Lichtheim, *Rückkehr*, pp. 90, 91, 84; interview with Dr. Siegfried Moses, 14.6.1971. See Table 6, "Presidents of the Zionistische Vereinigung für Deutschland." For an evaluation of the importance of these Zionist *Akademiker* for the movement, see Georg Herlitz, "Siegfried Moses' Entwicklung und Stellung im K.J.V." in Hans Tramer, ed., *In Zwei Welten: Siegfried Moses zum fünfundsiebzigsten Geburtstag* (Tel Aviv: Bitaon, 1962), p. 17.

13. Blumenfeld, *Erlebte Judenfrage*, pp. 43–44. See also Herlitz, *Mein Weg nach Jerusalem*, p. 54. An example of a syllabus for a history course for fraternity pledges is preserved in CZA: A231/1/1, "Kartellgeschichte [für] Fuxenunterricht. V.J.St. im B.J.C. zu Breslau," [c. 1910]. For one description of Zionist fraternity life, see Lichtheim, *Rückkehr*, pp. 88–90.

14. "Rundschreiben" of the Bundesleitung des Blau-Weiss (c. 1917), pp. 1–2, in Schocken Archive 536/34. See also the parallel statement in *Leitfaden für die Gründung eines Jüdischen Wanderbundes "Blau-Weiss"* (Berlin: Jüdischer Wanderbund Blau-Weiss, 1913), pp. 4–5, which suggests that the need for such rehabilitation was even greater for Jewish than Christian youth, since "our youth is in general physically less sound and more nervous than Christian youth." There are two recent studies devoted entirely to the various Jewish youth movements in Germany, including Zionist ones: Hermann Meier-Cronemeyer, "Jüdische Jugendbewegung," *Germania Judaica* 8 (1969), n.s. 27/28–29/30, entire; and Chaim Schatzker, "The Jewish Youth Movement in Germany between the Years 1900–1933" (Hebrew with English summary; Ph.D. diss., Hebrew University of Jerusalem, 1969). See also Chanoch Rinott, "Major Trends in Jewish Youth Movements in Germany," *LBIYB* 19 (1974):77–96; and Werner Rosenstock, "The Jewish Youth Movement," ibid., pp. 97–106. These articles survey much of the recent scholarship on this subject. See also Walter Laqueur, *Young Germany: A History of the German Youth Movement* (New York: Basic Books, 1962), ch. 9, "The Jewish Question," pp. 74–83; and Mosse, *The Crisis of German Ideology*, pp. 182–84. On the specific history of the Blau-Weiss, see Dolf Michaelis, "Mein 'Blau-Weiss' Erlebnis," *LBI Bulletin* 5, no. 17 (1962):44–67; and Tramer, "Jüdischer Wanderbund Blau-Weiss," pp. 23–43.

15. Georg Todtmann, "Was wir wollen," *Blau-Weiss-Blätter: Eine Flugschrift*, (1917?), p. 3; and idem, "Was wir wollen," *Blau-Weiss-Blätter* 2, no. 2 (May 1914):3. Also see Schatzker, "The Jewish Youth Movement," p. 56. Concerning the early history of the Blau-Weiss, see *Blau-Weiss Führer: Leitfaden für die Arbeit im Jüdischen Wanderbund "Blau-Weiss"* (Berlin: Die Bundesleitung, 1917), pp. 26–27; and "Bericht der Bundesleitung des 'Blau-Weiss,' Bund für jüdisches Jugendwandern in Deutschland an die Zentralkomitee-Mitglieder der ZVfD" (10.6.1914), copy in Schocken Archive 536/34.

16. "Das Bundesgesetz von Prunn," *Blau-Weiss-Blätter: Führerzeitung* 3, no. 2 (December 1922):26, 30. (The *Bundestag* that adopted the constitution was held at Schloss Prunn.) The *Jüdische Rundschau*'s evaluation is quoted in Hermann Meier-Cronemeyer, "Jüdische Jugendbewegung," p. 64. See also Gershom Scholem's criticism of the Blau-Weiss in "With Gershom Scholem," pp. 13–14. On the Blau-Weiss workshop in Palestine and its various difficulties, see "Memorandum an die Wintertagung des Blau-Weiss, Dresden, Winter 1925," in YIVO (New York) Archives: Germany, General, no. 136.

9. Jewish and Arab Nationalism in Palestine

1. The Balfour Declaration, contained in a letter from British Foreign Secretary Arthur James Balfour to Lord Rothschild (2.11.1917), is quoted in Böhm, *Die zionistische Bewegung,* 2:592.
2. On the relationships between Zionism and Arab nationalism, see Esco Foundation for Palestine, *Palestine: A Study of Jewish, Arab, and British Policies,* 2 vols. (New Haven: Yale University Press, 1947); Walter Laqueur, *A History of Zionism* (New York: Holt, Rinehart and Winston, 1972), especially ch. 5, "The Unseen Question;" Amos Elon, *The Israelis: Founders and Sons* (New York: Holt, Rinehart and Winston, 1971), especially ch. 7, "Innocents at Home"; and Böhm, *Die zionistische Bewegung,* passim. On the Arab nationalist movement, see Yehoshuah Porath, *The Emergence of the Palestinian Arab National Movement, 1918–1929* (London: Frank Cass, 1974).
3. For an example of this view, see Arthur Ruppin, "Das Verhältnis der Juden zu den Arabern," *Der Jude* 3 (1918/1919):453–57.
4. Quoted in Esco, *Palestine,* 1:139, 143.
5. Lelewer, *Was will der Zionismus?* p. 43; emphasis in original. See also Esco, *Palestine,* 1:178–79.
6. *Stenographisches Protokoll der Verhandlungen des XII. Zionisten-Kongresses* (1921), p. 769. See also Esco, *Palestine,* 1:269ff.
7. Quoted in Esco, *Palestine,* 1:140.
8. Lelewer, *Was will der Zionismus?* p. 43.
9. Weltsch, "Anträge zur Araberfrage" (1921), in Jewish National and University Library, Jerusalem (JNUL): ms. var. 350 (Buber Archive)/800.2; Hugo Bergmann to Rabindranath Tagore (26.6.1921), JNUL: ms. var. 350/800.2 (filed in Weltsch file).
10. See Robert Weltsch, "Deutscher Zionismus in der Rückschau," in Tramer, ed., *In Zwei Welten,* p. 39; and Lichtheim, *Geschichte des deutschen Zionismus,* pp. 236–41.
11. Robert Weltsch, "A Tragedy of Leadership (Chaim Weizmann and the Zionist Movement)," *Jewish Social Studies* 13, no. 3 (July 1951):223. See also idem, "Politische Neujahrsbetrachtung," *JR* 29, no. 77/78 (26.9.1924):552; and Weltsch, introduction to Buber, *Der Jude und sein Judentum,* pp. xxx–xxxi. Information also from Weltsch interview, 21.6.1971. For an interesting parallel in the earlier French Zionist renunciation of French nationalist chauvinism and its stress on the benign nature of Jewish nationalism, see Marrus, *The Politics of Assimilation,* pp. 264–65.
12. CZA: A167/17, Robert Weltsch to Felix Rosenblüth (1.2.1929), p. 4; *JR* 31, no. 66/67 (27.8.1926):477; Robert Weltsch, "Die Legion (Anlässlich des XII. Zionistenkongresses, 1921)" (August 1921), in Hans

Kohn and Robert Weltsch, *Zionistische Politik: Eine Aufsatzreihe* (Mährisch-Ostrau: R. Färber, 1927), p. 248. See also Susan Lee Hattis, *The Bi-National Idea in Palestine during Mandatory Times* (Haifa: Shikmona, 1970), passim.

13. [Brith Shalom], *Memorandum by the "Brith Shalom" Society on an Arab Policy for the Jewish Agency* (Jerusalem, 1930), para. 4. The Brith Shalom statutes are quoted from the English version given in Aharon Kedar, "Brith Shalom, 1925–1933" (M.A. thesis, Hebrew University of Jerusalem, 1969), appendix 1. For a German text and a description of Brith Shalom by one of its leading members, see Artur Ruppin, "Brith Schalom," *JR* 31, no. 52 (6.7.1926):381–82. See also Hattis, *The Bi-National Idea*, pp. 38–64; and Kedar, "Brith Shalom," passim. The Hebrew words *brith shalom* mean "covenant of peace." On the founding of the Arbeitsgemeinschaft für zionistische Realpolitik, see "Ergebnis Protokoll einer Besprechung . . . in der Wohnung von Herrn Dr. Robert Weltsch . . ." (8.9.1929), and "Resumee . . ." (16.9.1929), in LBI, New York, Weltsch Collection, II (1066), which also contains no. 1 of the *Korrespondenzblatt der Arbeitsgemeinschaft für zionistische Realpolitik*. Other material on this group is contained in the Schocken Archive 538/8.

14. Robert Weltsch, "Zion als unendliche Aufgabe," *Der Jude: Sonderheft für Martin Bubers fünfzigsten Geburtstag*, Special Issue no. 5 (1928), p. 37.

15. Robert Weltsch, "Was wir Buber danken," *JR* 33, no. 11 (7.2.1928): 76; emphasis added. For a fuller account of Buber's views on Zionism, see Hans Kohn, *Martin Buber, Sein Werk und seine Zeit: Beitrag zur Geistesgeschichte Mitteleuropas, 1880–1930.* ("Nachwort: 1930–1960," by Robert Weltsch), 3d rev. ed. (Cologne: Melzer, 1961), passim; and Ernst Simon, "Nationalismus, Zionismus und der jüdisch-arabische Konflikt in Martin Bubers Theorie und Wirksamkeit," *LBI Bulletin* 9, no. 33 (1966):21–84.

16. CZA: A167/17, Robert Weltsch to Felix Rosenblüth (1.2.1929), p. 3.

17. Lichtheim speaking at the 1926 *Delegiertentag*, quoted in *JR* 31, no. 66/67 (27.8.1927):480. See also the essay by Fritz Stern, "The Political Consequences of the Unpolitical German," in his collection *The Failure of Illiberalism: Essays on the Political Culture of Modern Germany* (New York: Knopf, 1972), pp. 3–25.

18. For the details of this dispute and the subsequent disturbances, see Esco, *Palestine*, 2:595–614; and Porath, *The Emergence of the Palestinian Arab National Movement*, ch. 7.

19. Great Britain, *Parliamentary Papers*, "Report of the Commission on the Palestine Disturbances of August, 1929," Cd. 3530, 1930, p. 65. This was called the "Shaw Commission Report." after its head.

20. Robert Weltsch, "Die blutigen Kämpfe in Palästina," *JR* 34, no. 68 (30.8.1929):435–36.

21. JNUL: ms. var. 350/880.5, Weltsch to Hugo Bergmann (31.8.1929), pp. 2, 4. For a parallel statement, see also JNUL: ms. var. 350/800.5, Weltsch to Felix Rosenblüth (1.9.1929). Additional documents revealing Weltsch's views on the events of 1929 and the problem of relations with the Arabs may be found in the especially rich material, which unfortunately covers only the years from 1929 to 1931, in the still uncatalogued collection of Weltsch's papers at the Leo Baeck Institute in New York. See, for example, the "Memorandum to the Zionist Executive" (16.9.1929) by Weltsch et al.; and the letter from Moritz Bileski and Weltsch to the Zionist Executive (15.10.1929), both in folder II (1066).

22. JNUL: ms. var. 350/800.5, Weltsch to Felix Rosenblüth (1.9.1929); and ibid., Weltsch to Hans Kohn (2.9.1929).

23. Calvary, "Deutsche Juden in Erez-Israel," *JR* 34, no. 83 (22.10.1929): 556; emphasis in original.

24. The Tel Aviv meeting was held on 27.10.1929, and the declaration was forwarded to the ZVfD Executive Committee on 31.10.1929. A copy may be found in CZA: A206/17 (October 1929). It was printed as "Erklärung führender Zionisten in Erez Israel," in [ZVfD], Gruppe der unabhängigen allgemeinen Zionisten [Gruppe Kollenscher], *Materialien zum Jenaer Delegiertentag der Zionistischen Vereinigung für Deutschland* (n.p.: December 1929). A statement of support for Weltsch from German Zionists in Palestine may be found in LBI, New York, Weltsch Collection, II (1066), "An den geschäftsführenden Ausschuss der ZVfD" (31.10.1929). Weizmann to Blumenfeld (13.11.1929) in Weizmann Archive.

25. Weltsch's speech is reported in *JR* 35, no. 2 (7.1.1930):14. The text of the resolution on the Arab question and the vote of confidence in Blumenfeld are reported in *JR* 35, no. 1 (3.1.1930):1. See also Blumenfeld, *Erlebte Judenfrage,* pp. 186–89. Weltsch also won a vote of confidence on his editorial stance in favor of binationalism at the 1926 *Delegiertentag.* See *JR* 31, no. 66/67 (27.8.1926):477.

Despite the display of unity between Weltsch and Blumenfeld in 1929, later a serious gap seems to have developed between them regarding accommodation with the Arabs. During a trip to Palestine in the summer of 1930, Blumenfeld expressed sharp disagreement both with Weltsch and with the tactics of Brith Shalom, though not with its basic program. See Gerda Arlosoroff to Weltsch (5.6. 1930), LBI, New York, Weltsch Collection, III (1067)/1, and Weltsch to Blumenfeld, (19.6.1930), ibid., III (1067)/2. After his return to Germany, Blumenfeld considered resigning the presidency of the ZVfD. See "Protokoll der 20. Sitzung des Geschäftsführenden Ausschusses vom 1. Juli 1930," and Weltsch to Bileski (23.6. 1930), both in ibid., III (1067)/1.

26. Weltsch, "Deutscher Zionismus in der Rückschau," pp. 39–40.

27. Weltsch, introduction to Buber, *Der Jude und sein Judentum*, p. xxxiii.
28. Robert Weltsch, "Wir und die Araber," *JR* 33, no. 16 (24.2.1928):12; emphasis in original.

10. Conclusion

1. Concerning the last years of the Weimar Republic, see Kurt Loewenstein, "Die innerjüdische Reaktion auf die Krise der deutschen Demokratie," in Werner E. Mosse, ed., *Entscheidungsjahr 1932*, 2d rev. ed. (Tübingen: J.C.B. Mohr, 1966), pp. 349–403. On the Nazi period, see Abraham Margaliot, "The Political Reaction of German Jewish Organizations and Institutions to the Anti-Jewish Policy of the National Socialists, 1932–1935 . . ." (Hebrew with English summary; Ph.D. diss., Hebrew University of Jerusalem, 1971); and Lichtheim, *Geschichte des deutschen Zionismus*, ch. 9, "Der Nationalsozialismus und die Liquidation der ZVfD."
2. Information from the respective articles in Patai, ed., *Encyclopedia of Zionism and Israel.*
3. One example of this was the "Zionist orientation to the nationalist trends of our time" outlined by Gustav Krojanker in his *Zum Problem des neuen deutschen Nationalismus: Eine zionistische Orientierung gegenüber den nationalistischen Strömungen unserer Zeit* (Berlin: Jüdische Rundschau, 1932). Concerning Blumenfeld, see Loewenstein, "Die innerjüdische Reaktion," pp. 379–81. Concerning Weltsch, see Lichtheim, *Geschichte des deutschen Zionismus*, pp. 259–60, and Weltsch's editorials in the *JR* from 1933, including that quoted below. A selection of these editorials was collected in [Jüdische Rundschau], *Ja-sagen zum Judentum: Eine Aufsatzreihe der "Jüdischen Rundschau" zur Lage der deutschen Juden.* (Berlin: Jüdische Rundschau, 1933).
4. *JR* 37, no. 73/74 (16.9.1932):351.
5. *JR* 38, no. 27 (4.4.1933):131–32; emphasis in original.

BIBLIOGRAPHY

The research for this book was done primarily at the Harvard University Library, and at the Central Zionist Archives and the Jewish National and University Library in Jerusalem. I have also used the library and archives of the Leo Baeck Institute in New York. Unless otherwise noted, published materials cited may be found in one of these libraries.

The Bibliography that follows lists the books that I have consulted that proved to be useful. It is not a comprehensive listing of works on Zionism, nor does it include the vast number of occasional publications, pamphlets, and books generated by the German Zionist movement that I consulted, but which did not prove directly relevant to this study. A list of the abbreviations used can be found on page 184.

General Works on Zionism, German Jewry, and German Zionism

With regard to German Jewry the publications of the Leo Baeck Institute (Jerusalem, New York, and London) deserve special mention, including the *Year Book* (vol. 1, 1956 et seq.), the *Schriftenreihe wissenschaftlicher Abhandlungen*, the *LBI Bulletin*, and the annual *Lectures*. A step toward a synthetic history of German Jewry, one goal of the institute's program, has been taken with the publication of two important symposium volumes, both edited by Werner E. Mosse: *Deutsches Judentum in Krieg und Revolution, 1916–1923.* Tübingen: J.C.B. Mohr, 1971; and *Entscheidungsjahr 1932: Zur Judenfrage in der Endphase der Weimarer Republik.* 2d ed., rev. and enl. Tübingen: J.C.B. Mohr, 1966.

Böhm, Adolf. *Die zionistische Bewegung.* 2 vols. Tel Aviv: Hozaah Ivrith, 1935, 1937.

Elbogen, Ismar and Sterling, Eleonore. *Die Geschichte der Juden in Deutschland: Eine Einführung.* Frankfort on the Main: Europäische Verlagsanstalt, 1966.

Elon, Amos. *The Israelis: Founders and Sons.* New York: Holt, Rinehart and Winston, 1971.

Esco Foundation for Palestine. 2 vols. *Palestine: A Study of Jewish, Arab and British Policies.* New Haven: Yale University Press, 1947.

Graupe, Heinz Mosche. *Die Entstehung des modernen Judentums: Geistesgeschichte der deutschen Juden, 1650–1942.* Hamburg: Leibniz, 1969.

Halpern, Ben. *The Idea of the Jewish State.* Cambridge, Mass.: Harvard University Press, 1961.

Hertzberg, Arthur, ed. *The Zionist Idea: A Historical Analysis and Reader.* Cleveland: World, 1960.

Jüdisches Lexikon: Ein enzyklopädisches Handbuch des jüdischen Wissens. Berlin: Jüdischer Verlag, 1927–1930.

Kampmann, Wanda. *Deutsche und Juden: Studien zur Geschichte des deutschen Judentums.* Heidelberg: Verlag Lambert Schneider, 1963.

Katz, Jacob. *Out of the Ghetto: The Social Background of Jewish Emancipation, 1770–1870.* Cambridge, Mass.: Harvard University Press, 1973.

Laqueur, Walter. *A History of Zionism.* New York: Holt, Rinehart and Winston, 1972.

Lichtheim, Richard. *Die Geschichte des deutschen Zionismus.* Jerusalem: R. Mass, 1954.

Lowenthal, Marvin. *The Jews of Germany: A Story of Sixteen Centuries.* New York: Longmans, Green, 1936.

Meyer, Michael A. *The Origins of the Modern Jew: Jewish Identity and European Culture in Germany, 1749–1824.* Detroit: Wayne State University Press, 1967.

Philo-Lexikon: Handbuch des jüdischen Wissens. Berlin: Philo Verlag, 1934.

Pierson, Ruth Louise. "German Jewish Identity in the Weimar Republic." Ph.D. dissertation, Yale University, 1970.

Reinharz, Jehuda. *Fatherland or Promised Land: The Dilemma of the German Jew, 1893–1914.* Ann Arbor: University of Michigan Press, 1975.

Primary Sources

ARCHIVES

Central Zionist Archives, Jerusalem (CZA)
  (A) Private archives
      A8   Adolf Friedemann
      A11   Arthur Hantke
      A15   Max Bodenheimer
      A22   Jakob Wagner
      A48   Theodor Zlocisti
      A69   Aron Sandler
      A94   Max Jungmann
      A102 Hugo Schachtel
      A126 Leo Motzkin
      A135 Sammy Gronemann
      A142 Alfred Klee
      A146 Heinrich Loewe
      A167 Robert Weltsch (a fragmentary collection)
      A206 Julius Berger
  (A) Nonofficial Zionist bodies and other Jewish national organizations
      A187 Brith Shalom
      A231 Kartell jüdischer Verbindungen
      A265 Herzl Bund
  (DD) *Ossef divre d'fus* (Miscellaneous printed matter)
      Zionistische Vereinigung für Deutschland
  (F) Files of territorial Zionist organizations and collections of documents pertaining to the history of Zionism in various countries
      F4   Germany (a fragmentary collection)
  (Z) Central offices of the World Zionist Organization and of the Jewish Agency for Palestine abroad
      Z1   Vienna, 1897–1905
      Z2   Cologne, 1905–11
      Z3   Berlin, 1911–20
      Z4   London, 1917–55
Houghton Library, Harvard University. bMsGer91. "Life in Germany Contest."
Institute of Contemporary Jewry, The Hebrew University of Jerusalem. Oral History Collection, no. 990. Kurt Blumenfeld.
Jewish National and University Library, Jerusalem (JNUL). Ms.var.350. Papers of Martin Buber.
Leo Baeck Institute, Jerusalem. Memoirs of Max Kollenscher.

Leo Baeck Institute, New York. (C) Memoirs Robert Weltsch Collection.
Schocken Library, Jerusalem. Papers of Salman Schocken.
Weizmann Archive, Weizmann Institute, Rehovot. Papers of Chaim Weizmann.
YIVO Institute for Jewish Research Archives, New York. Germany, General, 139.

MEMOIRS AND DIARIES

Auerbach, Elias. *Pionier der Verwirklichung: Ein Arzt aus Deutschland erzählt vom Beginn der zionistischen Bewegung und seiner Niederlassung in Palästina kurz nach der Jahrhundertwende.* Stuttgart: Deutsche Verlags-Anstalt, 1969.
Blumenfeld, Kurt. *Erlebte Judenfrage: Ein Vierteljahrhundert deutscher Zionismus.* Stuttgart: Deutsche Verlags-Anstalt, 1962.
―――――. "Ursprünge und Art einer zionistischen Bewegung." *LBI Bulletin,* no. 4 (July 1958):129–40.
―――――. Oral History Collection, Institute of Contemporary Jewry, The Hebrew University of Jerusalem, no. 990. Biographical interview.
Bodenheimer, Max Isidor. *So wurde Israel: Aus der Geschichte der zionistischen Bewegung, Erinnerungen von Dr. M.I. Bodenheimer.* Edited by Henriette Hannah Bodenheimer. Frankfort on the Main: Europäische Verlagsanstalt, 1958. English translation: *Prelude to Israel: The Memoirs of M. I. Bodenheimer.* Translated by Israel Cohen. New York: Yoseloff, 1963.
Friedemann, Adolf. Diary in Central Zionist Archives. CZA:A8/2(6), original manuscript; A8/2(7) typescript transcription.
Goldmann, Nahum. *The Autobiography of Nahum Goldmann: Sixty Years of Jewish Life.* New York: Holt, Rinehart and Winston, 1969.
Goldstein, Moritz. "German Jewry's Dilemma: The Story of a Provocative Essay." *LBIYB* 2 (1957):236–54.
Gronemann, Sammy. *Zichronot shel Yekeh.* Vol. 1 (no more published). Tel Aviv: Am Oved, 1946. A Hebrew translation of the first volume of the typescript memoir cited in the next item.
―――――. "Erinnerungen." Typescript. 2 vols. N.p., n.d. Copies of this typescript may be found in the Central Zionist Archives, CZA: A135/44; and in the Leo Baeck Institute, New York, C/137.
Herlitz, Georg. *Mein Weg nach Jerusalem: Erinnerungen eines zionistischen Beamten.* Jerusalem: R. Mass, 1964.
Herzl, Theodor. *The Complete Diaries of Theodor Herzl.* Edited by Raphael Patai, translated by Harry Zohn. New York: Herzl Press, 1960.
Jungmann, Max. *Erinnerungen eines Zionisten.* Jerusalem: R. Mass, 1959.
Kollenscher, Max. "Erinnerungen [Memoirs]." Typescript. Leo Baeck Institute, Jerusalem.

Kohn, Hans. *Living in a World Revolution: My Encounters with History.* New York: Trident, 1964.

Lichtheim, Richard. *Rückkehr: Lebenserinnerungen aus der Frühzeit des deutschen Zionismus.* Stuttgart: Deutsche Verlags-Anstalt, 1970.

"Life in Germany Contest." Houghton Library, Harvard University. bMsGer91.

Meyer, Max. "A German Jew Goes East." *LBIYB* 3 (1958):344–57.

Michaelis, Dolf. "Mein 'Blau-Weiss' Erlebnis." *LBI Bulletin* 5, no. 17 (1962):44–67.

Oppenheimer, Franz. *Erlebtes, Erstrebtes, Erreichtes: Erinnerungen.* 1st ed. Berlin: Welt Verlag, 1931. 2d ed. Düsseldorf: Melzer, 1964.

Preuss, Walter. *Ein Ring schliesst sich: Von der Assimilation zur Chaluziuth.* Tel Aviv: Martin Feuchtwanger, 1950.

Rosenbluth, Martin. *Go Forth and Serve: Early Years and Public Life.* New York: Herzl Press, 1961.

Sandler, Aron. "Erinnerungen [Memoirs]." Typescript. 2 vols. Israel, 1950. Copies in Central Zionist Archives, CZA: A69/2; and Leo Baeck Institute, New York, C/347.

Scholem, Gershom. "With Gershom Scholem" (Hebrew). Interview by Moki Zur. *Shdemot,* no. 55 (Winter 1974), pp. 8–34.

INTERVIEWS

(all held in Jerusalem)

Dr. Hannah E. Leszynsky-Steinfeldt, 23 March 1971.

Dr. Siegfried Moses, 29 June 1969, 23 July 1969, 14 June 1971.

Dr. Pinchas Rosen (Felix Rosenblüth), 15 June 1971.

Professor Gershom Scholem, 17 May 1971.

Dr. Robert Weltsch, 7 August 1969, 21 June 1971.

PERIODICALS

Die Arbeit: Organ der zionistischen volkssozialistischen Partei Hapoël-hazair, deutscher Landesverband der allweltlichen zionistischen Arbeitspartei Hitachdut. 1919–25.

Berliner Jüdische Zeitung. Published by the Berliner Zionistische Vereinigung. 1929–30.

Die B.Z.V.: Nachrichtenblatt der Berliner Zionistischen Vereinigung. 1922–23.

Blau-Weiss-Blätter. Published by the Bundesleitung des jüdischen Wanderbund Blau-Weiss. 1913–19, 1923–25.

Blau-Weiss-Blätter: Führerzeitung. 1917–23.

Die Blauweisse Brille. 1915–16.

Hechaluz: Monatsschrift des "Hechaluz," Deutscher Landesverband. 1924–25.

Israelitische Rundschau. See *Jüdische Rundschau.*

Der Jude. 1916–26.

Der Jude. Sonderhefte.
1. *Antisemitismus und jüdisches Volkstum.*
2. *Erziehung.*
3. *Judentum und Deutschtum.*
4. *Judentum und Christentum.*
5. *Sonderheft zu Martin Bubers fünfzigstem Geburtstag.*

Jüdische Jugend. Published by the Kartell jüdischer Verbindungen and the Jüdische Turnerschaft. 1919–20.

Jüdische Rundschau. 1901–33. Original title *Israelitische Rundschau.* Adopted as official organ of the ZVfD beginning with vol. 6, no. 20 (24 May 1901), at which time it also absorbed *Der Zionist,* published by the Breslauer Zionistische Vereinigung. Published under the title *Jüdische Rundschau* beginning with vol. 7, no. 40 (1 October 1902). Issued weekly until 15 November 1918, after which time it appeared twice weekly.

Der jüdische Student. 1902–33. Organ first of the Bund jüdischer Corporationen and after 1914 of the Kartell jüdischer Verbindungen.

Jüdische Welt: Zentral-Organ des Verbandes ostjüdischer Organisationen in Deutschland. 1929–30.

Der jüdische Wille: Zeitschrift des Kartells jüdischer Verbindungen. 1918–20.

Der junge Jude. Published by the Jung-jüdischer Wanderbund and the Merkas Hechaluz Deutschland. 1927–31.

Neue jüdische Monatshefte: Zeitschrift für Politik, Wirtschaft und Literatur in Ost und West. 1916–20.

Ost und West: Illustrierte Monatsschrift für modernes Judentum. 1901–23.

Der Schlemiel: Illustriertes jüdisches Witzblatt. 1903–05. Special Issues, 1907, 1908. Revived as *Der Schlemiel: Jüdische Blätter für Humor und Kunst.* 1919–21.

Die Welt: Zentralorgan der zionistischen Bewegung. 1897–1914.

BOOKS AND ARTICLES

Arbeitsgemeinschaft für zionistische Realpolitik. Zur politischen Krise des Zionismus: Materialien zu einer auf dem Prinzip des Binationalismus in Palästina beruhenden zionistischen Politik. Berlin: Arbeitsgemeinschaft für zionistische Realpolitik, 1931.

Arlosoroff, Victor Chaim. *Der jüdische Volkssozialismus.* Berlin: Hapoel Hazaïr, 1919.

————. *Leben und Werk. Ausgewählte Schriften, Reden, Tagebücher und Briefe.* Berlin: Hechaluz, 1936.

Blau-Weiss. *Blau-Weiss Führer: Leitfaden für die Arbeit im Jüdischen Wanderbund "Blau-Weiss."* Berlin: Die Bundesleitung, 1917.

————. *Die Karlsruher Siedlung: Plan einer Blau-Weiss Werkstätte in Palästina.* Munich, 1923.

————. Das Komitee der 50-Jahr-Feier des Blau-Weiss. *50 Jahre Blau-Weiss (Das Jubiläums Treffen des Blau-Weiss, Naharia, 18–19. Mai 1962).* Tel Aviv, 1962.

————. *Leitfaden für die Gründung eines Jüdischen Wanderbundes "Blau-Weiss."* Berlin: Jüdischer Wanderbund Blau-Weiss, 1913.

Blumenfeld, Kurt et al. *Beiträge zur Frage unserer Propaganda: Ein Briefwechsel zwischen Max Jacobsohn und Kurt Blumenfeld, nebst Äusserungen führender deutscher Zionisten.* Berlin: ZVfD, 1928. Copy in Schocken Archive 531/4.

Bodenheimer, Henriette Hannah, ed. *Im Anfang der zionistischen Bewegung: Eine Dokumentation auf der Grundlage des Briefwechsels zwischen Theodor Herzl und Max Bodenheimer von 1896 bis 1905.* Frankfort on the Main: Europäische Verlagsanstalt, 1965.

Bodenheimer, Max Isidor. *Wohin mit den russischen Juden? Syrien ein Zufluchtsort der russischen Juden.* Hamburg: Die Menorah, 1891.

Boehlich, Walter, ed. *Der Berliner Antisemitismusstreit.* Frankfort on the Main: Insel, 1965.

Brith Shalom. *Memorandum by the "Brith Shalom" Society on an Arab Policy for the Jewish Agency.* Jerusalem, 1930.

Buber, Martin. *Der Jude und sein Judentum: Gesammelte Aufsätze und Reden.* Cologne: Melzer, 1963.

————; Feiwel, Berthold; and Weizmann, Chaim. *Eine jüdische Hochschule.* Berlin: Jüdischer Verlag, 1902.

Cohen, Hermann. *Hermann Cohens Jüdische Schriften.* Edited by Bruno Strauss. Berlin: C. A. Schwetschke und Sohn, 1924.

Feiwel, Berthold, and Stricker, Robert. *Zur Aufklärung über den Zionismus.* Brünn: Jüdisch-akademische Verbindung Zephirah, 1898.

Fuchs, Eugen. "Referat über die Stellung des Centralvereins zum Zionismus in der Delegierten-Versammlung vom 30. März 1913." In Eugen Fuchs. *Um Deutschtum und Judentum: Gesammelte Reden und Aufsätze (1894–1919).* Frankfort on the Main: J. Kauffmann, 1919.

Goldstein, Moritz. "Deutsch-jüdischer Parnass." *Kunstwart* 25, no. 11 (Erstes Märzheft, 1912):281–94.

Great Britain. *Parliamentary Papers.* "Report of the Commission on the Palestine Disturbances of August, 1929." Cmd. 3530. 1930. (Known as the "Shaw Commission Report.")

Hasmonaea. *30 Jahre V.J.St. Hasmonaea.* Berlin: VJSt Hasmonaea im Kartell jüdischer Verbindungen, 1932.

Herzl, Theodor. *Altneuland.* Volume 5 of his *Gesammelte Zionistische Werke.* Tel Aviv: Hozaah Ivrith, 1935. English translation: *Old-New Land.* Translated by Lotta Levensohn. New York: Bloch, 1960.

———. *Zionistische Schriften.* 3d ed., rev. and enl. Tel Aviv: Hozaah Ivrith, 1934.

Herzl Bund. *Protokoll des II. ordentlichen Bundestages des Herzl-Bundes.* Berlin, 1919.

Holdheim, Gerhard, and Preuss, Walter. *Die theoretischen Grundlagen des Zionismus: Ein Leitfaden, mit einem Anhang: Die bedeutendsten jüdischen Organisationen und Institutionen.* Berlin: Welt, 1919.

Jüdische Rundschau. *Ja-sagen zum Judentum: Eine Aufsatzreihe der "Jüdischen Rundschau" zur Lage der deutschen Juden.* Preface by Robert Weltsch. Berlin: Jüdische Rundschau, 1933.

[Kartell jüdischer Verbindung]. Maccabaea (Königsberg), Verbindung jüdischer Studenten im KJV. *Rückblick und Besinnung: Aufsätze gesammelt aus Anlass des 50. Jahrestages der Gründung der Verbindung jüdischer Studenten "Maccabaea" im K.J.V. (Königsberg).* Tel Aviv: Präsidium des KJV, 1954.

Katzenberger, Naomi. "Dokumente zur Frage des Wahlrechts ausländischer Juden in den preussischen Synagogengemeinden." In Shlomo Simonsohn and Jacob Toury, ed. *Michael: On the History of the Jews in the Diaspora.* Tel Aviv: University of Tel Aviv, 1973, 2:191–203.

Keren Hayesod. *Bericht des Hauptbüros des Keren Hajessod an den . . . Zionisten-Kongress* (title varies slightly). London and Jerusalem, 1921–33 (biannual).

Keren Kayemeth Leisrael. *Report of the Head Office of the Keren Kayemeth Leisrael to the . . . Zionist Congress.* London and Jerusalem, 1921–33 (biannual).

Klatzkin, Jakob. *Probleme des modernen Judentums.* Berlin: Jüdischer Verlag, 1918. 2d enl. ed. published as *Krisis und Entscheidung im Judentum: Die Probleme des modernen Judentums.* Berlin: Jüdischer Verlag, 1921. 3d ed. identical to 2d, published as *Probleme des modernen Judentums.* Berlin: Lambert Schneider, 1930.

Kohn, Hans, and Weltsch, Robert. *Zionistische Politik: Eine Aufsatzreihe.* Mährisch-Ostrau: R. Färber, 1927.

Kollenscher, Max. *Binjan Haarez: Ein Wort an den XII. Zionisten-Kongress.* Berlin: Verlag des Binjan Haarez, 1921.

———. *Jüdische Gemeindepolitik.* Berlin: Zionistisches Zentralbureau, 1909.

———. *Zionismus und Staatsbürgertum.* 2d ed. Berlin: Zionistisches Zentralbureau, 1910.

Krojanker, Gustav. *Zum Problem des neuen deutschen Nationalismus: Eine zionistische Orientierung gegenüber den nationalistischen Strömungen unserer Zeit.* Berlin: Jüdische Rundschau, 1932.

Landauer, Georg. *Der Zionismus im Wandel dreier Jahrzehnte.* Epilogue by Robert Weltsch. Tel Aviv: Bitaon, 1957.

Lelewer, Hermann. *Was will der Zionismus?* Berlin: ZVfD, 1920.

Lessing, Gotthold Ephraim. *Nathan der Weise.* First published 1779.

Lichtheim, Richard. *Das Programm des Zionismus.* Berlin: ZVfD, 1911: 2d ed., rev. and enl., 1913.

———. *Was ist Zionismus? Ein Aufruf an die Wähler zum 17. Zionisten-kongress.* Berlin, 1931.

National-jüdische Vereinigung. "Der Nationaljude als Staatsbürger." *Flugblatt Nr. 2.* Cologne, 1897.

———. *Der Zionismus.* Cologne: n.d. [c. 1896].

Neue Jüdische Monatshefte. *Das deutsche Judentum, Seine Parteien und Organisationen: Eine Sammelschrift.* Berlin: Neue jüdische Monatshefte, 1919.

Riesser, Gabriel. *Börne und die Juden: Ein Wort der Erwiderung auf die Flugschrift des Herrn Dr. Eduard Meyer gegen Börne.* Altenburg: Hofbuchdruckerei, 1832. Reprinted in idem, *Gesammelte Schriften,* vol. 4. Edited by M. Isler. Frankfort on the Main: Verlag der Riesser Stiftung, 1868.

Rothschild, Eli, ed. *Meilensteine: Vom Wege des Kartells jüdischer Verbindungen (K.J.V.) in der zionistischen Bewegung: Eine Sammelschrift.* Tel Aviv: Präsidium des KJV, 1972.

Ruppin, Artur. *Dreissig Jahre Aufbau in Palästina: Reden und Schriften.* Berlin: Schocken, 1937.

Simon, Ernst. "Unser Kriegserlebnis." *Jüdischer Jugend* 1 (1919):39–45; reprinted in Ernst Simon, *Brücken: Gesammelte Aufsätze.* Heidelberg: Lambert Schneider, 1965, pp. 17–23.

Simonsohn, E. *Die jüdische Volksgemeinde.* Berlin: Jüdischer Verlag, 1919.

Sperlings Zeitschriften- und Zeitungs-Addressbuch: Handbuch der deutschen Presse. Leipzig: Börsenverein der deutschen Buchhändler zu Leipzig, 1908–35.

Statistik des Deutschen Reichs.

Tramer, Hans, ed. *In Zwei Welten: Siegfried Moses zum fünfundsiebzigsten Geburtstag.* Tel Aviv: Bitaon, 1962.

———, and Loewenstein, Kurt, eds. *Robert Weltsch zum siebzigsten Geburtstag von seinen Freunden.* Tel Aviv: Bitaon, 1961.

Weltsch, Robert. "Buber's Political Philosophy." In Martin Buber, *The Philosophy of Martin Buber,* ed. Paul A. Schilpp and Maurice Friedman. La Salle, Ill.: Open Court Press, 1967, pp. 435–49.

———. "Deutscher Zionismus in der Rückschau." In Hans Tramer, ed. *In Zwei Welten: Siegfried Moses zum fünfundsiebzigsten Geburtstag,* pp. 27–42.

———. "Ein Feldpostbrief aus dem Osten." *Der Jude* 1 (1916/17):529–34.

———. Introduction to Martin Buber, *Der Jude und sein Judentum.* Cologne: Melzer, 1963, pp. xiii–xl.

———. "Entscheidungsjahr 1932." In Werner E. Mosse, ed., *Entscheidungsjahr 1932: Zur Judenfrage in der Endphase der Weimarer Republik,* 2d rev. ed.; Tübingen: J.C.B. Mohr, 1966, pp. 535–62.

———. "Siegfried Moses: End of an Epoch." *LBIYB* 19 (1974): vii–xi.

———. "A Tragedy of Leadership (Chaim Weizmann and the Zionist Movement)." *Jewish Social Studies* 13, no. 3 (July 1951):211–26.

———. See Kohn, Hans.

Zionist Congress. *Stenographisches Protokoll der Verhandlungen des . . . Zionisten-Kongresses.* 1–19, 1897–1935 (title varies slightly: vols. 1–4, . . . *Zionisten-Congresses*).

In addition to the indexes in each volume, the following more complete indexes have been published:

Heymann, Michael, ed. *Index to the Minutes of the . . . Zionist Congress.* Tel Aviv: Tel Aviv University, 1966–   .

Schachtel, Hugo. *Register zu den Protokollen der Zionisten Kongresse I–VI.* Berlin: Jüdischer Verlag, 1905.

———. *Register zum Protokoll des VII. Zionisten-Kongresses.* 1906.

Zionist Organization, Berlin Bureau. *Warum gingen wir zum ersten Zionistenkongress?* Berlin: Jüdischer Verlag, 1922.

Zionist Organization, Democratic Faction. *Programm und Organisations-Statut der Demokratisch-zionistischen Fraktion.* Berlin, 1902.

Zionistische Vereinigung für Deutschland. Beginning with the fifth *Delegiertentag* in 1901 the Proceedings of the *Delegiertentage* were printed in the *Jüdische Rundschau,* as was most of the material presented in the annual reports. Many of these proceedings and reports were published as separate pamphlets, which I have not listed here, as they essentially duplicate the material printed in the *Rundschau.* The printed protocols of the first, second, and fourth *Delegiertentag* may be found in the Central Zionist Archives, Collection of miscellaneous printed matter.

———. *Was will der Zionismus?* Berlin: Jüdische Rundschau, 1903; 2d ed. 1906. Author listed as Adolf Friedemann in *Zeitschrift für hebräische Bibliographie* 18, no. 4/6 (July/December 1915):99, item no. 376.

———. *Zionistisches A-B-C Buch.* Berlin: ZVfD, 1908.

[ZVfD], Gruppe der unabhängigen allgemeinen Zionisten (Gruppe Kollenscher). *Materialien zum Jenaer Delegiertentag der Zionistischen Vereinigung für Deutschland.* N.p., 1929.

———. "Unser Programm." *Flugblatt Nr. 4.* Cologne, c. 1898.

Secondary works

Adler-Rudel, Schalom. *Ostjuden in Deutschland, 1880–1940.* Tübingen: J.C.B. Mohr, 1959.

Angress, Werner T. "Prussia's Army and the Jewish Reserve Officer Controversy before World War I." *LBIYB* 17 (1972):19–42.

Asch, Adolph. *Geschichte des K.C. (Kartellverband jüdischer Studenten) im Lichte der deutschen kulturellen und politischen Entwicklung.* London: privately printed, 1964.

Asch, Adolph, and Philippson, Johanna. "Self-Defence at the Turn of the Century: The Emergence of the K.C. [Kartell-Convent]." *LBIYB* 3 (1958):122–39.

Baron, Salo. "Ghetto and Emancipation: Shall We Revise the Traditional View?" *Menorah Journal* 14, no. 6 (June 1928):515–26.

————. "Newer Approaches to Jewish Emancipation." *Diogenes,* no. 29 (Spring 1960):56–81.

Barzilay, Isaac E. "National and Anti-National Trends in the Berlin Haskalah." *Jewish Social Studies,* no. 21 (July 1959):165–92.

Baer, Jizchak Fritz [Yitzhak F.]. *Galut.* Berlin: Schocken, 1936. English translation: *Galut.* New York: Schocken, 1947.

Bein, Alex. "Franz Oppenheimer als Mensch und Zionist." *LBI Bulletin* 7, no. 25/28 (1964):1–55.

————. "Franz Oppenheimer and Theodor Herzl." *Herzl Year Book* 7 (1971):71–127.

Bennathan, Esra. "Die demographische und wirtschaftliche Struktur der Juden." In Werner E. Mosse, ed., *Entscheidungsjahr 1932: Zur Judenfrage in der Endphase der Weimarer Republic,* 2d rev. ed. Tübingen: J.C.B. Mohr, 1966, pp. 87–131.

Bodenheimer, Henriette Hannah. "The Three Delegates' Conferences of German Zionists (1897)." *Herzl Year Book* 7 (1971):175–82.

————, ed. *Toledoth Tochnith Basel* [History of the Basel Program]. Jerusalem: R. Mass, 1947.

Bolkosky, Sidney M. *The Distorted Image: German Jewish Perceptions of Germans and Germany, 1918–1935.* New York: Elsevier, 1975.

Borman, Stuart A. "The Prague Student Zionist Movement: 1896–1914." Ph.D. dissertation, University of Chicago, 1972.

Cohn, Henry J. "Theodor Herzl's Conversion to Zionism." *Jewish Social Studies* 32, no. 2 (April 1970):101–10.

Eliav, Mordechai. "Zur Vorgeschichte der jüdischen Nationalbewegung in Deutschland." *LBI Bulletin* 12, no. 48 (1969):282–314.

Engelman, Uriah Z. "Intermarriage among Jews in Germany, U.S.S.R., and Switzerland." *Jewish Social Studies* 2, no. 2 (April 1940):157–78.

Erikson, Erik H. *Young Man Luther: A Study in Psychoanalysis and History.* New York: Norton, 1962.

Esh, Shaul. "Kurt Blumenfeld on the Modern Jew and Zionism." *Jewish Journal of Sociology* 6, no. 2 (December 1964):232–42.

Felden, Klemens. "Die Übernahme des antisemitischen Stereotyps als soziale Norm durch die bürgerliche Gesellschaft Deutschlands (1875–1900)." Ph.D. dissertation, Heidelberg, 1963.

Friesel, Avyatar. *The Zionist Movement in the United States, 1897–1914* (Hebrew). Tel Aviv: University of Tel Aviv, 1970.

Gartner, Lloyd P. *The Jewish Immigrant in England, 1870–1914.* London: Allen and Unwin, 1960.

Gay, Peter. "Encounter with Modernism: German Jews in German Culture, 1888–1914." *Midstream* 21, no. 2 (February 1975):23–65.

Giebels, L.A.M. "Het onstaan van eew zionistische Beweging in Nederland . . . [The Rise of the Zionist Movement in the Netherlands . . .]." *Studia Rosenthaliana* 7, no. 1 (January 1973):90–115; 8, no. 1 (January 1974): 64–106; 8, no. 2 (July 1974):214–67; and 9, no. 1 (January 1975): 103–52. English summary in vol. 9, no. 1:148–52.

Goldstein, Walter. *Chronik des Herzl-Bundes, 1912–1962: Die Geschichte einer Zionssehnsucht.* Tel Aviv: Präsidium des Herzl-Bundes, 1962.

Gross, Walter. "The Zionist Students' Movement." *LBIYB* 4 (1959):143–64.

Gurevich, David. "Fifteen Years of Immigration to Palestine" (Hebrew). *Aliyah: Kovetz le-Inyane ha-Aliyah* 2 (1935): 43–62 and tables, pp. i–xlviii.

_____; Gertz, Aaron; and Bachi, Roberto. *The Jewish Population of Palestine: Immigration, Demographic Structure, and Natural Growth* (Hebrew with English summary). Jerusalem: Jewish Agency for Palestine, Statistical Department, 1944.

Habermas, Jürgen. "Der deutsche Idealismus der jüdischen Philosophen." In Thilo Koch, ed., *Porträts deutsch-jüdischer Geistesgeschichte.* Cologne: DuMont Schauberg, 1961, pp. 99–125.

Hamburger, Ernest. *Juden im öffentlichen Leben Deutschlands: Regierungsmitglieder, Beamte und Parlamentarier in der monarchischen Zeit, 1848–1918.* Tübingen: J.C.B. Mohr, 1968.

_____. "One Hundred Years of Emancipation," *LBIYB* 14 (1969):3–66.

Hattis, Susan Lee. *The Bi-National Idea in Palestine during Mandatory Times.* Haifa: Shikmona, 1970.

Herlitz, Georg. *Der Zionismus und sein Werk.* Berlin: Jüdische Rundschau, 1933.

Hertzberg, Arthur. *The French Enlightenment and the Jews.* New York: Columbia University Press, 1968.

Jüdischer Verlag Berlin. *Almanach: 1902–1964.* Berlin: Jüdischer Verlag, 1964.

Katz, Jacob. "The Term 'Jewish Emancipation': Its Origin and Historical Impact." In Alexander Altmann, ed., *Studies in Nineteenth-Century Jewish Intellectual History.* Cambridge, Mass.: Harvard University Press, 1964, pp. 1–25.

————. *Tradition and Crisis: Jewish Society at the End of the Middle Ages.* New York: Free Press, 1961.

————. "Was the Holocaust Predictable?" *Commentary* 59, no. 5 (May 1975):41–48.

Kedar, Aharon. "Brit Shalom, 1925–1933." M.A. thesis, Hebrew University of Jerusalem, 1969. Copy in possession of the Ben Zvi Institute, Jerusalem.

Klausner, Israel. *Opositsia le-Herzl* [The Opposition to Herzl]. Jerusalem: Achiever, 1960.

Knütter, Hans-Hellmuth. *Die Juden und die deutsche Linke in der Weimarer Republik, 1918–1933.* Düsseldorf: Droste, 1971.

Kohn, Hans. *Martin Buber: Sein Werk und seine Zeit: Ein Beitrag zur Geistesgeschichte Mitteleuropas, 1880–1930.* Epilogue: "1930–1960" by Robert Weltsch. 3d rev. ed. Cologne: Melzer, 1961.

Krohn, Helga. *Die Juden in Hamburg, 1800–1850: Ihre soziale, kulturelle und politische Entwicklung während der Emanzipationszeit.* Frankfort on the Main: Europäische Verlagsanstalt, 1967.

————. *Die Juden in Hamburg: Die politische, soziale und kulturelle Entwicklung einer jüdisches Grossstadtgemeinde nach der Emanzipation, 1848–1918.* Hamburg: Hans Christians, 1974.

Lamberti, Marjorie. "The Attempt to Form a Jewish Bloc: Jewish Notables and Politics in Wilhelmian Germany." *Central European History* 3, no. 1/2 (May/June 1970):73–93.

————. "The Prussian Government and the Jews: Official Behaviour and Policy-Making in the Wilhelminian Era." *LBIYB* 17 (1972):5–17.

Laqueur, Walter. *Young Germany: A History of the German Youth Movement.* New York: Basic Books, 1962.

Lessing, Theodor. *Der jüdische Selbsthass.* Berlin: Jüdischer Verlag, 1930.

Lestchinsky, Jakob. *Das wirtschaftliche Schicksal des deutschen Judentums: Aufstieg, Wandlung, Krise, Ausblick.* (Schriften der Zentralwohlfahrtsstelle der deutschen Juden und der Hauptstelle für jüdische Wanderfürsorge, no. 7.) Berlin, 1933.

Lewin, Kurt. *Resolving Social Conflicts: Selected Papers on Group Dynamics.* New York: Harper, 1948.

Loewenberg, Peter. "Theodor Herzl: A Psychoanalytic Study in Charismatic Political Leadership." In Benjamin B. Wolman, ed., *The Psychoanalytic Interpretation of History.* New York: Basic Books, 1971, pp. 150–91.

Loewenstein, Kurt. "Die innerjüdische Reaktion auf die Krise der deutschen Demokratie." In Werner E. Mosse, ed., *Entscheidungsjahr 1932,* 2d rev. ed. Tübingen: J.C.B. Mohr, 1966, pp. 349–403.

Lowe, Adolph. "In Memoriam Franz Oppenheimer." *LBIYB* 10 (1965): 137–49.

Margaliot, Abraham. "The Political Reaction of German Jewish Organizations and Institutions to the Anti-Jewish Policy of the National Socialists, 1932–1935 (until the Publication of the Nuremberg Laws)" (Hebrew). Ph.D. dissertation, Hebrew University of Jerusalem, 1971.

Markel, Richard. "Brith Haolim: Der Weg der Alija des Jung-jüdischen Wanderbundes (J.J.W.B.)." *LBI Bulletin* 9, no. 34 (1966):119–89.

Marrus, Michael R. *The Politics of Assimilation: A Study of the French Jewish Community at the Time of the Dreyfus Affair.* Oxford: Oxford University Press, 1971.

Massing, Paul W. *Rehearsal for Destruction: A Study of Political Anti-Semitism in Imperial Germany.* New York: Harper, 1949.

Meier-Cronemeyer, Hermann. "Jüdische Jugendbewegung." *Germania Judaica* 8, no. 1/2–3/4 (1969) (n.s. 27/28–29/30).

Meyer, Michael A. "Great Debate on Anti-Semitism: Jewish Reaction to New Hostility in Germany, 1879–1881." *LBIYB* 11 (1966):137–70.

Mosse, George L. *The Crisis of German Ideology: Intellectual Origins of the Third Reich.* New York: Grosset and Dunlap, 1964.

———. "German Socialists and the Jewish Question in the Weimar Republic." *LBIYB* 16 (1971):123–51.

———. "The Influence of the Volkish Idea on German Jewry." In *Germans and Jews: The Right, the Left and the Search for a "Third Force" in Pre-Nazi Germany.* New York: Grosset and Dunlap, 1971, pp. 77–115.

Mosse, Werner E. "Der Niedergang der Weimarer Republik und die Juden." In Werner E. Mosse., ed., *Entscheidungsjahr 1932: Zur Judenfrage in der Endphase der Weimarer Republik,* 2d rev. ed. Tübingen: J.C.B. Mohr, 1966, pp. 3–49.

Niewyk, Donald L. *Socialist, Anti-Semite and Jew: German Social Democracy Confronts the Problem of Anti-Semitism, 1918–1933.* Baton Rouge: Louisiana State University Press, 1971.

Paucker, Arnold. *Der jüdische Abwehrkampf gegen Antisemitismus und Nationalsozialismus in den letzten Jahren der Weimarer Republik.* 2d rev. ed. Hamburg: Leibniz, 1969.

Poppel, Stephen M. "Salman Schocken and the Schocken Verlag: A Jewish Publisher in Weimar and Nazi Germany." *Harvard Library Bulletin* 21, no. 1 (January 1973):20–49.

Porath, Yehoshuah. *The Emergence of the Palestinian Arab National Movement, 1918–1929.* London: Frank Cass, 1974.

Pulzer, Peter G. J. *The Rise of Political Anti-Semitism in Germany and Austria.* New York: John Wiley, 1964.

Rabinowicz, Oskar K. "Czechoslovak Zionism: Analecta to a History." In Society for the History of Czechoslovak Jews, ed., *The Jews of Czechoslovakia: Historical Studies and Surveys.* Philadelphia: Jewish Publication Society, 1971, 2:19–136.

Reichmann, Eva G. "Der Bewusstseinswandel der deutschen Juden." In Werner E. Mosse, ed., *Deutsches Judentum in Krieg und Revolution, 1916–1923: Ein Sammelband.* Tübingen: J.C.B. Mohr, 1971, pp. 511–612.

————. *Hostages of Civilization: The Social Forces of National Socialist Anti-Semitism,* Boston: Beacon, 1951.

Rinott, Chanoch. "Major Trends in Jewish Youth Movements in Germany." *LBIYB* 19 (1974):77–96.

Rinott, Moshe. *"Hilfsverein der deutschen Juden"—Creation and Struggle* (Hebrew). Jerusalem: Hebrew University School of Education, 1971.

Rosenberg, Hans. *Grosse Depression und Bismarckzeit: Wirtschaftsablauf, Gesellschaft und Politik in Mitteleuropa.* Berlin: De Gruyter, 1967.

Rosenstock, Werner. "The Jewish Youth Movement." *LBIYB* 19 (1974): 97–106.

Rosenthal, Erich. "Trends of the Jewish Population in Germany, 1910–1939." *Jewish Social Studies* 6, no. 3 (July 1944):233–74.

Rothholz, Julius. "Die preussischen Juden als Stadtbewohner." In *Statistik der Juden: Eine Sammelschrift.* Berlin: Jüdischer Verlag, 1918, pp. 61–66.

Ruppin, Arthur. "Die Juden als Stadtbewohner." In Albert Nossig, ed. *Jüdische Statistik.* Berlin: Jüdischer Verlag, 1903, pp. 424ff.

Schatzker, Chaim. "The Jewish Youth Movement in Germany between the Years 1900–1933" (Hebrew with English summary). Ph.D. dissertation, Hebrew University of Jerusalem, 1969.

————. "The Term 'Asemitism' in the German Youth Movement" (Hebrew). In A. Gilboa et al., eds. *Studies in the History of the Jewish People and the Land of Israel in Memory of Zvi Avneri.* Haifa: University of Haifa, 1970, pp. 267–85.

Scholem, Gershom. "Martin Buber's Hasidism: A Critique." *Commentary* 32 (1961):305–16.

Schorsch, Ismar. "Identity or Integration—Which?" *Judaism* 19 (1970): 373–77. Review of Tal's book listed below.

————. *Jewish Reactions to German Anti-Semitism, 1870–1914.* New York: Columbia University Press, and Philadelphia: Jewish Publication Society, 1972.

Schorske, Carl E. "Politics in a New Key: An Austrian Triptych." *Journal of Modern History* 39, no. 4 (December 1967):343–86.

Shapiro, Yonathan. *Leadership of the American Zionist Organization: 1897–1930.* Urbana: University of Illinois Press, 1971.

————. "The Zionist Faith." *American Jewish Archives* 18, no. 2 (November 1966): 107–27.

Sharot, Stephen. "Minority Situation and Religious Acculturation: A Comparative Analysis of Jewish Communities." *Comparative Studies in Society and History* 16, no. 3 (June 1974):329–54.

Silbergleit, Heinrich. *Die Bevölkerungs- und Berufsverhältnisse der Juden im Deutschen Reich.* Vol. 1: *Freistaat Preussen* (no more published). Berlin: Akademie Verlag, 1930. An analysis of the results of the census of 1925.

Simon, Ernst. "Martin Buber and German Jewry." *LBIYB* 3 (1958):3–39.

———. "Nationalismus, Zionismus und der jüdisch-arabische Konflikt in Martin Bubers Theorie und Wirksamkeit." *LBI Bulletin* 9, no. 33 (1966):21–84.

Simon, Walter B. "The Jewish Vote in Austria," *LBIYB* 16 (1971):97–121.

Stern, Fritz. "The Political Consequences of the Unpolitical German." In *The Failure of Illiberalism: Essays on the Political Culture of Modern Germany.* New York: Knopf, 1972, pp. 3–25.

———. *The Politics of Cultural Despair: A Study in the Rise of the Germanic Ideology.* Garden City, New York: Doubleday/Anchor, 1965. First published 1961.

Stonequist, Everett V. *The Marginal Man: A Study in Personality and Culture Conflict.* New York: Scribner's, 1937.

Strauss, Herbert. "The Jugendverband: A Social and Intellectual History." *LBIYB* 6 (1961):206–35.

Szajkowski, Zosa. "The Komitee fuer den Osten and Zionism." *Herzl Year Book* 7 (1971):199–240.

———. "The Struggle for Yiddish during World War I." *LBIYB* 9 (1964): 131–58.

Tal, Uriel. *Christians and Jews in Germany: Religion, Politics, and Ideology in the Second Reich, 1870–1914.* Ithaca: Cornell University Press, 1975.

Theilhaber, Felix A. *Der Untergang der deutschen Juden: Eine Volkswirtschaftliche Studie.* Munich: Verlagsbuchhandlung Ernst Reinhardt, 1911. 2d rev. ed. Berlin: Jüdischer Verlag, 1921.

Toury, Jacob. "The Judentag Plan and the Zionists in Germany" (Hebrew). *Hazionut* 1 (1970):9–56.

———. "Organizational Problems of German Jewry: Steps towards the Establishment of a Central Organization (1893–1920)." *LBIYB* 13 (1968):57–90.

———. *Die politischen Orientierungen der Juden in Deutschland: Von Jena bis Weimar.* Tübingen: J.C.B. Mohr, 1966.

Tramer, Hans. "Jüdischer Wanderbund Blau-Weiss: Ein Beitrag zu seiner äusseren Geschichte." *LBI Bulletin* 5, no. 17 (June 1962):23–43.

Urofsky, Melvin I. *American Zionism from Herzl to the Holocaust.* Garden City: Anchor Press, Doubleday, 1974.

———, and Henry L. Feingold, Howard M. Sachar, discussants. "Zionism: An American Experience." *American Jewish Historical Quarterly* 63, no. 3 (March 1974):215–43.

Weinberg, Jehuda Louis. *Aus der Frühzeit des Zionismus: Heinrich Loewe.* Jerusalem: R. Mass, 1946.

Wilhelm, Kurt. "The Jewish Community in the Post-Emancipation Period." *LBIYB* 2 (1957):47–75.

Yisraeli, David. *The Palestine Problem in German Politics, 1889–1945* (Hebrew). Ramat Gan: Bar Ilan University Press, 1974.

Zechlin, Egmont. *Die deutsche Politik und die Juden im Ersten Weltkrieg.* Göttingen: Vandenhoeck & Ruprecht, 1969.

Zeitschrift für Demographie und Statistik der Juden.

Zionist Organization, Palestine Zionist Executive, Immigration Department. *Ten Years of Jewish Immigration into Palestine, 1919–1929.* Jerusalem, 1929.

INDEX